R.G. DUN & CO.
1841~1900

Robert Graham Dun, 1826-1900. From a painting by Benjamin
Constant. *Courtesy of Dun & Bradstreet, Inc.*

R.G. DUN & CO. 1841-1900

The Development of Credit-Reporting in the Nineteenth Century

James D. Norris

Contributions in Economics and
Economic History, Number 20

GREENWOOD PRESS

WESTPORT, CONNECTICUT • LONDON, ENGLAND

Library of Congress Cataloging in Publication Data

Norris, James D
    R. G. Dun & Co., 1841-1900.

    (Contributions in economics and economic history;
    no. 20 ISSN 0084-9235)
    Bibliography: p.
    Includes index.
    1. Dun (R. G.) & Company, New York. I. Title.
HF5573.N63   338.7'61'33267   77-95359
ISBN 0-313-20326-1

Library of Congress Catalog Card Number: 77-95359
ISBN: 0-313-20326-1
ISSN: 0084-9235

First published in 1978

Greenwood Press, Inc.
51 Riverside Avenue, Westport, Connecticut 06880

Printed in the United States of America

10 9 8 7 6 5 4 3 2 1

TO NANCY

Contents

Illustrations   *ix*

Tables   *xi*

Series Foreword   *xiii*

Preface   *xv*

1   The Rise of Credit-Rating in the
    United States   3

2   Tappan & Douglass, 1849-58   36

3   The Civil War Years, 1858-65   59

4   The *Reference Book* Years, 1866-76   89

5   The Coming of Age, 1876-94   124

6   The End of an Era, 1894-1900   153

Notes   *165*

Bibliography   *193*

Index   *199*

Illustrations

Robert Graham Dun, 1826-1900   Frontis

1   Dorr's Building, Hanover and Exchange
streets, New York   13

2   Lewis Tappan, 1788-1873   15

3   Benjamin Douglass, 1816-1900   38

4   Arthur Tappan, 1786-1865   39

5   John M. Bradstreet, 1815-63   50

6   Elizabeth Douglass Dun, 1817-82   64

7   James Angus Dun and R. G. Dun, c. 1870   65

8   "Dunmere," the R. G. Dun summer home,
Narragansett, Rhode Island   102

9   Mary (Minnie) Bradford Dun, 1848-1910   103

10   1885 Report on T. R. McGurn,
Storey County, Nevada   137

11   R. G. Dun Building at 290 Broadway, New York   160

Tables

1	Mercantile Agency Branch Offices, 1849-57	43
2	B. Douglass & Co. Profits, 1855-59	47
3	1859 *Reference Book* Key to Markings	55
4	R. G. Dun & Co. Profits, 1859-65	69
5	R. G. Dun & Co., Profits by Branch Offices, 1859-65	75
6	R. G. Dun & Co., *1864 Rating Key*	84
7	R. G. Dun & Co. Net Profits, 1866-77	98
8	Branch Offices Established, 1858-76	108
9	Firms Reported on in the *Reference Book*	110
10	1878 Specimen Contract	141
11	R. G. Dun & Co. Profits, 1874-1900	143
12	R. G. Dun & Co. Branch Offices, 1877-1901	157

Series Foreword

In drawing a distinction between the kinds of problems different historians face, Robin Winks wrote that the Americans begin by asking questions and then seeking answers from a wide variety of sources. The Europeans, who for the most part have fewer documents and related evidence upon which to draw, begin with them and then ask what they tell. The American, then, controls his destiny because, as Winks puts it, "He will have more data, more evidence, more rewarding journeys, than any other national historian." The European, in contrast, is at the mercy of his material: "Here are the private papers of Joseph Chamberlain, or of Gladstone, or of Disraeli. What do they tell me of British politics? Of Queen Victoria? Of the Jameson Raid? Of the development of British tariff policy? Of Colonial affairs? Of Ireland?"

James Norris has had to face many perplexing riddles and overcome obstacles in the research and writing of this book, for as Winks might have put it, he has tried to write an American-style book with a European variety of sources. The reader will find suggestions of this dilemma in the body of the work but would be better prepared if he or she would go through the bibliography first. It is a comparatively short list and essay for so important an undertaking, but business historians familiar with the subject will understand that the author has done a thorough and admirable job.

Little has been written on the role credit played in the development of American business, although no one denies that without these instruments in the nineteenth century, there scarcely could have been anything more than local or perhaps regional production and distribution. Dun & Bradstreet, the premier company in the field and one of the most important corporations in the land, has been the subject of only one published book-length work, *Seventy-Five Years of the Mercantile Agency: R.G. Dun &*

Co., 1841-1916, by Edward N. Vose, which was released over sixty years ago, and, as the title indicates, is quite limited in scope. The Vose book is generally unavailable and in any case does not answer many of the questions almost anyone interested in the subject would want to ask. Owen A. Sheffield's "Dun & Bradstreet, Inc." is an encyclopedic work that with proper editing could be pruned from its present four volumes to a single one. But it remains unpublished and is on file at D & B's New York headquarters.

Several years ago, while engaged in research there, I came across these volumes by accident and discovered their existence was known to only a few individuals in the company. As Norris writes, Sheffield had been secretary there and had completed his work around 1965. He was interested primarily in the gathering of material he rightly felt might be lost to future scholars. Sheffield did little by way of interpretation or synthesis; this he left to others he felt might be better equipped by training and temperament for the task. The D & B secretary had unearthed a major vein, which James Norris has refined, augmented, organized, and presented. In no way does it distract from this book to say that a good deal of it could not have been written as well or as completely as it has been without the raw material gathered by Sheffield.

Of course there was much more to the research than material to be found at D & B. Professor Norris has gone down all the alleys, the blind as well as the fruitful, in his search for materials and evidence. He has performed well the double task of analyzing the role credit reporting played in the nineteenth century and the ways proprietors and managers of the leading firm in the industry fashioned their operations to meet the evolving requirements of clients. That such a book hadn't been written years ago is regrettable but also understandable, given the paucity of sources and the kinds of questions historians tried to ask of them—the two simply didn't appear to go together. James Norris has demonstrated that the task could be done and has filled an embarrassing gap in the literature in the process. Perhaps he next will undertake an equally important task, and in a second volume continue his history to the present.

Robert Sobel
Professor of Business History
Hofstra University

on personal knowledge. In the absence of such information, letters from local attorneys, merchants, and clergy attesting to the
good character and sound business habits of the applicant usually sufficed for the granting of modest credit.

In a stable community, these informal avenues of credit
information provided the creditor with the necessary data to
balance the risk against the potential loss of profits if credit were
not granted. As American settlement pushed westward into the
Mississippi Valley and economic growth accelerated after the
War of 1812, it became increasingly difficult for eastern wholesalers to obtain accurate and current information on which to
base credit decisions. Moreover, every merchant knew that simply restricting credit to known customers would cost him a substantial portion of his business. Encouraged by the expanding
economy in the 1820s, which culminated in the boom during the
mid-1830s, eastern wholesalers granted extremely liberal credit
on woefully inadequate information. Even before the panic of
1837 provided marked proof of the need for an effective method
of obtaining adequate, accurate, and timely credit-reports, there
had been abortive attempts to establish credit-reporting agencies
in the United States.

The founding of the Mercantile Agency in 1841 by Lewis Tappan was in response to this long-existing need for a credit-
reporting system suitable to the needs of a rapidly expanding nation and economy. Tappan's contribution, building on existing
but inadequate precedents, was to devise a scheme for providing
the necessary information about retail merchants for wholesale
houses to make informed decisions at affordable cost. Tappan,
like his successors Benjamin Douglass and Robert Graham Dun,
was primarily a merchant and visualized the function of the
Agency as one of promotion as well as protection of trade.

Tappan was a sedentary merchant who thought primarily in
terms of the New York market, while Benjamin Douglass, who
assumed ownership and control of the Agency after Tappan, had
wide experience as a commission merchant. Douglass began the
transformation of the institution from a regional house designed
to serve eastern wholesale firms into a national organization
capable of providing credit-reporting services throughout the

United States and much of Canada. To the organizational basis Tappan had provided, Douglass added vitality and a much broader vision of the role the Agency should play in the development of a national economy.

Building upon the contributions of Tappan and Douglass, Robert Graham Dun transformed the Mercantile Agency into a modern business fulfilling a necessary function in the American economy. From the time he purchased the Agency in 1858 until his death in 1900, Dun exerted the dominant influence in its development. The Mercantile Agency in the closing decade of the nineteenth century provided information on business firms of all descriptions throughout the world.

Of even greater significance was Dun's introduction of quantifiable measurements into credit-reports, thus changing the nature of the service from credit-reporting to credit-rating. Picking up John Bradstreet's innovation of printing credit-reports in a readily usable volume for subscribers, Dun greatly enhanced the scope and reliability of these reference books. He also substituted specific and comparable ratings for the formerly vague, impressionistic, and personalized information.

Recognizing the trends in the post–Civil War economy, Dun became an innovator in corporate credit-ratings. Although R. G. Dun & Co. credit-reports still contained analyses of the moral character and personal habits of businessmen, Dun insisted that reporters shift their emphasis to measures of capital worth, cash flows, debts outstanding, and other quantifiable data. Capitalizing on the huge volume of information collected by reporters for the Mercantile Agency, Dun provided his customers with statistics of business failures, economic conditions, and other information that he felt would enable them to make more rational decisions on credit transactions.

Robert Graham Dun was a manager par excellence. It was Dun who reorganized the management of the Mercantile Agency to make the channels of responsibility and authority more systematic, reasonable, and accountable. It was Dun who organized his office managers on a geographic basis with a headquarters staff that exercised both line and staff functions. He also insisted on formal lines of communication, defined responsibilities and authority, written rules and uniform procedures, and quality control and accountability. In short, Dun transformed Tappan's Mercantile Agency into a modern business.[2]

Despite the vital role that the credit system and credit-reporting played in the nineteenth-century American economy and R. G. Dun & Co.'s dominant position in credit-reporting, it would be a mistake to classify Dun among the so-called robber barons or captains of industry of the period. It is not simply the scale of his operations—he enjoyed a personal income exceeding a thousand dollars a day during the last twenty years of his life and left an estate of some six million dollars—that separated Dun from the Carnegies, Rockefellers, and Morgans; Dun was less a bold entrepreneur than a shrewd businessman. Although he adopted the life-style of the captains of industry and shared a rise from humble beginnings as a self-made man, he embraced none of their bold entrepreneurial characteristics and little of their social philosophy.[3]

That he did not rank with the business titans of his generation should not obscure the fact that Dun possessed one of the finest managerial minds in the late nineteenth century. Out of a bewildering array of credit-reporting firms entering and leaving the industry in the post–Civil War period, R. G. Dun & Co. emerged as the clear and dominant leader. No little portion of the credit for the Mercantile Agency's success is directly attributable to R. G. Dun's efforts and skills.

There can be no doubt that credit-reporting agencies performed a vital service in the expansion of the nineteenth-century American economy. As a contemporary observer noted, the credit-reporting agency in the beginning resulted from the credit system, but by the last quarter of the nineteenth century the credit system depended on the credit-reporting agencies. The primary role that R. G. Dun & Co. played in that transformation of the credit-reporting business makes it an ideal vehicle for an analysis of the firm and credit-reporting in nineteenth-century America.

In 1962 Dun & Bradstreet, Inc., deposited in the Baker Library at Harvard University some 2,580 volumes, consisting mostly of the credit-reports R. G. Dun & Co. collected from 1841 to 1890.

This collection, one of the largest of this type available for mid-nineteenth-century America, is only now beginning to be used extensively by business, economic and social historians. Hopefully, an analysis of R. G. Dun & Co. and credit-reporting in nineteenth-century America will enhance the usefulness of the Dun & Bradstreet collection in the Baker Library.[4]

My interest in R. G. Dun and the Mercantile Agency dates back nearly twenty years to when I worked with the James Collection at the University of Missouri-Columbia and encountered Dun's letters to his sister Lucy and her husband William James. In January 1973, as a result of the good office and efforts of Herbert West, president of the James Foundation, I received permission to use the Dun & Bradstreet archives for this study. I am also grateful to the James Foundation and Mr. West for a modest grant to assist my work in the summer of 1974. I wish to thank the officers of Dun & Bradstreet, Inc., for permission to use the archives and for their assistance. H. T. Redding, senior vice-president, responded to all of my requests for information with unfailing courtesy, and Mr. Redding and James J. Crenner, president, Dun & Bradstreet, Inc., read the entire manuscript in draft form and made numerous suggestions. Thomas P. Ivers, director of public relations and advertising, arranged for photographs for the manuscript. Shirley A. Forsberg, corporate secretary, helped me locate illustrations and photographs. Her efforts in collecting material for an historic collection of Dun & Bradstreet memorabilia at the New York office made the task not only easier but much more enjoyable.

Eugene D. Rigney, director of the Ross County Historical Society, Chillicothe, Ohio, allowed me to use his private office while working on the Dun papers in that collection and extended many kindnesses, which made my stay in Chillicothe much more profitable and pleasurable. I am grateful to Robert Lovett, manuscript division, Baker Library, Harvard University, for his thoughtfulness and his help. The staffs of the Ohio Historical Society in Columbus, Ohio, and the Thomas Jefferson Library at the University of Missouri-St. Louis provided the valuable aid one too often takes for granted from fine professionals, and I thank them.

Ford Hughes, director of the James Foundation in Missouri, encouraged me to undertake this study years ago, and his support has not wavered. Professors James Madison and John Gillingham read part of the manuscript in its initial stages and greatly sharpened my focus. Margaret Walsh and Lyle W. Dorsett read the entire manuscript and offered many valuable comments on style, organization, and content. For more than twenty years, I have enjoyed the wise counsel of James Neal Primm and Lewis E. Atherton as teachers, colleagues, and friends; both read the manuscript, and their suggestions greatly improved it. I am grateful for their advice and constant friendship. Mary Supranowich and Deborah Bohn typed and retyped a rough manuscript into final form. I am grateful to Doreen Buerck for lifting so many administrative burdens when I served as chairman of the history department, University of Missouri–St. Louis, thereby freeing my time to finish this manuscript.

I owe a special debt to Owen Sheffield, which is only partly acknowledged in my notes. Mr. Sheffield generously shared his notes, his knowledge, and his expertise, without which this would have been a much poorer study. Finally, the dedication only poorly indicates the extent of my wife Nancy's help.

I gratefully acknowledge all the assistance, but necessarily, I alone am responsible for the final product.

R.G. DUN & CO.
1841~1900

We stated at the beginning that the Mercantile Agencies were the outgrowth of our credit system. It may also be added that our present widely extended credit system is largely due to the labors of the Agencies, and that it is no longer a disputed question that they supply a want, and are indispensable to the public business.

P. R. Earling, *Whom to Trust: A Practical Treatise on Mercantile Credits* (1890)

1

The Rise of Credit-Rating in the United States

Credit-rating in one form or another has probably existed for as long as creditors have granted credit. One of the conditions of credit, an evaluation of the risk involved, presented few problems as long as the creditor had personal knowledge of credit-seekers. The problem was always one of obtaining accurate and complete information on which to make judgments.

Although the granting of mercantile credits by wholesale merchants to retail storekeepers preceded the discovery of the New World, the community in which credits were granted was much more geographically fixed and more stable than was to be the experience on the North American continent. Throughout the colonial period, English merchants provided American importers liberal credit, without which the colonial economy would have been seriously restricted. Indeed, with currency in chronic short supply, credit instruments, bills of exchange, and promissory notes became important substitutes for currency. Just as English merchants granted colonial importers generous credit, colonial wholesale merchants extended liberal terms to retail merchants in their locale, who in turn sold on credit to the local consumers. Usually both the retail and wholesale merchants knew their customers personally, and in this economic environment where seller knew buyer, each merchant reached his own conclusion as to the amount and terms of credit he might extend with reasonable safety.[1]

Certainly by the mid-eighteenth century, credit conditions and terms had become somewhat standardized. Importer-whole-

salers customarily extended twelve months credit, the agricultural marketing period, to their retail customers. As the volume
of trade increased, these practices became firmly entrenched.
While country merchants and wholesalers often discounted
prices to those willing and able to pay cash, they also willingly
extended credit. Prices tended to be higher for those wishing
credit over an extended term or for those deemed greater risks.
Despite the care and the personal knowledge that businessmen
used, risks were incurred in any extension of credit. Both English
merchants and colonial wholesalers had chronic problems with
delinquent debtors. Repayments were often sporadic and uncertain, and merchants found it difficult to collect from distant
debttors.[2]

The Revolutionary War introduced more uncertainty and risk
in domestic merchandising and largely curtailed foreign commerce. When colonial wholesalers found their sources of supply
disrupted, their lines of credit disturbed, and the domestic
economy uncertain at best, they naturally restricted credit to
retail merchants. Since many of the items handled by both
wholesale and retail merchants were imported, domestic merchants were faced with limited supplies and a booming demand.
In these circumstances, they shortened credit terms and offered
large discounts for cash purchases. After the Revolution, however, wholesale merchants returned to the customary liberal
terms of credit for country storekeepers.

Although the terms of trade were well developed, the extent of
the market had not increased greatly in its geographic scope. The
first census in 1790 revealed that the center of population for the
nearly four million inhabitants of the new nation lay some
twenty-three miles east of Baltimore, Maryland. Despite the fact
that American settlement had been characterized by a westward
migration almost from the establishment of the first permanent
colonies, until after the War of 1812, the bulk of the population
remained crowded along the eastern seaboard, and the great
Mississippi Valley remained largely unsettled and undeveloped.[3]

The decades that followed the end of the War of 1812, particularly after the panic of 1819, witnessed a remarkable burst of expansion and development in American society. By 1860 East and

West Florida had been acquired by treaty, Texas annexed, a war with Mexico won, the Mexican cession secured, and the United States empire completed to the Pacific. In the same period the entire area east of the Mississippi River had been carved into states, and eight states west of the river had been admitted into the Union. The population had increased eightfold from 1790 to 1860, to approximately 31.4 million. Immigration accelerated from approximately 700,000 in the two decades between 1820 and 1840 to over four million between 1840 and 1860. Natural increase remained the main source of population growth throughout the period, however, and as it grew, it shifted westward. By 1860 the center of population lay a few miles east of Chillicothe, Ohio, and there were 160 cities in the United States with a population of more than 2,500 inhabitants as opposed to only 26 in 1820.[4] The disproportionate population growth of the West and its growing urbanization illustrated what some eastern merchants had long realized: the Mississippi Valley represented a large internal domestic market for imported and eastern goods.

The growth of American internal commerce in the period between 1815 and the Civil War resulted from a variety of interrelated factors, of which population and settlement was only one. During the same period, the nation developed a transportation system capable of sustaining that commerce. First roads and turnpikes and later, and far more important, a canal system connected eastern seaports with the western hinterland. By the Civil War a network of railroads covered the United States east of the Mississippi River, transforming the entire area into one large market.

The stimulus to economic development provided by the growing population and expanding transportation network was heightened by technological developments, an expanding foreign trade, a growth of domestic manufacturing, a booming world market for the South's cotton, and the commercialization of agriculture in the Mississippi Valley. Several different indicators revealed the dimensions of this rapid growth in domestic internal commerce. Perhaps the two most significant measurements were the value of westward traffic on the Erie Canal and the value of receipts from the interior at New Orleans. The first increased from about $15 million annually from 1825 to 1830 to a peak of $94 million in 1853. (After that, much of the traffic was carried by railroads.) The second climbed from $15 million in 1821–22 to $185 million in 1860.[5] The leading authority on western and southern merchandising in the antebellum period estimated that the annual western market from eastern whole-salers probably exceeded $15 million before 1840, and the southern market was even larger:

> A contemporary source in 1849 estimated that the South had pur-chased more than $76,000,000 worth of merchandise in New York alone during that year. In 1859 the estimate was $131,000,000. . . . Much of it was purchased in New York City by country and interior storekeepers who made personal trips in order to supervise directly all the stages of acquiring the yearly supply of goods . . . recogni-tion is deserved by the storekeeper for his extension of store credit to farmers and small planters. The latter operated for a full twelve months on provisions, dry goods, and tools furnished on a credit basis from the larger wholesale centers through the channels of the country interior stores.[6]

The same authority noted, moreover, that internal trade uni-versally depended on the credit system, which "was character-ized by the liberality with which it was extended, especially on the part of eastern wholesalers."[7] Prior to the panic of 1837, ex-perienced clerks who obtained letters of introduction from their locality testifying to their general character and ability could secure a stock of merchandise from most eastern wholesale houses. For example, Arthur Tappan and Co. of New York City advertised in southern newspapers in 1829 that it welcomed re-quests for credit from country storekeepers who presented "re-spectable letters" and moreover could introduce such merchants to other New York houses.[8] Before the panic few New York wholesale houses heeded the advice, "It is better to cry over goods than cry after them."[9]

The rapid expansion of the market and volume of trade after 1815 produced subtle but important shifts in the market organi-zation. Since the colonial period, the dominant figure in the domestic market had been the all-purpose merchant. He bought and sold goods of all kinds; he imported and exported; he acted as agent, wholesaler, retailer, individual, and partner. He was a vital factor in the economy. His techniques differed little from those employed by sedentary merchants in the Middle Ages.[10] These merchants were very adaptable to changing economic conditions, with wide knowledge of prices, shipping, insurance, domestic and foreign markets, credit instruments, and sources of capital.

> Equally necessary was a knowledge of the credit standing of commercial correspondents (normally other all-purpose merchants). Business conducted in many places across vast distances had to be based upon faith in one's creditors, for the forceful collection of overdue bills was difficult if not impossible. The merchant's traditional solution to this problem was to restrict his dealings to a network of people known to be trustworthy. Often this group was bound together by ties of kinship or religion.[11]

Until the rapid expansion of the domestic market in the United States these sedentary merchant-capitalists continued to operate substantially as they had since the colonial period. From their headquarters in port cities, they bought and sold a wide variety of products in markets throughout the world. As the market expanded after 1815, many merchants specialized in a function or commodity line.

The increased volume of trade, as well as the constantly expanding geographical area over which trade was conducted, meant that it was impossible for merchants to confine their activities to a network of correspondents about whom they had adequate knowledge to base credit decisions. Generally the merchant-capitalist responded to this challenge in one of two ways. A significant number of those who concentrated on wholesaling became commission merchants and selling agents; rather than taking title to the goods they handled, they bought and sold items for a commission or fee, thereby reducing their needs for operating capital, as well as avoiding the risk of credit dealings with distant and unknown customers. Other merchants moved into the gap between commission merchants, importers, and retailers and became jobbers in one or more specialized lines of commodities. Porter and Livesay in their study of nineteenth-century marketing argued that the jobbers "assumed a prominent role in the American distribution system" after 1815 in such commodities as hardware, groceries, shoes, plumbing and building materials, dry goods, and drugs.[12] Jobbers, handling a wide variety of goods within commodity lines, permitted the small retail merchant from the interior to purchase all of his goods from one source rather than shopping from merchant to merchant. With the advent of auctions in New York City as a major means of disposing of imported and domestic goods, the jobber saved the retail merchant time and money by buying in large lots when the goods were offered at auction, and he also provided the credit that auctioneers could not extend.

In the optimistic and expansionist period following the panic of 1819, commission merchants, wholesalers, jobbers, importers, manufacturers, and retailers freely granted credit to their customers. In the rapidly expanding domestic trade, both in terms of the volume of trade and in the wider geographic area served, merchants, jobbers, manufacturers, and retailers found it impossible to restrict transactions to their old network of customers. The booming economy of the late 1820s and early 1830s persuaded most merchants, when faced with the alternative of granting credit on the basis of inadequate information or losing sales to more liberal competitors, to extend the credit and hope for the best.

The panic of 1837 and the subsequent depression convinced many hard-pressed merchants who survived of the need for more accurate information upon which to base their credit decisions, as well as the need for some mechanism for creditors to collect delinquent accounts from distant debtors.

Even before the panic, a few of the more cautious wholesale merchants had realized the need for more information about credit risks than letters of reference could provide. Lewis Atherton has pointed out that as early as 1806 Robert Whyte, a Nashville lawyer who collected debts for Philadelphia wholesalers, regularly responded to requests from those merchants for information on particular storekeepers in the Nashville area.[13] Some of the larger New York houses undoubtedly followed the same procedure, and a few of them employed traveling salesmen or agents who toured the South and Midwest collecting accounts, securing new customers, and investigating the reliability of old, new, and potential customers. By 1827 a group of New York houses had hired Sheldon P. Church to tour the country collecting information, making reports, and publishing them annually for the benefit of his employers.[14] Unfortunately these early abortive schemes were neither complete, systematic, nor timely in providing credit-reports. Merchants needed information on a regular basis in the spring and fall when country storekeepers normally made their trips to secure supplies for the coming seasons. In addition current information about old customers as well as potential new customers had to be readily available since decisions to advance or deny credit had to be made while the customer was still in the city.

In 1829 Thomas Baring of London's Baring Brothers and Company contracted with Thomas Wren Ward, a retired, wealthy merchant from Boston, to serve as special agent for Baring Brothers and Company in the United States. Baring Brothers was one of a small group of London banking houses active in financing and marketing American bonds. During the boom years of the late 1820s and early 1830s, their American business vastly expanded. Their success as credit brokers depended on the reliability and financial responsibility of their correspondents in the United States. From 1829 to 1853, Ward submitted credit-reports relying on private conversations, inquiries, and travel, on thousands of American businessmen. These ratings were organized and systematized in the "Private Remarks Book." Each firm listed was assigned a number so that both Ward and the London office could correspond without revealing the names of the firms involved. Ward even devised a rating code with which he divided the houses into eleven classifications. Foreign firms were listed as no. 1 without reference to size or character, whereas American houses received ratings from 2 to 11, with each of the categories having specifically agreed upon definitions. The system proved most effective for the Barings, who continued it for over thirty years.[15]

The system utilized by Baring Brothers and Company, the activities of Sheldon Church, and urban merchants' increasing reliance upon lawyers or prominent storekeepers for credit-reports indicated the merchants' growing awareness of the need for timely, systematic, and reliable credit information. Prudent merchants realized that in too many cases, doubtful credit was being freely granted under the existing system, but the general prosperity tended to hamper the adoption of any stringent credit-reporting system.[16]

Traditionally historians have credited Lewis Tappan with establishing the first systematic scheme and organization for credit-reporting. Although Edward Vose stated, "The first mercantile agency in the world was established in the City of New York in 1841," later writers have been more cautious.[17] Generally they have assumed that Tappan's "Mercantile Agency" was the first credit-reporting firm in the United States to embody the unique feature of utilizing attorneys as unpaid correspondents. These country lawyers furnished information on storekeepers in their communities and in return were recommended to subscribers as agents to collect delinquent debts in their locale.[18] In all probability, Tappan copied the plan and organization for his agency directly from the earlier New York credit-reporting agency of Griffen, Cleaveland and Campbell.[19]

In June 1835 Griffen, Cleaveland and Campbell asked William Jessup, a lawyer in Montrose, Pennsylvania, to serve as their correspondent from Susquehanna County. The New York firm claimed that it had already organized the state of New York and was now expanding into the surrounding states. According to the agency's plan, local lawyers, whom it selected, would serve as collecting attorneys for New York merchants who subscribed to the service. The attorneys received fees for their work and were guaranteed that all claims the Agency received would be forwarded to them. In return the local attorneys agreed to furnish the names, residences and business standing of every merchant in their districts who purchased goods in New York. The reports were to be made twice a year, timed to arrive in New York prior to the semi-annual purchasing trips by local merchants. In addition, individual reports were to be submitted whenever the attorney felt changes in the standing of a local merchant warranted it.[20] Griffen, Cleaveland and Campbell claimed over one hundred firms as patrons and confidently predicted that many more would subscribe.[21]

Jessup also received a printed circular from Griffen, Cleaveland and Campbell with confidential instructions for correspondents detailing the kind of information required, providing examples of good and poor credit-reports, and explaining exactly how the scheme was to work. Information for credit decisions, the correspondent was reminded, needed to be specific and based on sound evidence. Essential information included the full name and complete address of the businessman being reported, a history of his firm, and, they hoped, answers to such questions as "Is he a man of fair character and good business habits?" "Was he educated to merchandise?" "What is he worth, and has he able friends?" "Is he engaged in any other business, and if so, what?" "Is he a man of family, and has he ever failed in business?"[22] Correspondents were urged to give the names and addresses of all merchants in their areas, even those too small to journey to New York, because this information too was valuable to subscribers. Old, respected, and wealthy merchants, officers of banks, and sheriffs were cited as the best sources of information.[23]

Jessup was assured that merchants who were not subscribers and had not agreed to assign all debt collection to the Agency's correspondents would have no access to the records. Subscribers could inquire about the standing of any country merchant at the office, but information was never volunteered and was considered confidential. The Agency also assured Jessup that despite the substantial initial effort required of him, subsequent updatings would not be so time-consuming. His reward, they reminded him, would be a monopoly of collection demands in his assigned area and all the subsequent fees, commissions, and charges for collecting and forwarding debts. They assured Jessup, "We have not engaged in this business for any temporary purpose, or for any limited period of time. And we do believe that the enterprise will be highly beneficial to the merchants in this city, and cannot therefore fail to be profitable to our correspondents, as well as ourselves."[24]

In one important respect Griffen, Cleaveland and Campbell's

system differed from that organized some six years later by Lewis Tappan: subscribers to its service received information on any merchant they requested provided he was already included in the appropriate correspondent's report, with the data being current as of the last semi-annual report. If subscribers desired information not in the current files, Griffen, Cleaveland and Campbell forwarded the request to the appropriate attorney, who would make the report at a "reasonable charge" to the subscribers. In the Tappan firm such requests were handled at the agency's expense.[25]

It is clear that Tappan knew of Griffen, Cleaveland and Campbell and that he probably knew its operating procedures. The New York business community during this period was still relatively small, with most establishments clustered in the Lower Manhattan area. Arthur Tappan & Co. fronted on Pearl Street, with its rear entrance on Water Street, just a few doors from Sheldon P. Church's establishment. Lewis Tappan opened his agency at 7 Dorr's Building, at the corner of Hanover and Exchange streets, near his brother Arthur's firm, which was just south of Griffen, Cleaveland and Campbell's location at 44 Wall Street. In such a small business community, it is extremely unlikely that Tappan would not have been familiar with the new credit-reporting firm.

Indeed the first printed circular that Tappan distributed to solicit subscriptions noted, "A few years since a plan was commenced and prosecuted in this city for obtaining information respecting the responsibility of country merchants for the use of merchants here." Tappan suggested that although the plan had not proven successful because of some "errors in the plan or its promotors," nevertheless, he felt that a judicious scheme, "managed so as to have the countenance of legal gentlemen of the first respectability, and respectable merchants in this city would be of great advantage to all interested in it."[26]

Tappan was being a bit unfair in his remarks. The plan he spoke of too closely resembled that of Griffen, Cleaveland and Campbell to have been a coincidence. Edward E. Dunbar, at one time a partner of Lewis Tappan, gave a more balanced assessment of the status of the credit-reporting business prior to Tappan's entry.

1.Dorr's Building, Hanover and Exchange streets, New York, where Lewis Tappan opened the Mercantile Agency. *Courtesy of Dun & Bradstreet, Inc.*

> In June, 1841, Mr. Lewis Tappan commenced the business of the Mercantile Agency in the City of New York. He purchased the books and papers that had been used in the establishment of Messrs. Griffen and Campbell, and was more successful in systematizing the business, and bringing it into general notice, than those who had before engaged in the same enterprise.[27]

No records survive to measure the success or failure of the Griffen, Cleaveland and Campbell firm or to provide an explanation for its demise. Within a short time after it was founded in 1835, Cleaveland withdrew from the firm, which became Griffen and Campbell. The successful operation of a mercantile credit-reporting agency required skills and experience in administration and commerce not ordinarily found in the legal profession. As the originators of the concept of general credit-reporting to the New York mercantile business community and legal profession, the firm undoubtedly encountered much resistance. Their timing was another negative factor. The Agency opened in the boom period just before the panic of 1837, when most New York merchants readily extended credit on the basis of letters of reference from leading citizens of the storekeepers' community. With the onset of the panic and for several years thereafter, merchants were naturally reluctant to spend money on an untried service.

By the time Tappan opened his Agency in 1841, Griffen and Campbell had been in business six years, and much of the novelty of their service had undoubtedly worn off. Economic conditions in the East had improved materially, but memories of the panic remained fresh enough to encourage New York merchants to seek more reliable and systematic information about the financial standing of their customers.

If the time was opportune in 1841 to establish a mercantile credit-rating firm to serve the needs of the New York business community, Lewis Tappan embodied the characteristics and experience essential for successful operation of such an undertaking. Born in Northampton, Massachusetts, in 1788, Lewis Tappan descended from early English settlers in that colony. His father, Benjamin, a one-time goldsmith, operated a modest general store in Northampton and apparently exerted little en-

2. Lewis Tappan, 1788-1873. *Courtesy of Dun & Bradstreet, Inc.*

during influence on his sons. Sarah Homes Tappan, Lewis Tappan's mother, was the dominant force in the family. A strong-willed, intelligent woman, she was a stern but loving mother. She encouraged her children to make the most of their opportunities, to achieve, to be independent—except in matters of religious convictions. An uncompromising, rigidly orthodox Calvinist, Sarah "required the children's loyalty to the family religion, and she pursued them on this topic with a vehemence that betrayed at least a powerful inclination to dominate."[28]

When Lewis and his older brothers, John and Arthur, fell under William Ellery Channing's influence and temporarily embraced Unitarianism, Sarah spent the remainder of her life urging her wayward sons to return immediately to orthodoxy. Shortly after the death of his mother in 1828, Lewis Tappan did so. It was, however, an evangelical orthodoxy, which would lead Lewis and Arthur Tappan to enlist in most of the social reform movements that were sweeping the United States in the second quarter of the nineteenth century.[29]

Not all of the reform movements that the Tappans crusaded for and provided financial support enjoyed popular support. Indeed in 1834 Lewis's home was sacked and his furnishings burned by a mob outraged by his abolitionist activities. While not as violent in its reaction, New York's staid and conservative business community nevertheless generally disapproved of Tappan's involvement in the antislavery movement. Despite the fact that Arthur and Lewis Tappan not only joined and supported unpopular reforms and at a time and in a manner to attract attention to themselves and their activities, no one in the business community doubted their moral character or business integrity. For the founder of a successful mercantile credit-rating agency, a widespread reputation for uncompromising business integrity was essential.

Lewis and Arthur were also widely respected for their business acumen. At the time he launched the Mercantile Agency, Lewis Tappan was an experienced merchant, having established his own business in Boston in 1809, after five years as a clerk in the mercantile firm of Sewall and Salisbury in that city. In August 1827 Lewis liquidated his Boston firm and joined his brother as a partner in Arthur Tappan & Co.[30] Within ten years the firm be-

came one of the largest of the New York mercantile houses, en-
joying a profit of nearly a million and a half dollars during the
period. To offset the loss of southern business, alienated by the
Tappans' abolitionist activities, Arthur Tappan began to extend
long-term credit without increasing his prices to make up for the
bad debts and additional capital requirements. Forced to borrow
money almost daily during the summer of 1836, the firm could
only hope for a large cash inflow in the fall. It never happened.
On May 1, 1837, faced with demands from their creditors and
unable to make collections, the firm announced a general suspension.[31]

Despite staggering debts of over a million dollars, the Tappans' reputation for integrity and ability enabled them to stay in
business. Creditors were pursuaded to accept interest-bearing
notes, which were paid as they matured. Nevertheless, Lewis was
convinced that the firm would never regain its former prosperity
and decided to leave the firm.[32]

On July 20, 1841, the following public notice appeared in the
New York Commercial Advertiser and was repeated through July
31, 1841.

> DISSOLUTION—The co-partnership heretofore existing between
> the subscribers, under the firm of Arthur Tappan & Co. was dissolv-
> ed on the first instant by mutual consent.
>
> New York, July 20, 1841
>
> Arthur Tappan,
> Lewis Tappan,
> Alfred Edwards,
> W. E. Whiting.

> COPARTNERSHIP—The undersigned will continue the business
> under the same firm at the old stand, No. 122 Pearl Street.
>
> Arthur Tappan,
> Alfred Edwards,
> W. E. Whiting.

LEWIS TAPPAN, Mercantile Agency, No. 7 Dorr's Building, corner
of Hanover and Exchange streets, in rear of Merchants' exchange.

This agency has been established with the concurrence of many
experienced merchants in this city and in the country, for the purpose of obtaining, in a proper manner, intelligence of the responsibility of merchants visiting the market from different parts of the
country to purchase goods from time to time—the same to be in-
spected, with proper limitations and restrictions, to such merchants and others as may be disposed to patronize the agency, and
become subscribers thereto. The terms, and the plan and greater
detail, will be made known on application as above. Merchants interested in such sales are respectfully invited to visit the office.[33]

Lewis Tappan never revealed what induced him to launch the
Mercantile Agency as a credit-reporting service in 1841. In his
1916 treatment of the Agency, Edward Vose argued that "the
panic of 1837 . . . not only led directly to the establishment of the
Mercantile Agency, but was largely responsible for its early success."[34] Vose, however, overemphasized both the effect of the
panic and the early success of the Agency. Later interpretations
of Tappan's decision to found the firm, although more modest in
their claims, continued to stress the impact of the panic and the
subsequent collapse of the credit structure.[35] Without entirely
neglecting the role of the panic in Tappan's actions, several other
factors certainly shaped his decision.

No doubt the problems encountered by Arthur Tappan & Co.
encouraged Lewis to study critically the mercantile credit
system, and he may well have contemplated means to improve
it. But Tappan was first and foremost a merchant and thought
primarily in terms of sales. The problem could not be alleviated
simply by avoiding risks. An economy dominated by agriculture
and chronically short of capital depended upon the extension of
credit. The individual merchant who reduced or restricted credit
faced an almost certain loss of sales. With his over thirty years of
experience as an importer and wholesaler, Tappan knew that as
the season progressed, sellers would be increasingly concerned
that they had lost more from good business turned away than
had been saved by bad business declined. Confronted with un-

certainty, the sellers were inclined to take greater risks toward the end of the season. As a merchant, Tappan sought not just the safest credit risks but those with the greatest sales potential within reasonable limits of risk. From his own experience, Tappan must have known that the great value of his proposed credit-reporting agency lay in up-to-date information, which would allow subscribers to seek not just the safest but the most profitable accounts. The Agency was intended to promote as well as protect trade, and to suggest that it was produced primarily by the panic of 1837 is to underestimate Lewis Tappan's experience as a merchant.

Lewis Tappan knew, or should have known, that the system of mercantile credit then being followed throughout the United States had little or nothing to do with the panic of 1837. The best credit-reporting agency and the most stringent mercantile credit probably would not have reduced the onslaught of the panic, although it might have lessened its impact on cautious individual merchants. One authority has noted that the tremendous rate of bankruptcy among country storekeepers during the panic indicated that dishonesty was not the major problem. Wholesalers and country merchants were more the victims than the cause of the depression.[36]

The announcement in the *New York Commercial Advertiser* on July 20, 1841, did not represent a precipitous decision on Lewis Tappan's part. He combined his visionary reform sentiments with hardheaded Yankee practicality. Before publishing his intentions, Tappan estimated the income necessary to meet the expenses involved, devised a rate schedule for prospective subscribers, sought advice from merchants and possible correspondents, and had even begun to solicit subscribers.

On April 19, 1841, Tappan mailed a copy of his prospectus to Seth M. Gates, a congressman from Le Roy, New York. Gates, an antislavery Whig who served in the twenty-sixth and twenty-seventh congresses (1839–43), was an attorney and a former editor of the *Le Roy Gazette*, known to Tappan through their mutual involvement in the antislavery movement. Tappan sought Gates's advice about the broad outlines of his plan for the credit-reporting agency. He told the congressman that a "good collecting attorney" would be selected in each county to report on local merchants who visited New York to purchase goods. The attorney would assess each storekeeper's character, habits, business capacity, and capital, would gather other pertinent information, and would revise his report every six months. In return he would handle all subscribers' debt collections in his district. Tappan assured Gates that there would be several hundred subscribers. Tappan would maintain an office in New York and serve as agent for the attorneys and the subscribers. Information in the reports would be available only to subscribers who pledged to give the corresponding attorneys all their collection business. Finally Tappan asked Gates's advice and solicited his services as a correspondent. The proposal Tappan outlined to Gates closely resembled the earlier Griffen, Cleaveland and Campbell scheme.[37]

On July 7, 1841, armed with a small notebook in which he had written the terms of contract and itemized his budget, Tappan set out to enlist subscribers. Despite collection problems and Tappan's glowing public advertisements, New York merchants strongly resisted Tappan's plan for their salvation.[38] Only eleven firms, including Arthur Tappan & Co., subscribed during the first five months of the operation. In January 1842 Tappan lowered his subscription rates and acquired the files of the defunct Griffen and Campbell firm. In response to this change and perhaps better business prospects, thirty-three new customers subscribed that month.

The rates charged were based on the subscriber's annual sales without reference to the number of his service requests.

Firms with sales of:		annually
	$100,000 or less...	$100
	100,000 to 200,000	150
	200,000 to 350,000	200
	350,000 to 500,000	250
	over 500,000	300

the entire amount payable in advance

Firms with sales of:		annually
	$ 50,000	$ 50
	50,000 to 100,000	100
	100,000 to 125,000	125
	125,000 to 200,000	150
	200,000 to 300,000	200
	300,000 to 400,000	250
	over 400,000	300

Payable: ½ in advance and balance in six months

The agency's initial estimated expenses:

Office	$ 650
Expenses	200
Clerk hire	2500
Office Boy	150
Postage	2000
6 Agents @$1000	6000
Traveling expenses	6000
	17500
Family expenses	3500
	$21000[39]

Tappan's contracts carried an automatic renewal clause, subject to a three-month notice by the merchant that he did not intend to renew. In addition the charges to the subscriber were subject to adjustment; the first year's fee was based on the previous year's sales, and if the current year's sales rose or fell, the charge was adjusted accordingly.

Probably most of the thirty-three signing in January 1842 came in at the minimum $50 rate. Since Tappan did not have a hundred subscribers until August or September 1842, most of whom came in at the minimum $50 rate, he could not have realized even his minimum budget of $9,000 during his first year.[40]

Tappan had promised his subscribers reports on merchants residing in the "States of New York, Ohio, Michigan, Indiana, Illinois, the New England States, New Jersey, parts of Missouri and Pennsylvania, and the Territories of Iowa and Wisconsin."[41] To accomplish this, he immediately began to recruit correspondents in each county in these areas. Tappan preferred attorneys whose only compensation would be their fee charged to subscribers for collections; thus educated and knowledgeable reporters would be employed at no expense to the Agency beyond the postage.

Tappan also employed a few traveling reporters who concentrated primarily on recruiting new correspondents and opening up new territories. Often they assisted new correspondents with their original reports. On rare occasions the traveling agents reported on districts already covered, enabling the New York office to check the correspondents for accuracy and coverage. Tappan claimed that resident reports were both less expensive and more desirable because "the local agent . . . having his eye upon every trader of importance in his county, and noting it down, as it occurs, every circumstance affecting his credit, favorably or unfavorably, becomes better acquainted with his actual condition than any stranger can be."[42]

Tappan assured his subscribers that nearly all of the correspondents were attorneys and that a special effort had been made to enlist only those who were "honest, capable, faithful and prompt." Therefore it was to the merchant's own best interest and vital to the Agency that all claims be turned over to those attorneys for collection. The more business that subscribers entrusted to Agency attorneys, the greater inducement for them to be diligent in their reporting. Finally, Tappan threatened to withhold information from subscribers who did not turn over all claims for collection to the Agency correspondents, reminding them that the survival of the Agency depended on the services of these otherwise unpaid reporters. Tappan contended that "the sum paid to me is a bare remuneration for the heavy expenses of the office in this city, and the great labor bestowed in acting as a medium of communication between subscriber and attorneys."[43]

Despite his efforts, Tappan found it impossible to enforce this last provision of his contract with subscribers. He repeatedly reminded them of the obligation and even inserted a clause in the contract that bound merchants who did not utilize the Agency's corresponding attorney to pay him a fee of five dollars for each claim collected by non-Agency attorneys, plus a small percentage of the amount collected (0.5 percent for the first thousand dollars and 0.25 of the excess of one thousand dollars).[44] These penalties notwithstanding, some merchants continued to place their claims in the hands of customers or acquaintances living in the vicinity of the debtors.[45] By the summer of 1843, Tappan had decided that good sense and persuasion would be more effective with New York merchants than pledges or penalties.[46]

In May and November of each year, the Mercantile Agency provided its corresondents with a printed circular containing instructions for the preparation of their semi-annual reports. Correspondents were required to start complete coverage of their respective counties early in May and again in early November. The May canvass, to be available for the fall trade, had to reach New York by the end of June; the second report was due in late December to be ready for the spring business. The agents were reminded of the need for complete coverage on every revision — a mere "no change" would be unacceptable. After his first report, each correspondent was supplied with a list of merchants he had reported on previously. In addition to the instructions, the pamphlet assured the correspondents of the success of the Agency and of Tappan's efforts to be certain they received all of the collecting business in their county.

Tappan selected his agents with care and evidently made every effort to assure the correspondents that he valued their services. The semi-annual circulars often contained discussions of business conditions or other timely public topics, although none took a position on the question of slavery, and the entire tone of these communications indicated that an established relationship existed between the Agency and the correspondent. The much more impersonal letters sent to bank officials, merchants, postmasters, and professional men occasionally selected for information in special cases were of an entirely different nature.[47]

Correspondents were expected to report local business news, court cases, changes in existing firms, and complete information on new merchants entering business in their area during the months between the semi-annual revisions. Tappan often requested his correspondents to send him occasional copies of their local newspapers so that he might keep posted on business and economic conditions in various parts of the country. He reciprocated by sending the agents copies of the New York papers and occasionally purchased subscriptions for them to magazines or journals.[48]

Tappan urged his correspondents to include in their reports the names of the New York houses where merchants from their counties normally made their purchases. According to Tappan, this information allowed the Agency to supplement the correspondents' reports with opinions and data from trade sources. (One suspects, however, that the sales-minded Tappan was more interested in using the names to solicit subscriptions.[49])

Since the Agency paid postage both ways, correspondents were urged to use folio paper, write on both sides, continue one report after another, and combine reports whenever possible. Tappan complained that carelessness on the part of correspondents increased his postage. "On one occasion I paid a dollar and twenty-five cents on two large sheets mailed together . . . if they had been mailed separately, the postage would have been only fifty cents."[50] Continuous writing on folio paper saved postage but greatly increased labor costs in the New York office; still, labor was cheaper than postage. Nevertheless correspondents were admonished to write clearly, to leave margins on their reports for the use of the clerks, and, most important, to give the full names of the firms on which they reported. The procedures the New York office followed during the first two years are not clear. However, after the first branch office opened in Boston in 1843, the incoming reports were laboriously copied off into large bound volumes and the original reports sent on to Agency branches to be copied. The New York office always received the originals first.[51]

The pattern that Tappan initiated and expanded gradually was to report only on merchants who came to New York to make their purchases in person. In a few years, country merchants utilizing Boston, Philadelphia, and Baltimore markets were added as branches of the Agency opened in these cities in 1843, 1845, and 1846, respectively. By restricting the reporting to country merchants, Tappan confined his service almost entirely to wholesalers and jobbers. Most of his subscribers were dry goods merchants who included hardware, guns and ammunition, shoes, leather goods, and certain items not available in the interior (such as salt and spices) in their stocks. Since country merchants usually used local suppliers for food items, the Agency could not include the wholesale food merchants in the city as potential customers.

The Mercantile Agency did not report on its own subscribers, the wholesalers and importers, until English and European exporters demonstrated an interest in the service and began to ask for reports on customers in this country. Although as early as the mid-1850s the Agency had persuaded a number of banks and insurance firms to subscribe, no attempt was made to serve manufacturers or commission houses whose customers would have been the wholesale firms. When the Agency decided to expand into local city reporting, the service was covered by a separate agreement, and additional full-time staff members were hired to handle the reporting. Tappan undertook some tentative expansions of the service during his management, but the major growth of the Agency's services did not take place until just prior to the Civil War. For the most part, Tappan's vision of the Agency's scope remained limited.[52]

Subscribers, unless one of the few out-of-town clients, received no written reports or information. To obtain information on a customer, the subscriber or his designated "confidential clerk" called at the Agency office, and the information he required was read to him by one of the Agency clerks. Under no circumstances could the subscriber send a messenger for the report. Unless the information was so unfavorable as to be potentially libelous, the subscriber could copy the information as the clerk read it. Each time the subscriber sought information, he signed an inquiry ticket and entered his subscription number. If subsequent reports on the same storekeeper contained important new information, the subscriber received an "invitation ticket" to inquire at the office if interested. Upon presenting the ticket and signing it, the subscriber would be read the new information.

No charge was levied for inquiries, and each subscriber could avail himself of the service as often as he chose. The cost was apportioned to the annual sales of the subscriber, as closely as Tappan could determine that figure, on the theory that the charge was related to the potential needs and not the actual use the subscriber made of the Agency services.

Subscribers were admonished repeatedly to keep all information confidential; indeed, Tappan requested that they not even inform customers that they subscribed to the Agency. Tappan soon discovered that despite all his efforts, subscribers could not keep the information to themselves. Some merchants revealed details of Agency reports to nonsubscribers; others divulged the contents of reports to the country storekeepers themselves. Tappan could only continue to plead and hope that in time the merchants would perceive that their own self-interest required confidentiality. Part of his concern about confidentiality undoubtedly stemmed from wanting all who utilized the information to subscribe, part from his fears of potential libel suits, and a good deal from a desire to protect the identity of his correspondents.[53]

The operation of the Mercantile Agency required superior managerial talent. Tappan had to keep his subscribers and his correspondents satisfied, he had to ensure prompt and accurate reporting, and he had to see that the reports were properly copied and that the subscribers received timely and courteous service. Lewis Tappan was an efficient and capable administrator who apparently enjoyed the work. In 1843 he told a relative that "the M[ercantile] Agency is quite popular here . . . . It checks knavery, & purifies the mercantile art."[54] Indeed Tappan's major biographer claimed that while he enjoyed solving administrative problems and devising a smoothly running, efficient operation, Tappan disliked routine management: "Once he had laid down the patterns, their repetition grew irksome."[55] With the Mercantile Agency the problems were seldom routine and certainly were never-ending.

The success of the Agency encouraged competition, and rival firms sought to exploit the Mercantile Agency's lack of southern coverage. Tappan had decided, perhaps because of his anti-slavery zeal, to make no reports on southern merchants and solicit no subscribers in the South.[56] The decision seriously handicapped the Agency and left it extremely vulnerable to competition.

The rapidity with which competitors sprang up reflected the success of the Mercantile Agency and, perhaps more important, a basic need for its service in the expanding economy. In August 1842, only a year after Tappan started in business, the Commercial Agency began operation. Although Tappan dismissed its proprietors, William A. Woodward and William Coxe Dusenbery, as younger men "in whom I have no great confidence," he was clearly concerned about the threat of the rival agency to his business.[57] Apparently Woodward and Dusenbery copied Tappan's operation exactly and made no innovations or developments in techniques of credit-reporting on their own. They did, however, cover the southern trade.[58]

In the summer of 1844, Warren A. Cleaveland, one of Tappan's employees who had served as manager in Tappan's occasional absences from the Agency, left the employment of the Mercantile Agency after a disagreement with Tappan and immediately established his own credit-reporting firm in the same building. Cleaveland claimed that like the Commercial Agency, he could provide complete coverage of the United States and also correspondence with foreign countries. Not only did Cleaveland adopt Tappan's scheme, he also attempted to utilize many of Tappan's correspondents. The threat of competition spurred Tappan into action.[59]

Lewis Tappan had never conceived of the Mercantile Agency as a national organization—that is, as a single closely knit firm covering the entire nation. When the threat of competition forced him to widen his concept of the Agency, he sought to expand by opening branches in various geographic locations to serve eastern wholesale merchants. In February 1843 he proposed to Edward E. Dunbar, probably through mutual friends in abolitionist societies, that the latter establish a branch of the Mercantile Agency in Boston. Why Tappan chose Boston is not known. Although he had relatives and close friends in the business community in that city, and Boston would allow him to expand without covering the southern markets, it is more likely that he realized that the existing network of correspondents for the New York market would suffice for Boston without significant addition.

In July 1843 Tappan sent a circular to his correspondents announcing that under the name of Edward E. Dunbar & Co., "I have established a Branch of the Mercantile Agency in Boston. . . . Copies of your reports to be sent by me to Boston and the Boston subscribers to send their collecting business to you."[60] Unlike those in New York, Boston subscribers would not be required to pledge to send all their collection claims to Agency attorneys. Tappan and many of his correspondents had already decided that the pledges caused more trouble than they were worth and would soon abandon the requirement in New York. He assured his correspondents that he would continue to do everything possible to encourage merchants to transact their collecting business through the Mercantile Agency, and since the new Boston branch would result in little additional work for the correspondents, they stood only to gain from the expansion.[61]

Under Tappan's management the branches of the Mercantile Agency were more like franchises than parts of a single business firm. Although Tappan usually secured a participating income from the three branch offices established during his proprietorship, he was not a proprietary owner and they operated under entirely different names — Edward E. Dunbar & Co. in Boston, William Goodrich & Co. in Philadelphia, J. D. Pratt & Co. in Baltimore. In Boston, for example, Tappan owned no interest in the office but collected a percentage of the profits as a return for sharing the credit reports. In the relationship between various branches of the Agency, Tappan established a policy that remained constant throughout the nineteenth century. Within its prescribed geographical area, each branch was expected to generate its own income. The interchange with other branches, including the New York office, was both a privilege granted and an obligation imposed. The interchange of information was completely reciprocal and free even to the postage, and there was no provision for striking credit and debit balances among the branches.

The free exchange of reports, while it may have been understandable and equitable in the beginning, became a serious hardship on the smaller western branches in the last half of the century. The arrangement worked no real hardship on any one branch, as long as the branches were confined to the Atlantic seaboard markets, all serving much the same market-jobbers and wholesalers of finished goods, often imported from Europe. In the latter half of the century, the rapid growth of domestic manufacturing and the development of important markets in western cities like Cincinnati, St. Louis, Chicago, and San Francisco created an important manufacturing clientele for the Agency. With these developments, the smaller branches often had vast territories to report and relatively limited sources of revenue. Offices in the larger centers of distribution had ample revenue and comparatively small geographical areas to report.

Within a few months after the Dunbar branch opened in Boston, Tappan's concern about competition from rival agencies led him to suggest that Dunbar consider leaving the Boston branch to join the parent firm in New York. Dunbar demurred, arguing that abandoning the Agency's first branch would damage the entire firm. By the spring of 1844, Dunbar's business had greatly improved, and the Boston office seemed assured of profits that year. Despite the apparently bright future of Dunbar & Co., Tappan's pleas of competitive pressure and advancing age prevailed, and Dunbar joined the New York office as a partner.[62]

Upon his arrival in New York, Dunbar discovered that rival agencies were luring subscribers away from the Agency primarily because of Tappan's refusal to cover the southern states. By the fall of 1844 Dunbar had convinced Tappan of the necessity of expanding into the South. Tappan wrote a friend, "Rival agencies have sprung up and unless we went ahead, we should go astern."[63] Hoping to catch the spring trade, Dunbar, William

Goodrich, and three other Agency reporters left New York for the South in January 1845.

The plan called for the reporters to tour the South to gather information and recruit resident correspondents. They recognized that most southern attorneys would be unwilling to correspond openly with the notorious abolitionist Lewis Tappan, and arrangements were made for correspondence to be addressed to Edward E. Dunbar. However, the local reporters were to be informed that Tappan remained a member of the firm.

Tappan had underestimated the hostility his name would engender in the South. Goodrich and the other agents soon found it nearly impossible to obtain reputable correspondents in many southern communities. Two of the New York reporters quickly gave up the task and returned, disheartened and frightened. Realizing that the Mercantile Agency needed the southern coverage if it was to compete in the credit-reporting business, Tappan suggested that Dunbar "converse with attorneys in your own name, as if the Mercantile Agency were your own."[64]

Dunbar later claimed that Tappan meant to deceive the southern attorneys, a charge Tappan denied. Dunbar apparently insisted on disclosing Tappan's connection, but he did suggest that the reports be addressed to Edward E. Dunbar alone. However, Goodrich and the other agents often failed to divulge Tappan's connection with the Agency.

Discouraged by the reports he received from the agents who returned to New York, Lewis Tappan wrote to Dunbar that the southern coverage seemed necessary and yet appeared impossible to arrange as long as the Tappan name remained connected with the Mercantile Agency. He suggested that either they divide the Agency, with Dunbar taking the southern business and Tappan retaining the northern, while continuing to share an office and clerks, or that Tappan sell his interest to some person agreeable to both parties.[65] Dunbar assured Tappan that prospects were not as gloomy as the returning agents had depicted. In May 1845 Dunbar and the other agents returned to New York after completing a preliminary survey and arranging a correspondence throughout most of the southern and southwestern states in time for the spring trade.[66] Dunbar took charge of the southern business in the New York office and conducted all the correspondence in his own name. Indeed an effort was made to separate Tappan's name from the "Southern Department."

In June 1845 Dunbar and William Goodrich formed a partnership and established a branch of the Mercantile Agency in Philadelphia under the name of William Goodrich & Co. Tappan agreed to relinquish his share in return for a sizable cash settlement. Dunbar would later call Tappan's demand "onerous." According to Tappan, he had allowed the partners to establish a branch of the Mercantile Agency, with access to all the available information, and had also furnished much of the necessary capital for the new firm. The agreement had specified that William Goodrich & Co. and Lewis Tappan & Co. would share all information on an "equal, equitable and reciprocal term."[67] They had also agreed to share the responsibility for securing information and reports from the southern states, with the New York office retaining the eastern and northern territories.

Later in 1845, the aggressive Dunbar approached Tappan with a proposal to establish a branch in Baltimore. Tappan agreed, under the condition that he would be a partner in the venture. But both Dunbar and Goodrich insisted that Tappan's notorious antislavery connections constituted an insurmountable barrier to success in that southern city. Dunbar, whose relations with Tappan had been steadily deteriorating, told Tappan he would be a "dead weight" on the business. Stung by the remark, Tappan agreed to allow William Goodrich & Co. to open the Baltimore branch in return for a large cash payment. Already deeply in debt to Tappan, Dunbar and Goodrich refused his proposition.[68]

On December 31, 1845, while on one of his periodic visits to the Boston branch, Dunbar wrote Tappan that "my candid opinion is, and has been for some time, that the arrangement I made with you in New York would prove foolish and unfortunate for me, and I think you have discernment enough to see that it has been my desire that it should terminate rather than continue."[69] Dunbar argued that Tappan's unpopularity in the South gave rival credit-reporting agencies an unfair edge both in the South and in New York. Apparently he suggested that Tappan sell his interest in the firm to his son-in-law, Hiram Barney, and then continue working on a set salary. Tappan, undoubtedly upset by Dunbar's remarks about his "personal unpopularity," replied that he felt "no special obligations to my partners on this score," adding, "My reputation is a thing upon which I place no value, and I shall never do anything to bolster it up or compensate for its loss."[70] To Dunbar's surprise, Tappan readily agreed to dissolve the partnership.[71]

Relations between the partners, who were unable to settle their affairs amicably, grew steadily worse, and in early 1846 they filed cross-actions in court to dissolve the firm. Both Tappan and Dunbar agreed to arbitration, and on June 8, 1846, the decree was entered effective as of March 1 of that year.

Lewis Tappan emerged from the arbitration a clear victor. In return for a modest cash settlement, he obtained sole possession of the New York office, including the southern department, which Dunbar had conducted under his own name. Most important, except in Boston and Philadelphia where he retained his partnership interest, Dunbar was enjoined from entering or engaging in any business similar to the credit-reporting agency until the original partnership agreement expired in 1849. Dunbar then disposed of his interests in both William Goodrich & Co. in Philadelphia and Edward E. Dunbar & Co. in Boston, published a long, detailed account of the controversy, and left for California.[72]

No doubt Dunbar had grievances, real and imagined. Lewis Tappan could not have been an easy man to get along with, and soon he would retire from the Agency for reasons of age and health. Most important was Dunbar's claim that business had suffered because of Tappan's unpopularity. From a high of about 280 in mid-1844, the subscribers to the New York branch had declined to 170 at the time of dissolution of the partnership. At the same time, the coverage had improved and been extended to include the slave-owning states. In early 1843, prior to the opening of the Boston office, the Agency had approximately 180 correspondents covering New England, the mid-Atlantic states, and the Northwest. By March 1846 New York had over 350 correspondents, Boston 115, and the new Philadelphia office had 212, a total of over 670 reporters with all states covered. Although the coverage and service improved, primarily because of Dunbar's efforts and persistence, income was declining and competition was making inroads in the Agency's business.[73]

During the controversy, William Goodrich and a number of the Agency's employees had supported Dunbar. Even after the settlement Goodrich noted that although he and Dunbar had dissolved their former partnership, he still had "full confidence" in Dunbar. He insisted that the dissolution of the Tappan-Dunbar partnership had terminated all agreements between William Goodrich & Co. and Lewis Tappan & Co. Tappan responded by circulating a letter among all the correspondents in Goodrich's territory inviting them to correspond directly with him or address his son-in-law "Hiram Barney, Esq., Attorney at Law, this city."[74] Previously when competitors had approached his correspondents, Tappan had insisted that they correspond only with the Mercantile Agency. "We shall decline corresponding," Tappan warned the local reporters in 1845, "with any attorney or law firm that sends copies of reports to any agency in New York, Boston, Philadelphia or Baltimore, in which we, or one of us, are not concerned."[75] In June 1846 Tappan assured correspondents that his antislavery views did not harm the Agency:

> Certain malicious persons have circulated reports that it was impossible for me, on account of my opinions on the subject of slavery, to obtain the confidence of merchants here who deal with Southern merchants, or establish and maintain mercantile correspondence with Southern lawyers, as if legal men at the South allowed the private opinioins of a merchant, on any subject, to interfere with matters of business; and as if sagacious merchants at the North did not look mainly at the capacity and general character of those whose agency they desire in the management of their business rather than at their opinions on other subjects. SUCH REPORTS ARE UNFOUNDED.[76]

Goodrich must have known that as long as Tappan controlled the New York Agency, he had the upper hand and that more would be gained by compromise than confrontation. Even Goodrich's claim that the dissolution of Lewis Tappan & Co. changed the status of the relationship between the branches rested on dubious grounds since the arbitrators had specified that the agreements and understandings between the Boston, Philadelphia, and New York firms were still binding. By the end of the year, normal relations had resumed among the various branches, and Tappan had reinstated Jubez Pratt, whom he had fired for supporting Dunbar, and allowed him to establish a Baltimore branch under the name of J. D. Pratt & Co.

The Agency emerged from the disruption caused by the controversy in a strong and competitive position, primarily for two reasons. First, Tappan realized that complete coverage of the southern markets was absolutely necessary, and second, he turned the day-to-day management of the Agency over to Benjamin Douglass, who enjoyed excellent southern mercantile connections. A much younger and more vigorous man, Douglass also had the advantage of residence in the South.[77] It was because of Douglass's popularity and hard work, Tappan admitted, "that my business had increased so much since Dunbar quit."[78]

The New York office subscriptions began to increase again after Douglass's arrival, and by 1851, the Mercantile Agency had easily eclipsed all rival agencies in that city. Most important, regardless of the association with Lewis Tappan, the agency dominated the southern credit-rating business and enjoyed a reputation in the South for accuracy and competence above that of any other credit-rating firm.[79] With the Agency on a solid and profitable basis and an estimated personal income from investments of $15,000 a year, Tappan decided to retire.

Notwithstanding Douglass's characterization of his title from 1846 to 1849 as "clerk," he undoubtedly had an agreement with Tappan that part of his compensation would be a participating share of the profits, which he applied toward the purchase of a one-third ownership in the firm. On May 31, 1849, Lewis Tappan agreed to sell the Agency on the condition that his brother Arthur, who had fallen on hard times, be included as a partner. Douglass, knowing Arthur's "dour personality, crotchety business habits, poor health and growing introspection," agreed only on the condition that he would be an equal partner and that he would have the right to buy Arthur out at a specified later time.[80]

Although he would be drawn back two years later as a defendant in a libel suit, Lewis Tappan's formal connection with the Mercantile Agency ceased. Traditionally evaluations of Tappan's contribution to credit-reporting have stressed the originality of his scheme and his creation of the Mercantile Agency. Actually Tappan borrowed the details of his business from the older Griffen, Cleaveland and Campbell concern, and his Agency was neither the first nor the sole credit-reporting firm in the United States. But Tappan's contribution was that he made the system work. His contribution reflected his character. He grappled with the incredibly numerous details, he developed a workable organization, he infused the entire project with an air of unquestionable integrity, and, most importantly, he persevered.

Perhaps R. G. Dun most clearly indicated Tappan's contribution some years later, except for the novelty of the idea, when he wrote:

> When this office was started 22 years ago its object was novel and embraced what to many were objectionable and unpopular features. It encountered much prejudice and opposition and it was only by a plain unmistakable demonstration of its practical benefits that it overcame these obstacles and became (as it is now) an indispensable adjunct of the credit system.[81]

By the time Lewis Tappan retired from the Mercantile Agency, the concept of credit-reporting agencies, although still facing major legal, political, and public opinion barriers, had won widespread acceptance from the business community that it served. Even the influential *Hunt's Merchants' Magazine* would admit on the tenth anniversary of the founding of the Agency that its former fears and prejudices had been alleviated by the performance of the Mercantile Agency. "Confidence," the article concluded, "is the life of credit, and knowledge is the life of confidence."[82] Tappan's contribution was to provide confidence.

2

Tappan & Douglass, 1849-58

Business, like politics, makes strange bedfellows. When Lewis Tappan sold his brother a half-interest in the Mercantile Agency, Arthur Tappan was in his mid-sixties and in poor health. His firm, Arthur Tappan & Co., after weathering the suspension during the panic of 1837, had been forced into bankruptcy following Lewis's departure from it. Arthur Tappan, having earned and lost a sizable fortune, found himself the rather "shabbily" treated partner in a mercantile firm controlled by younger men.[1] Although Lewis insisted that Arthur be an equal partner in the new firm of Tappan & Douglass, he admitted that his brother never played more than a minor role in the business affairs of the firm. "The weight of the business," he wrote, "falls on Mr. Douglass, who has an iron constitution, and who loves to labor very hard."[2]

Benjamin Douglass possessed in abundance those qualities lacking in his partner. He was only thirty-three years old, he was in superb health, energetic, hardworking, and vigorous, and he was alive with ambition. Despite his youth Douglass had acquired a wide acquaintance and a thorough knowledge of commerce and the merchandising business before he joined Lewis Tappan & Co. in 1846.

Benjamin Douglass was descended from Scottish-Presbyterian settlers in Charles County, Maryland. His father, George, had engaged in the West Indies trade with an older brother Richard. In 1824 the brothers dissolved their partnership, and George moved his family and business from Baltimore to New York, where for more than fifteen years he conducted a commission trade with the West Indies. By the time Benjamin Douglass joined the Mercantile Agency, his father had begun reducing the volume of his mercantile business.

In 1832 George Douglass took Benjamin into business as a partner and reorganized the firm as George Douglass & Co. Like his father, the younger Douglass had a commanding presence. The tall, broad-shouldered, and erect Douglasses were accustomed to being treated with respect. Benjamin Douglass had received more than the usual formal education and shared with his father a deep and lasting intellectual curiosity and a flair for literature. During his years at the Mercantile Agency, for example, Douglass employed a neighboring Jewish rabbi to teach him Hebrew and Arabic, and he became proficient in both languages.

The entire Douglass family was deeply committed to the Presbyterian church. George Douglass's grandfather, James Douglass, had been a distinguished Glasgow minister, and George and Benjamin Douglass shared an interest in religious literature. R. G. Dun, himself of Scottish Presbyterian origins, called them "religious fanatics."[3]

The Douglasses were important and influential merchants in New York, and the Tappans probably knew and appreciated their deep religious convictions; however, they did not share the Douglass's views on slavery and state sovereignty. On a visit to Baltimore during the Civil War, George Douglass took an oath that he would never cut his beard until Maryland's sovereignty had been restored (he died with the beard intact). When his New York minister prayed for a northern victory, the elder Douglass left his church and even talked of leaving the Presbyterian faith, saying the war was "like Cain against his brother."[4] During the war Benjamin Douglass, who shared his father's convictions, wrote letters and pamphlets defending slavery and the South.[5] While Lewis Tappan may have strongly disapproved of Douglass's views, he no doubt valued his wide acquaintances and business experience in the South and West.

In 1838, after several years as a junior partner in his father's firm, Benjamin Douglass opened his own commission house in Charleston, South Carolina, with capital advanced by his father.

3.   Benjamin Douglass, 1816-1900. *Courtesy of Dun & Bradstreet, Inc.*

4. Arthur Tappan, 1786-1865. Although the original photograph or painting was not dated, this is presumably a photograph taken late in life. A
copy appears in Lewis Tappan's book on Arthur, and the autograph on
the photograph evidently was addressed to Lewis. *Courtesy of Oberlin
College.*

Shortly thereafter he moved to New Orleans, where he operated as a cotton factor and commission merchant, buying and selling throughout the Mississippi and Ohio valleys. In his travels in the Mississippi Valley, he acquired experience and knowledge that made him especially valuable to the Mercantile Agency. Perhaps more important, Douglass became convinced that the region had great commercial potential, a vision he would carry into his conduct of the Agency.

On these trips through his trading territory, Douglas became acquainted with the Dun families in Chillicothe, Ohio. Like Douglass, the Duns were Scots, and they attended a local Presbyterian church. George William Dun and his brother John were among the wealthier members of the community and had impressive commercial backgrounds, but Douglass courted and married Elizabeth Dun, whose father, Robert, had been an impoverished storekeeper.

After his marriage in 1842, Douglass returned to New Orleans. However, because of recurring epidemics, especially of yellow fever, he became convinced that the city was not a healthy place in which to raise a family, and in late 1844 he returned to New York. For the next eighteen months, young Douglass's family lived with Benjamin's father while Benjamin looked for a business opportunity. In June 1846 he entered the Mercantile Agency.[6]

Douglass's youth and vigor were valuable assets to the firm, but he brought much more. He was a seasoned merchant whose travels had acquainted him with the vast potential of the interior markets and the opportunities for profits it offered for the Mercantile Agency. Although it would take him eight years to gain full ownership, Douglass quickly became important to the Agency. Lewis Tappan turned all of the Agency's correspondence over to him, and Douglass, who referred modestly to himself as "chief clerk," noted, "I attended generally to the business of the Agency. I had the principal charge."[7]

Within three years, Douglass, utilizing the income from his participating shares of the Agency's profits, had purchased a one-third proprietary interest in the business. On June 1, 1849, Lewis, who held the remaining four-sixths ownership, sold his brother, Arthur, three-sixths for $25,000 and the remaining one-sixth to Douglass for $12,500, making the two equal partners. Both Arthur and Douglass agreed to pay for their respective shares from future profits. Although Douglass paid a higher price for his shares and paid interest on his indebtedness and Arthur did not, he won the right to purchase Arthur's shares at the end of five years for $18,000.

Five years later, having paid in full for his shares, Douglass exercised his option to purchase Arthur's one-half interest. He argued that Arthur had already drawn out more than his half of the profits and therefore was not entitled to the full $18,000 originally agreed upon. After a long negotiation, a lawsuit, and arbitration, Douglass paid Arthur Tappan $12,000 and became the sole owner of the Mercantile Agency.[8]

Douglass entered the Mercantile Agency at a propitious time. The depression of 1837–43, one of the most severe in U.S. history, had run its course. An economic slowdown in 1847–48 quickly ran its course, and by 1849 the economy was riding a wave of expansion, which was to continue uninterrupted, except for the financial panic of 1857, until Douglass left the credit-rating business. The discovery of gold in California, the rapid natural increase in population, immigration, the expanding settlement of the Mississippi Valley, the growing importance of manufacturing in the economy, and the accelerating domestic trade all contributed to this remarkable decade of economic growth.

The U.S. population grew from seventeen million in 1840 to twenty-three million in 1850 and increased more than eight million in the next decade. The natural increase was augmented by more than four million immigrants who poured into the nation in the twenty years following 1840, with immigration reaching its single-year peak of 369,980 in 1850. Perhaps as important as the population increase was its uneven distribution. In the 1840s more than 40 percent of the population growth occurred in the West, and the South and West together accounted for five-sixths of the increase during the decade. Of the more than eight million population growth in the 1850s, the West accounted for more than half; its percentage of the national population increased from about 29 percent in 1840 to nearly 38 percent in 1860.

Americans were also moving into cities. The increase nationally was about 35 percent for the decades of the 1840s and 1850s, but the urban population increased 92 percent in the 1840s and 75 percent during the 1850s. In 1820 there had been only five cities with populations of more than 25,000; twenty years later there were twelve such cities, and by 1860, thirty-five cities had exceeded this size.[9]

Between 1819 and 1859 the nation's real money supply nearly doubled each decade at a time when prices in agriculture, manufacturing, and transportation displayed secular declines. The price declines in the face of an increased money supply reflected the increased demand for money by a growing population and expanding economy and indicated the greatly increased volume of trade.[10] In the 1849–59 decade per capita real income showed the largest increase for any similar period during the nineteenth century, growing from $235 to $296. During this period, trade experienced the largest increase of any sector of the economy.[11]

The expanding volume of trade, the rapid development of the South and West, and the building of a transportation network that significantly extended the market area presented the Mercantile Agency with unusual challenges and opportunities during the decade of Benjamin Douglass's control. Although Douglass did not become sole owner of the Agency until 1854, he exercised effective control during the entire decade after Lewis Tappan's retirement. It was probably fortunate that Douglass, not Tappan, guided the firm during the 1850s. Tappan's view of the Agency had never extended beyond a credit-reporting service for New York City dry goods merchants. Even when branches were organized in other cities, Tappan had been content with arrangements for reciprocal exchange of information and small participating shares of the profits. Douglass, on the other hand, envisioned a national or even international organization, controlled by one person, that provided a variety of services for the business community.

Douglass's first major move after assuming control in 1849 was to expand the Agency's branches in the West and South. With the exception of those in Richmond and Petersburg, Virginia, all of the new branches were wholly owned and controlled by Douglass. In 1855, after William Goodrich's refusal to provide reports on Philadelphia merchants on the grounds that it would be unethical for him to report on subscribers or potential subscribers had led to a lawsuit, Douglass bought full control of the Philadelphia office. By 1857, with the exception of the E. Russell & Co. branch in Boston and J. D. Pratt's Baltimore and Richmond branches, Douglass had attained full ownership and control of the Mercantile Agency operations. Throughout the decade, he centralized his control, hoping to render the Agency a more profitable organization. The New York office reemerged as the dominant or head office, with decision making concentrated in Douglass's hands.[12]

In addition to expanding the geographic coverage of the Mercantile Agency, Douglass broadened the services provided. During the late 1840s and early 1850s, the Agency began to enroll

Table 1

MERCANTILE AGENCY BRANCH OFFICES, 1849-57

1849	Cincinnati	W. B. Pierce & Co.
1850	Louisville	W. B. Pierce & Co.
1850	St. Louis	Charles Barlow & Co.
1851	Charleston, S.C.	B. Douglass & Co.
1851	New Orleans	B. Douglass & Co.
1852	Pittsburgh	B. Douglass & Co.
1852	Richmond, Va.	Pratt & Getty
1854	Chicago	B. Douglass & Co.
1856	Petersburg, Va.	W. F. Getty
1856	Detroit	B. Douglass & Co.
1856	Cleveland	B. Douglass & Co.
1857	Milwaukee	B. Douglass & Co.
1857	London, England	B. Douglass & Co.
1857	Montreal, Canada	B. Douglass & Co.

Source: The Mercantile Agency Directory (Dun & Bradstreet, 1934), file 3, Dun & Bradstreet Archives, New York.

more banks and fire insurance companies as subscribers, and
during the later period manufacturers and commission houses.
Douglass quickly recognized the changes that were occurring in
the economy which made credit information essential to manufacturers and commission merchants, as well as dry goods
houses. Credit data moved between cities other than New York
with increasing frequency. Beginning in July 1851, Douglass insisted that branch office managers report on customers in their
respective districts for the benefit of other offices. This policy
brought protests from the various branch managers that their
customers would resist and resent this inclusion of their financial
status. But Douglass insisted, and he even brought legal action
against William Goodrich when he refused to comply with the instructions.[13]

Although Douglass revised the schedule of prices to accom-
modate subscribers using only the city service, he did not make
the necessary revisions to adjust the charges to different types of
users. The basic principle of the Agency—that the charge to
subscribers should be based on potential need and not actual
use—remained. The problem lay in its application. In 1853
Douglass revised the schedule. He changed the top price of $300
for firms where sales exceeded $400,000 to a sliding scale,
starting with a $50 minimum for those using only the city service
and $75 for both the city and the country. In addition to the mini-
mum charge, a fee of one dollar for each thousand dollars in
sales was levied, based on the previous year's sales. Beginning in
1854, when R. G. Dun became a participating partner, the Agency kept a count of the requests made by individual subscribers.
But no charge was levied against subscribers, and the record appears to have been used only in soliciting renewals, though occasional marginal notes implied that the Agency would "not renew
unless they pay more money."[14] Douglass proved successful in
attracting new clients, but the price schedule remained essentially unchanged.

Douglass's first duties with the Agency had been to conduct
the correspondence with reporting attorneys. The correspondence system was the vital link in the credit-reporting system, and
his responsibilities included organizing and administering it. He

maintained a close personal relationship with the individual reporters, secured replacements when needed, and occasionally visited a region to recruit correspondents or to assist and advise a local reporter. He also served as liaison between correspondents and subscribers. Douglass's semi-annual letters to correspondents were less formal than Tappan's. In addition to the usual warnings about competitors trying to use the Agency's correspondents, Douglass carefully used words like "we," "our association," "our interests," and even "our mutual association," seeking to lead the reporters to identify their interests with those of the Agency.[15]

The Mercantile Agency's routine business communications with correspondents, particularly after 1854, also contained economic news and business information. In November 1852, for instance, the New Orleans office noted in its semi-annual communication that "there has been considerable merchant distress in many parts of the south, in consequence of the shortness of crops for the past two years" and that many of the local merchants feared a "revulsion" in trade.[16] Reporters were urged to be as complete as possible in their information so as to protect the interests of the subscribers. The New York office, for example, in 1852 expressed "gratification" for the "wonderful degree of prosperity which a kind Providence has visited upon our country at large."[17] In May 1854, when soliciting fall reports due on June 1, the Cincinnati office warned the local reporters of the "severe pressure in our money markets . . . . Unless relief comes soon, more or less failures are inevitable."[18] Later that year the Philadelphia office commented on the "unusually disturbed state" of commerce.[19] In May 1855, the Charleston, South Carolina, branch blamed the currently large number of financial embarrassments on "the almost unprecedented drought," which had caused widespread fear that the crops would fail. They warned their reporters that credit had been widely and liberally overextended in that section, that the credit system had "been stretched to its upmost tension," and that "everything depends upon the agricultural interests of the country."[20] All of these predictions and warnings were accompanied by exhortations to the reporters to be unusually complete and careful because of the conditions affecting trade and credit. Although each office mailed its own circulars to correspondents in its district, the semi-annual circulars were approved, as well as printed, by the New York office.[21]

In addition to the economic and business news furnished to correspondents, the Agency collected statistical information on mercantile failures in the United States and Canada.[22] In 1856 the *New York Independent*, in its regular column on commerce and finance, began to publish articles on business failures and supplemented these with weekly summaries of contemporary failures supplied by the Mercantile Agency. The following year *Hunt's Merchants' Magazine* printed a brief summary of business failures for the preceding year. The journal noted that the reports had been "made up at the Mercantile Agency, and we have no doubt are correct. The facilities which that institution has at its command keep it well posted."[23] The article, which noted over 2,700 failures during 1856, undoubtedly encouraged businessmen to subscribe to a service that might keep them informed about such an astounding number of failures.

The January 1858 circular issued by the Agency to its subscribers reported 5,123 failures for the period December 25, 1856, to December 25, 1857, compared with only 2,705 for the previous year. The circular placed the total liabilities of the failures at nearly $300 million and estimated that the loss to creditors would exceed $140 million. The failures were reported by states and major cities and the rate of failures compared to the existing "number of stores." In addition, the failures were classified as "ordinary failures," "swindling and absconding debtors," "not classed dishonest, but will pay little or nothing," and "likely to pay in full." Not only did the Agency supply its subscribers with a statistical analysis of business failures from what was commonly acknowledged to be the most accurate information in the country, it also offered an explanation for the causes of the panic. "We entertain the common opinion, that the officers of four or five of our strongest banks was [sic] the chief cause of the great disasters of the season." The remedy, according to the circular, was a more stringent banking law for the state of New York, where the largest banks were located.[24] Al-

Table 2

B. DOUGLASS & CO.
PROFITS, 1855-59

	New York Subscribers	Profits from Making Collection in New York	Profits from Addressing Circulars	Total Profits
1855	1,181	$ 351.71	$ 370.74	$43,434
1856	1,398	1,610.90	1,451.76	51,552
1857	1,357	2,928.42	609.60	58,269
1858	1,147	4,052.23	1,667,02	14,302
1859	1,195	3,702.15	4,054.87	32,659

Source: Complied from Owen A. Sheffield, "Dun & Bradstreet, Inc.: The Mercantile Agency Since 1841 . . ." (1965), II-4. There is some discrepancy between the figures compiled by R. G. Dun around the close of the Civil War and those later prepared by the accounting department of R. G. Dun & Co. Like Sheffield, I am inclined to accept Dun's earlier figures.

though the format of the annual circulars varied over the next few years, the basic content remained relatively constant. A statistical analysis of failures was compared to those of previous years, followed by a review of business conditions during the period, and occasional calls for legislation or other remedies for what the Agency considered weaknesses or abuses in the economy and business system.

In early 1852, in the same semi-annual circular in which Douglass informed correspondents that Robert Graham Dun was now his confidential clerk, he suggested that for some time the Agency had contemplated establishing collection offices. Douglass assured the reporters that this step was intended to obtain more business for the collecting attorneys and also to protect the confidential relationship between the local correspondent and the Mercantile Agency. In November of the same year the subject of collection offices was again broached to the correspondents. The Agency suggested that it handle all the correspondence concerning claims and solicited the views of the reporters.[25] Evidently their response discouraged Douglass from installing this procedure nationally. Nevertheless Douglass's accounts indicate that no later than 1855, almost as soon as he assumed full ownership, a collection department was established in New York. The decision to operate a collection department within the Agency in New York City reflected a shift in reporting that area from corresponding attorneys to Agency employees. Douglass felt that some debts were rather routine and could be easily collected without the services of an attorney. On the other hand, the reluctance to expand the collection system throughout the Agency revealed the unwillingness of the branch offices to jeopardize their relationship with their reporters.

Not only did the Mercantile Agency broaden its coverage both geographically and by categories of business firms reported, it also increased the services it offered. The greatest innovation was the use of its lists of business firms for direct mail advertising for its subscribers, perhaps the first time this had been done in the United States. Apparently Douglass initiated this service during his first year as sole owner of the Mercantile Agency. His accounts that year showed an income of $370 for addressing circulars, and during the next four years, this income from the New York office increased to over $4,000 (see table 2). The Agency never adopted a uniform procedure for its direct mail service. Each job was contracted separately, and the material to be mailed was delivered in bulk to the Agency. Clerks selected names and addresses from the report books and addressed the material by hand, delivering the addressed material to the post office. R. G. Dun, although he may have suggested this service to Douglass, was not impressed by its results and abandoned the practice after the Civil War.[26]

From the time he joined the Mercantile Agency, Douglass worried about potential competitors. The semi-annual circulars to the corresponding attorneys, although claiming "to speak kindly of parties who set themselves up as our competitors," repeatedly urged, warned, and cajoled the reporters not to deal with competitive firms.[27] In November 1852, for example, the Agency warned reporters that the new and smaller firm of O. R. Potter, formerly W. A. Cleaveland, Esq., was heavily in debt and suggested that local reporters have nothing to do with it.[28] Two years later the Cincinnati office reminded its correspondents that the owner of the Bradstreet Agency was "formerly a retail trader in Cincinnati and failed."[29] In 1855 Douglass explained why he continued to discredit his competitors to corresponding reporters: "The imitation Agencies continue, we find, their importunate applications to our friends. Aware that our correspondents are selected for their high character and business qualifications, they approach the leading members of the Bar under various pretexts and promises . . . . We think it desirable, indeed necessary, to keep the matter before you, so that you may not unwittingly do us injury by helping them to information that they have no other means to procure."[30] Douglass realized that the success of the Mercantile Agency depended on the reliability of its information and the coverage it offered. Soon after assuming full ownership, he informed corresponding attorneys that the Agency insisted on "the right to the exclusive advices of our correspondents, as regards other agencies."[31]

Douglass's major innovations—the expansion of the Agency's service into the West and South, the unification of the various branch offices under his control, and the introduction of collection and direct mail services—had all been designed to forestall possible competition and increase the Agency's profits. His last, and in many ways his most significant, innovation resulted from a drastic drop in profits and was forced on the reluctant Douglass by an aggressive competitor.

In 1855 John M. Bradstreet, who was to prove the Agency's most formidable competitor, moved his headquarters from Cincinnati to New York. No doubt Bradstreet had found it difficult to penetrate the New York market. Because of Douglass's efforts, the Mercantile Agency had provided nationwide coverage and enjoyed an enviable reputation for accuracy in its reports.[32] To succeed, Bradstreet had to find a way to make his credit-rating service more attractive than Douglass's.

The major weakness in the Agency's operation was its inconvenience to subscribers. In theory each subscriber was entitled to unlimited report service once his charge had been fixed by a measure of his total sales. He could, if he chose, check the

5. John M. Bradstreet, 1815-63. *Courtesy of Dun & Bradstreet, Inc.*

rating of each of his customers at any time he wanted. In addition, when an Agency clerk recorded information he deemed important, a ticket went out to each subscriber who had checked the previous report, inviting him to call at the Agency. The problem was that the subscriber or a designated "confidential clerk," not just a messenger, had to call at the Agency for information not always as important as the Agency clerk had thought. Under this system, subscribers did not receive the benefit of the great volume of information flowing into the office on a daily basis.[33]

Recognizing this weakness, Bradstreet filled the gaps in information delivery by means of a reference book. As early as 1852 Bradstreet had supplied his customers with abstracts of reports printed on loose sheets arranged alphabetically according to towns and cities, with the reports given in abbreviated words and codes. Periodically change sheets supplied subscribers with new information, and revisions of complete sheets helped clear up accumulated changes. While Bradstreet's innovation was sound, it proved too cumbersome to attract subscribers. In August 1857 he replaced the looseleaf system with a bound volume, *Bradstreet's Book of Commercial Reports*.

Bradstreet apparently had intended his new publication simply as a bound version of his previous summaries of reports, complete with listing of name, line of business, and a detailed report in code. But at the last minute, he replaced the coded reports in the latter portion of the book with a system of ratings. In subsequent issues, the entire listings of the *Reports* were converted to ratings. The original key to the reports, bound separately in both the 1857 and 1858 volumes, contained a list of phrases that could be inserted into the report by their respective number. For example, Thomas B. Carter & Co., wholesale dealers in dry goods and clothing of Chicago, received a credit listing of "good". By consulting the key, a subscriber could learn that the numerical code 1 6 8 11 14 17 21 25 following the dealer's name stood for: "making money," "economical," "business not too much extended," "does not pay large interest," "good moral character," "credits prudently," and "not sued." Bradstreet's decision to switch to symbolic ratings, which were more vague and generalized than detailed reports, may have been strongly influenced by fears of libel suits.[34]

Certainly Douglass had used the threat of libel suits to explain why the Mercantile Agency would not publish its credit reports. In December 1851 Douglass had served twenty days in jail for contempt of court because he refused to give the court the name of a corresponding attorney.[35] The libel suit of *Beardsley* v. *Tappan* was still pending against the Agency in higher courts when Bradstreet published his first bound volume.[36] Even more important, in late 1854, following lengthy appeals, the courts had awarded two Columbus, Mississippi, firms $5,000 each in a libel suit against S. P. Church & Co. Douglass hastened to inform his correspondents that the case in no way affected the Mercantile Agency because "the peculiar features of these cases, and those which operated against him in the ruling of the Court, were that he *printed* his reports, and *sold them* in book form to Eastern merchants; thus giving information (libelous or otherwise) to the purchasers of the book about men in whom they *had no interest.*"[37] Douglass assured his reporters that his Agency operated in conformity with the law in order to protect the interests of "our friends . . . correspondents and subscribers."[38]

No amount of bluster or ridicule of Bradstreet's *Reports* could lessen their devastating impact on Douglass's profits and their serious threat to the future of the Mercantile Agency. Agency profits, already reduced by the panic of 1857, dropped from $48,269 in 1857 to $14,302 in 1858, the first year of competition from the *Reports*. It lost over two hundred subscribers. True, the New York business community experienced a mild recession in 1858–59, but it is unlikely that it accounted for the sharp reversal of the Agency's fortunes.[39]

Douglass did not act precipitously. He and Dun waited a year and a half before deciding to issue a book of credit-ratings. Exactly how much of the decision was Douglass's and how much Dun's is impossible to determine. As early as April 1858, Douglass considered retiring from the business, and Dun, who had been a participating partner since Douglass had acquired full proprietorship of the firm in 1854, expected to become the principal owner.[40] Actually Douglass and Dun had little choice. If the Mercantile Agency was to survive, they had to meet the challenge posed by Bradstreet's *Reports*. In view of Douglass's strong objections to a reference book and since it appeared in

February 1859, only three months before he formally relin-
quished ownership to R. G. Dun, it seems probable that he agreed
to the preparation of such a book immediately after the terms of
the transfer were arranged.[41]

On February 1, 1859, *The Mercantile Agency's Reference
Books, of the United States and British Provinces: Containing
Ratings of the Principal Wholesale Merchants (Together with
Some Retailers) and Manufacturers for the Year 1859* appeared on
the market. The 519-page volume contained the names of 20,268
rated firms arranged alphabetically by town and state. In addition, an index of towns and cities and a separate index of firms
aided the subscriber in finding entries. The listed firms received a
maximum of three ratings and a summary of these ratings, for the
following reasons:

> We have found three ratings necessary: one for Bankers, one for
> Commission Merchants, and a third for the common benefit of Im-
> porters, Manufacturers and Jobbers. . . . The Banker loans his
> money on interest. Having no other consideration, it should be a
> fundamental principal with him, in all cases to be secure. His
> judgement should be rigid. The Commission Merchant, however,
> has other inducements than that of interest on his capital — he has
> two commissions. His guarantee charge creates a fund out of
> which to meet losses, not, however, sufficient to justify much
> hazard; for which reason his judgement should be highly conser-
> vative. But with the Importer, Manufacturer and jobber, under the
> stimulus of good profits, a larger liberality is expected. Holding
> these views, we have adapted our markings accordingly.[42]

Even more than Bradstreet, Dun and Douglass wished to avoid
factual rating codes, and so the 1859 rating key was strongly symbolic. Almost no personal information about the proprietor of
the firm being reported appeared in the key.[43] Apparently the
key was copied completely from a London credit-reporting firm,
Sedy's (it, in turn, strongly resembled the key found in Lloyd's
Register of Ships). Not only did the Mercantile Agency borrow
the rating key, it also wrote into the contract an indemnity clause
similar to Lloyd's. The contract obligated the subscriber to keep
the book on the designated premises of the firm, in a secure
place, available without notice on the call of the Agency repre-

sentative, and to surrender the book at the end of the year's subscription to the Agency. Not only did the subscriber agree to
keep the book secure, he also pledged to keep the information
confidential. Douglass even equipped the volumes with lock and
key. Clearly he worried about possible violations of the rather
strict interpretation of the law regarding conditions of privileged
communications.[44]

Bradstreet sold his book for $50 for nationwide coverage or
$25 for New York City alone. Since his *Commercial Reports* were
abstracted from his more detailed reports, he made copies of the
full reports available to purchasers without limit or charge. He
also supplied all subscribers with weekly notification sheets containing corrections to the book ratings and in numerical code all
the important and unfavorable items received on each firm. Only
in cases where the information was so unfavorable or its authen-
ticity so questionable as to make publication hazardous were
subscribers instructed to "inquire if interested."[45] Bradstreet's
single fixed price was the opposite of the Mercantile Agency's
philosophy that an equitable differential should be maintained
in respect to subscription prices between large and small firms.

Douglass and Dun priced their book at $200 per year with but
one edition per year. The book covered all of the United States
and part of Canada and in coverage alone was far superior to
Bradstreet's *Commercial Reports*. A notification system kept the
book up to date, and purchasers of the book were not required to
subscribe to the report service. Neither did subscribers to the
general report service have to purchase the *Reference Book*. Although some took both, others dropped the office service and
subscribed only to the book and notification system. Those who
subscribed only to the book had no privilege of going to the office to obtain full reports on firms. On the other hand, the weekly
notification system Douglass and Dun developed to keep subscribers posted on incoming reports required the book to identify
the subject of each item.[46]

In the 1859 issue of the *Reference Book* and in the following
two editions, each page contained a list of firms, and each business was given a number, starting with one. A maximum of forty-
two names appeared on a page. By combining the page and firm
number, readers could identify a particular listing. For example,

Table 3

1859 *REFERENCE BOOK*
KEY TO MARKINGS

A   NO. 1   of long standing; good antecedents; business
               (comparatively) devoid of hazard; ample means
               in, and large wealth out of business; *credit un-*
               limited.

NO. 1   Unquestioned
1½   Strong
2   Good   Taking into view capital; the
2½   Very fair   nature, extent and hazard of busi-
3   Fair   ness; business qualification;
3½   economy with past success & etc.
4   (plus) strengthens; — (minus) weak-
                      ens. Explanation of abbreviations
                      used

D. dissolved   F. Failed.   A. Assigned
              L. Liquidating   S. Suspended

Source: *The Mercantile Agency's Reference Book* (New York, 1859). Note:
          Ratings of 3½ or 4 were undesirable credit reports, and subscribers
          were advised to call at the offices.

S. S. Grant, leather business, was the fifth name on page 466. To a
book subscriber the code 466-5 meant S. S. Grant, an Illinois
leather merchant. Each day the Agency purchased space in a
New York daily newspaper and listed the *Reference Book* code
numbers of the names on which important new information had
been received. The subscriber could check the numbers against
his copy of the book to see if they referred to one of his accounts. If they did, he or his designated clerk could check at the
Agency. Subscribers to the book only were denied this additional
information.[47]

Although this mechanism appeared to work satisfactorily, it
was not as convenient as Bradstreet's weekly change and notifi-

cation sheets. When a Bradstreet customer received his weekly sheet, there was no need to check the numbers to identify a name nor did he have to make a trip to ascertain the nature of the information. The weekly change sheet contained the name, location, and information received on each firm.

Douglass and Dun ridiculed Bradstreet's book and correction sheets, pointing out, correctly, that the Mercantile Agency's *Reference Book* offered a much wider coverage and stressing their Agency's enviable reputation for accuracy. Douglass's income, which had suffered so severely in 1858, did show a marked improvement the following year. Apparently the New York office alone sold over $24,000 worth of the *Reference Books* in the first five months after it appeared.[48]

However, no matter how Douglass and Dun ridiculed Bradstreet's book and his agency, the fact remained that for the first time the Mercantile Agency faced serious, solid, and sustained competition. The excuses the Agency offered for not issuing printed changes did not improve their cumbersome notification system. Douglass and Dun stressed the need to protect themselves and the corresponding attorneys from possible libel suits, claiming that the Agency had by far the better coverage and charging that Bradstreet would pirate the information if the Agency printed the material.

Bradstreet's system gave him the advantage, especially with smaller houses that subscribed only to his book and hence had little opportunity to judge the merits of the two reporting systems in their entirety. Bradstreet's firm grew at the Mercantile Agency's expense, and as it grew, Bradstreet improved the extent and quality of his service.[49] Clearly the situation demanded further adjustments by the Agency.

With its resources and established reputation, the Mercantile Agency probably could have seized the initiative from Bradstreet and totally dominated the credit-reporting business in the United States. In January 1858 the *Banker's Magazine and State Financial Register*, a journal devoted to financial news, claimed that the usefulness of the Agency was "unquestionable. Without it, the credit system, in a country like ours, with vast distances between seller and buyer, would make mercantile pursuits the most uncertain of all."[50] By 1858 Douglass had neither the energy nor the inclination to meet the competition, and his interests had turned elsewhere. He had made large investments in New York real estate and felt that still greater wealth was within his reach in that field without tying himself down as much as details of the Agency's business demanded. He had also realized nearly a $250,000 profit from the Agency. These profits, invested primarily in New York real estate, provided more than enough income to allow him to devote his time and talents to other pursuits. In early 1858 he decided to leave the credit-reporting business, promising his brother-in-law, Robert Graham Dun, who already enjoyed a participating share of the business, the opportunity to purchase the major proprietory interest in the firm.

Douglass actually sold his entire interest in the Agency to Dun. While neither the contract nor any other details of the terms of sale survive, it is safe to assume that since Dun had little or no available funds, Douglass agreed to allow him five years to pay. The price included a fixed "promissory" amount plus a contingent claim against profit during the five-year period June 1, 1859, to May 31, 1864. Although Douglass apparently agreed to extend the payment period, Dun later reminded his brother-in-law, "You sold me the business, 'tis true, but on no more favorable terms than you had offered it to others; and you must acknowledge that by economy—even to the future detriment of the business—and desire to squeeze out all I could for you in the five years profits, you realized largely more than you would have done had it fallen into other hands."[51] In December 1864 Dun wrote his brother, James Angus Dun, "I still owe him [Douglass] about $20,000."[52] Less than a year later, he noted, "I have about paid Mr. Douglass off in full—at all events I can't owe him to exceed a few hundred dollars."[53] Dun calculated the profits for the first six years he owned the Agency at $160,817 after paying himself $15,000 a year "clerk hire."[54] Since Dun had no funds for paying Douglass other than those earned by the Mercantile Agency and since profits for the business accelerated during the latter part of the six-year period, it seems likely that during the five years while Douglass was being paid, profits amounted only to slightly over $100,000.[55]

Although Douglass left the Mercantile Agency at a time when it faced severe competition, some twelve years earlier he had

entered the business when it was in a sharp decline and had reversed the tide, perhaps saving the Agency from failure. Under
his direction the Mercantile Agency again clearly dominated the
field of mercantile credit-rating. Realizing the great economic
growth of the West and South, Douglass expanded the Agency's
coverage to include almost all of the United States and parts of
Canada and the United Kingdom. In addition to credit-reporting,
he experimented with collecting debts directly through the Agency and with providing direct mail services. Most important, anticipating the shift in the American economy from mercantile to
finance capitalism, he expanded the categories of businesses reported to include banks and manufacturers.[56] The Agency
Douglass sold to Dun was vastly improved and expanded from
the one he purchased from Lewis and Arthur Tappan.

In a recent study Glenn Porter noted that one of the dis-
tinguishing characteristics of "giant enterprise" was that whereas
early "mercantile, commercial, and financial enterprises usually
involved only a few partners and a handful of clerks," big business required an elaborate administrative structure "with various
levels of managers making and implementing both long-range
planning for the venture as a whole and the day-to-day operations of its far-flung divisions."[57] During Douglass's tenure, the
Mercantile Agency had taken major steps in the transition from
small to big business. In acquiring the various branch offices,
Douglass began the process of welding the firm into a unified national business. Through periodic inspection tours of the
branches and improved internal communications, he sought to
secure both accountability and uniformity from the branch
managers. All of this is not to argue that in 1858 the Mercantile
Agency represented "giant enterprise," but certainly at a time
when such concerns were relatively rare, it was among the few
national business organizations. Along with the railroads it
pioneered in the art of business administration. For all his innovations Douglass viewed the Mercantile Agency almost entirely as
a source of income and had little desire to build an institution.
R. G. Dun, on the other hand, despite his claims to be in the business for money, proved even more forceful in building a modern
business institution. The transformation from small to big
business, begun by Douglass, was completed by Dun.

A relatively short man, Robert Graham Dun was heavily built with stout sloping shoulders and muscular arms. His receding dark hair and heavy mustache tended to accent his deep-set and penetrating eyes. Despite his rather formidable appearance, Dun possessed a quick wit and a keen and ready sense of humor. Like Douglass, he was descended from Scottish-Presbyterian immigrants.

Dun's father, Robert Dun, was born in 1784 in Kilsyth, Sterlingshire, Scotland, the son of the Reverend James Dun of Kilsyth and the former Elizabeth Graham of Tamraer Castle, Sterlingshire. Although educated to the ministry, Robert Dun refused ordination and became a clerk in a local store. Prior to the American Revolution, Robert Dun's uncle, John Graham, migrated to Virginia and established a prosperous tobacco export business. After the Revolution, Graham, by then a leading Richmond merchant, began to purchase Revolutionary War land warrants. In 1811 he sent his nephew, Walter Dun, who had come to Virginia from Scotland in 1801 to Chillicothe, Ohio, to look after his real estate holdings.

No sooner had Walter Dun arrived in Chillicothe than his brother, Robert, began to chafe about his own life in Scotland, writing to Walter, "I am living and clerking and I might add too discontented and unhappy. Will I never see Virginia?"[2] Soon thereafter Robert informed his brother that he was preparing to join him because "in consequence of the revocation of the British Orders in Council, great shipments are making from this country to New York, & etc., the merchants here not doubting that the differences between the two countries will be made up."[3] When Dun's prediction proved wrong and the captain of his ship deposited him in New London, Canada, rather than risk impoundment in Richmond, Dun informed his brother that he expected the captain to pay for his transportation to Richmond, adding, "I can now say that one of the many things in this world that I am not very fond of is a voyage across the Atlantic."[4]

It was good that Robert Dun simply added Atlantic voyages to a list of things he did not like—the list would grow. In 1816, with $5,000 borrowed from his uncle, John Graham, Robert Dun opened a general merchandise store in Chillicothe, Ohio. Two years later he married Lucy Wortham Angus, the sister of his brother Walter's wife.[5] When Robert opened his store in Chillicothe, a younger brother, George William, joined him with the intention of becoming a partner. The two brothers, although fond of each other, quickly discovered their incompatibility as business colleagues. As George later remarked, "Robert is stiff and confident in his own judgement and more bent upon governing than common partners would like."[6] George then started a woolen import business in Philadelphia with another younger brother, John, who remained in Scotland for several years as the contact man with the mills.[7]

All of the Dun brothers but Robert prospered. In 1833 Walter Dun estimated that the value of his real estate holdings alone exceeded $188,000.[8] While neither John nor George William Dun acquired landed estates as large as Walter did, they were among the wealthiest men in southern Ohio when they retired to Chillicothe in the late 1830's.[9] In 1828 Robert complained that despite his efforts, "my stock has increased just nothing in 5 years."[10] Two years later he noted that John was worth over $25,000, adding, "I wish I could meet with such good luck in Chillicothe."[11] Less than a month before his death in February 1835, Robert Dun wrote his brother Walter still another long letter lamenting his situation and asking for advice and assistance. He concluded, "I should like to be able to live along decently in Chillicothe. . . . But to live as we have done for some time I would rather live in purgatory, for there we would at least have some hope for deliverance."[12] During the whole of his discontented life, Robert Dun remained an unsuccessful small-town storekeeper with grandiose dreams, frustrated all the more because of the success of his uncle and brothers.

Robert Dun's death left his family impoverished. His brothers settled his estate, paid his debts, and assumed responsibility for caring for his family. Walter Dun took the widow and children into his home, but the arrangement quickly proved unsatisfactory. Mrs. Dun then returned to Chillicothe where her brothers-in-law supported her on a annual allowance of $500.[13] Robert Graham Dun, his three sisters, and his brother James thus spent their childhood as poor relations of one of the wealthiest families in southern Ohio.[14] Even though this was apparently a happy arrangement and R. G. Dun remained fond of his uncles and cousins all of his life, there is no doubt that the experience left a lasting impression on him.

The death of his father, on the other hand, seems not to have affected the young Dun seriously, although he was over nine years old at the time. In over forty years of extensive correspondence, Dun never mentioned his father, and his mother only rarely and then in tender but oblique fashion. Although his father had been a business failure and a Unitarian in a community of Calvinists, he had also been among the best educated and well-informed men in the community. During his lifetime his children were well started on their formal education—the local academy for the boys and seminary for the girls—and they were reared in a home that valued books, periodicals, music, and art. While R. G. Dun's formal education may have been cut a little short, in his own home and those of his uncles and friends, he was exposed to a literate and cultured society. Such association with the social elite of the region led R. G. Dun to absorb their manners, bearing, and tastes.[15]

In one way the early death of his father and his mother's impoverishment and dependence upon the Dun family seems to have left a lasting impression on R. G. Dun: he remained unusually close to his immediate family, particularly his sisters and his brother. In spite of his frequent disclaimers that kinship had no effect on his business decisions, he could never bring himself to deny them any reasonable request for assistance. For a number of years he made a place in R. G. Dun & Co. for his younger sister Jane's husband, even though he was obviously not qualified and the salary was secretly charged against Dun's personal account. When Jane remarried after the death of her first husband, Dun employed her second husband, Jay Lugdin, even after Lugdin had provoked Dun on several occasions to the point of exasperation. Dun willingly loaned his brother money, knowing full well that James could never repay the loans. Periodically he would cancel James's debts and indicate his willingness to make further "loans" should they be needed. Dun's deep and continued financial involvement in the Ozark Ironworks, against his better judgment, stemmed from his desire to aid his sister Lucy's husband, William James. When William was forced into bankruptcy, Dun willingly assumed the responsibility of supporting Lucy and her family for the remainder of his life. Throughout his life, Dun enjoyed playing the benevolent patriarch to his brother, sisters, and nephews.

At the age of sixteen, his formal education completed, R. G. Dun became a clerk in the Chillicothe firm of Hospenteller & Turner, the largest general merchandising store in the area. He quickly gained experience in all aspects of merchandising, from sweeping the floor to buying and selling, bookkeeping, and pricing items. In 1847, having reached twenty-one and demonstrated his energy and talents, Dun was elevated to the status of "partner." Since his name never appeared in the firm, it was in all likelihood a participating and not proprietary partnership, with the young Dun sharing in the profits but not in the ownership of the firm. So far his career had followed a familiar western pattern.[16] If he had stayed with Hospenteller & Turner, Dun could have reasonably looked forward to a full partnership or even to owning a general merchandise store.

Perhaps the specter of his unsuccessful father, the urgings of his discontented mother, and his uncles' successes convinced Dun to seek his fortune in other areas. In any event he and his older brother, James, readily accepted the offer of their brother-in-law, Benjamin Douglass, to join the Mercantile Agency. In 1850 they became resident reporters for the Agency in Milwaukee. Impressed by his young brother-in-law's talents, in May 1851 Douglass promoted R. G. Dun to the position of confidential clerk in the New York office. James Angus Dun, bored by the routine of the Agency, disliking the Milwaukee winters, and lured by the prospects of sudden riches, joined the gold rush to California.[17]

R. G. Dun enjoyed a warm and close personal relationship with his brother-in-law. On his arrival in New York, Douglass invited Dun to live in his home. Three years later his sister Elizabeth Dun Douglass died in childbirth, leaving five sons ranging in age from eleven years to nineteen months. Douglass's sister Elizabeth then moved into the home to care for the children and manage the

6. Elizabeth Douglass Dun, 1817-82, first wife of R. G. Dun. Photograph by W. Kurtz, of Paris and Vienna, about 1878. *Original in Ross County Historical Society, Chillicothe, Ohio. Courtesy of Dun & Bradstreet, Inc.*

7. James Angus Dun and R. G. Dun, c. 1870. *Courtesy of the Old Album Collection, James Foundation, St. James, Missouri.*

household. In the fall of 1855, Douglass married Julia Hayes, daughter of the manager of the Chicago office of the Mercantile Agency, and Dun married Elizabeth Douglass.[18]

While Dun remained close to Douglass and valued his advice, he was careful not to allow Douglass to take advantage of their relationship. Late in the summer of 1856, Douglass ordered him home from a short vacation in Saratoga Springs to care for the Douglass children and manage the Agency while Douglass conducted his annual tour of the branch offices. Dun quickly replied that Douglass presumed too much, adding, "I do not conceive your invitation to stay at Ft. Washington, during your expected absence, a very courteous one—to say the least in asking so great a favor."[19] Furthermore, Dun assured Douglass that the latter's concern that Dun might be spending too much money was unwarranted, "as I am principled against any such imputation."[20] To soften his reply, Dun assured Douglass that he would take the letter as an expression of concern and kindness; indeed R. G. Dun could never remain angry with any member of his family.

When Dun purchased the Mercantile Agency in 1859, he had more than nine years of experience in commercial credit-reporting, having served as a resident reporter, confidential clerk, and, during Douglass's frequent absences, as manager of the New York office and coordinator of the affairs of the entire operation. Dun's great strength as a businessman was his extraordinary grasp of and attention to details and his outstanding organizational ability. Neither as bold nor as expansionist as Douglass, Dun was much more methodical and systematic in his management of the Agency. He realized from the beginning that the key to success for the Agency lay in molding the association into a tightly organized and centrally directed business, which would allow him to exploit the individual branch offices for the good of the whole and to take advantage of the Agency's already enviable reputation for honesty and accuracy in credit-reporting.

Although Dun frequently solicited Benjamin Douglass's advice on business matters, especially during the five years that Douglass received a portion of the income as payment for the business, he quickly established his own authority. When he took over the Agency, Dun may have expected some resistance from some of the older and more experienced employees. Perhaps to mollify them but primarily to rationalize the administrative structure of the Agency, he named four—Robert R. Boyd, Charles Barlow, Matthias B. Smith, and William Reilly—as "partners," each with separate areas of responsibility. None participated in profits or owned any shares of the Agency. They were simply salaried employees with no fixed tenure of office, whose compensation of $2,400 per year about equaled that of the managers of larger branch offices.[21]

Robert Boyd, who was honored by inclusion in the firm's name in New York—Dun, Boyd & Co.—served as the New York city manager and took charge of the *Reference Book.* Boyd had been with the firm for some nine years when Dun bought the Agency, and including his name in the firm title undoubtedly was an advantage to Boyd and the firm in handling the New York office and business.

Responsibility for the country business rested with Charles Barlow, a Yorkshireman who had been with the Mercantile Agency since he arrived in the United States in 1844 at the age of nineteen. After working as a copyist and clerk in the New York office, Barlow in 1850 had supervised the opening of a branch office in St. Louis under the name of Chas. Barlow & Co. The branch's name was changed to B. Douglass & Co. two years later, but Barlow continued as manager until 1857, when he returned to the New York office. As country manager Barlow supervised reports from all parts of the country not covered by the New York office, handled all correspondence with reporters, and coordinated all credit-reporting activities outside New York. Keeping the reports flowing and dealing with a virtual army of reporters required uncommon tact and diplomacy, and it was appropriate that Dun referred to Barlow as "my secretary of state."[22]

If Barlow was secretary of state, Matthias Smith was secretary of the treasury. Smith, who was somewhat older than Dun, had been with the Agency for many years. He served as head accountant, auditor, and inspector of the branch offices. Unlike Douglass, Dun seldom toured the branch offices; rather he sent Smith on a yearly tour of them. Smith audited books, offered advice to the branch managers, informed Dun of local developments, and evaluated the managers.

The last of the four, William Reilly, had served as manager of the Cincinnati office before moving to New York, where he devoted his time and efforts to selling Agency subscriptions and reference books.[23]

Even though Dun assured Daniel Webster, the manager of the New Orleans office, that his partners were "mere salaried clerks," he relied heavily on their advice and granted them the necessary authority for their spheres of responsibility.[24] With Boyd supervising the home office, Barlow responsible for country reporting and correspondence, Smith in charge of bookkeeping and auditing the branches, and Reilly handling sales, Dun had taken a major step in rationalizing the administration of Agency business. Moreover the Mercantile Agency's *Reference Book* issued during Douglass's last year had helped restore profits lost after Bradstreet's intrusion into the New York market. Net profits, which had dropped from more than $48,000 in 1857 to $14,302 in 1858, rebounded to more than $30,000 in 1859.[25] Assuming continued improvement in the economy after the brief 1857 panic and recession, Dun undoubtedly expected profits to continue to rise.

Encouraged by the reception of the first volume of the *Reference Book*, Dun quickly turned his attention to producing an expanded second edition. The 1860 edition was improved in two important respects. First, it divided merchants into six groups: shipping and commission; silk, cotton, and woolen goods; boots and shoes; hardware, founders, metals, and house furnishings; booksellers, publishers, and stationers; hats, caps, furs, and straw goods. Subscribers could order each part bound separately or combined in one large volume, Second, Dun ceased including outside markings, or credit-reports, given for banks and lending institutions, arguing that these were "creating confusion."[26] The larger 1860 volume listed some 558 private bankers, a category not included in the first edition. While Dun never separated sales of the reference books in his personal accounting, that item undoubtedly accounted for much of the healthy increase in profits for the year.

Encouraged by the success of the book, Dun planned further improvements in the 1861 volume. Admitting that even under his elaborate classification system many country merchants defied

Table 4

R. G. DUN & CO.
PROFITS, 1859-65

Year	Net Profit, New York	Net Profit, All Branches	Total Net Profit
1859–60	$36,071	$31,151	$67,222
1860–61	11,168	18,608	29,776
1861–62	1,618	6,358	7,971[a]
1862–63	2,024	21,739	23,764
1863–64	(13,146)	16,841	3,695[b]
1864–65	(2,664)	25,744	23,079[b]

[a]*It is probable that low net profits from New York resulted from Dun's deducting $15,000 salary under "clerk hire" although it is not indicated in the originals. Dun nevertheless must have had some arrangement with Douglass to allow a fair salary for his (Dun's) services before figuring "net profits."*
[b]*In both 1863–64 and 1864–65 there is a notation "R.G.D. $15,000" under "clerk hire" in the New York office.*

Source: *R. G. Dun letter book III, reproduced in Owen A. Sheffield, "Dun & Brad-street, Inc.: The Mercantile Agency Since 1841 . . ." (1965), II-5; 20A –20H. These figures should be used with some care since the originals are extremely faded, and in some cases Dun's figures, which he probably prepared as part of the settlement with Benjamin Douglass, appear in-consistent.*

clear classification, Dun dropped the subdivision system. Believ-ing that small traders safely could be rated only by consulting complete records in the appropriate branch offices, he excluded them from the published volumes. "We have," he concluded, "adapted the present work to that class of merchants who grant credit as bankers, money-lenders and wholesale dealers."[27]

Dun revised the rating key into five basic groups: A-1, strong, good, fair, and limited or undesirable. With the exception of A-1, which was reserved for large firms with unlimited credit, each group, by a system of pluses, minuses, and fractions, contained gradations. The new key allowed over fifteen possible ratings as compared to seven under the older scheme.[28] Dun, who had always been more concerned than Douglass about the *Reference Book*, was beginning to modify its form, but he still retained Douglass's awkward notification system and pricing scheme. Before the distribution of the 1861 *Reference Book* had been completed, the economic disruptions of the Civil War had hit the Mercantile Agency with a devastating impact. (See table 4.)

In his annual circular to subscribers in January 1862, Dun discussed business conditions and offered a statistical analysis of business failures during the past year. He also provided an educated commentary on the major events that would probably affect commerce during the coming year. He assured his subscribers that conditions in the North had not been as bad as generally believed. In fact, he pointed out that while in 1861 there had been 5,935 business failures involving an indebtedness of slightly over $178 million in the northern states, the panic of 1857 had produced 4,255 failures with an indebtedness of nearly $266 million.[29] Both years had been abnormal, with the number of failures nearly double the 1858-60 average and their total indebtedness three to four times the annual loss during the same period.[30]

In the 1857 financial panic, banking houses and larger importing and commission firms had been the principal sufferers; the impact of the war, however, had fallen most severely on the smaller jobbers and wholesale houses. For this reason there were more failures but a lower total indebtedness. Moreover, he noted that failures in the southern states during the first four months of 1861 had exceeded a thousand firms with a total loss of $25,578,257, compared to 675 firms with an indebtedness of $25,932,000 for the whole of 1857. The circular suggested that the much higher rate of southern failures during the previous year had been intentional, with the firms depending on secession to allow them to evade their northern debts. Secession and the subsequent annulling of all northern claims by southern states followed by war convinced Dun that the entire southern indebtedness had been swallowed up in the war, "involving a general bankruptcy there."[31]

In response to what he insisted were requests from many leading merchants for reliable statistics on the "*mercantile* indebtedness of the South to Northern merchants," Dun published an analysis, which he and others claimed to be the most accurate available. Southern indebtedness in 1861 amounted to nearly $300 million, with dry goods wholesalers alone holding nearly one-third of the bad debts. New York firms suffered the most severe loss with $159,800,000, followed by Philadelphia, $24,600,000, Baltimore, $19,000,000, and Boston, $7,600,000.[32] It was not surprising, Dun concluded, that there was a high rate of failures among northern wholesalers. After the initial shock, northern business failures in commerce fell to record lows in 1862, especially during the latter months of that year. Dun attributed this dramatic improvement to the abundance of money in the economy and reform in the credit system, which he had previously advocated.[33]

Even before he bought control of the Agency, Dun had consistently warned merchants against the all too common practice of granting extended credits during periods of prosperity. Because of an improved transportation system and an abundant supply of money, Dun suggested that merchants shorten rather than increase the grace period granted debtors. Just as hazardous, he insisted, was the jobbers' practice of carrying country merchants on open accounts rather than demanding notes payable at a specific bank at a specific time. Jobbers in turn had given manufacturers, importers, and commission merchants notes payable on demand, and Dun insisted the entire procedure jeopardized the credit system of the country. In 1864 he noted with satisfaction that the general prosperity in the North, the abundance of money in the economy, and the high demand of goods had for the most part ended these abuses of commercial credit. The war's disruption had produced one substantial benefit. The failure of so many small, poorly financed firms during the first year of the war had left commerce concentrated in "the hands of comparatively few" with ample capital, thus even further reducing business failures.[34] Dun argued that the high demand for goods and the ample currency supply had so restricted credit terms that many country merchants feared that they would no longer be granted credit in New York. While he still recommended prudence and conservative terms, Dun reminded his subscribers that denying proper credit could result only in a loss of business. The message was clear: the wise and prudent merchant would avail himself of the Mercantile Agency's detailed reports until a more stable political climate made the issuance of a new *Reference Book* possible.

More than a year earlier, Dun had pointed out in an annual circular that the many failures and liquidations of small wholesale and commission houses had increased the concentration of domestic trade in the hands of a relatively few larger firms, which had had a marked effect on his own business.[35] Although the subscription price supposedly varied in proportion to the individual subscriber's sales volume during the previous year, the Mercantile Agency, like almost all other nineteenth-century businesses, had engaged in a great deal of bargaining. Dun periodically reviewed the position of subscribers and established minimum prices below which he advised managers not to accept subscriptions, but he usually left the haggling up to the individual managers. In the New York office this task usually fell to Robert Boyd, but with very large customers such as A. T. Stewart, one of the largest merchant houses in the country, Dun personally negotiated renewals. In December 1862 Dun illustrated for A. T. Stewart the effect of "the concentration of business in your hands which had formerly been diffused thro' many smaller Houses" on the operations of the Mercantile Agency. During the previous year the Agency had responded to nearly 10,000 inquiries from A. T. Stewart, more than double those of any former year. The 1861 subscription had cost A. T. Stewart $1,500. Dun pointed out that had the inquiries been "divided among smaller houses whose united business would not have exceeded" A. T. Stewart's, the Agency would have received $20,000 in subscriptions.[36] He argued that the Agency could not accept Stewart's subscription for less than $5,000, but he finally agreed to take $3,000.

While Dun's argument with A. T. Stewart & Co. was character-
istic of good nineteenth-century haggling, it also reflected a major transformation occurring in the American economy. Even
before the war, Dun had recognized the growing dominance of
specialized jobbers in the domestic trade of the United States; in
part the abortive effort in the 1860 *Reference Book* to classify
merchants had been designed to meet the needs of jobbers for
credit information on customers and potential customers in a
more convenient form. The war accelerated both the trend
toward specialized functions and the growth in the size of the
jobbing firm. Not many firms could give better witness to this
transformation than the Mercantile Agency, particularly after
early 1864 when it began to gather statistics on the capital worth
of mercantile houses.[37]

The process of gathering capital worth data cast additional
light on still another related phenomenon in the American
economy: the growth of corporate business. In a circular letter of
instruction to managers on preparing ratings, Dun urged them to
give special attention to the growing number of incorporated
companies. The transformation of the American economy
through increased specialization, the growing concentration of
business, and the growth of corporate enterprise Dun well knew
would force commercial credit-reporting agencies to make substantial modifications in their methods of operation.

While his analysis of business conditions dealt extensively
with the political economy, Dun had no taste for personal involvement in politics, though he found it fascinating to watch.
Early in 1858, in a humorous letter to his brother, James, Dun protested the charge that he lacked "political ardor," noting that
"my name was conspicuous as a *Vice-President* at the Anti-Le-
compton meeting held in this city a few evenings since."[38] True,
he added, he had not attended the meeting; nevertheless, "they
had my name & sympathies with them."[39] James Angus Dun undoubtedly thought it peculiar that his apolitical brother had
openly supported any faction, much less the Anti-Lecomp-
tonites, organized in opposition to the pro-slavery Kansas state
constitution. It would be the last time R. G. Dun would support
any antislavery group.

In a letter written in April 1861, Dun told a Scottish relative that the dreaded war had come. He sympathized with the South, but he blamed both sides for being too "hot headed and hasty in their actions." Business in New York, which had been poor since Lincoln's election, was paralyzed, and Dun added, "My business of course suffers with other mercantile interests, but have never felt the times as much as at present."[40] No doubt the impact of the war on Agency business was a factor in Dun's bitter opposition to the war and the Republican administration. To his uncle John Dun in Ohio, he admitted that the war was "playing the h——l with us all here," adding that it had cut his receipts over a hundred thousand dollars in the past year.[41]

The loss in revenue told only part of the story. All four of the southern branch offices had immediately closed. While Dun had never calculated the profits on the Nashville and Richmond offices under separate accounts, the loss of the New Orleans and Charleston offices deprived the Agency of its fourth and fifth most profitable branches. The loss of revenue from New Orleans and Charleston did not concern Dun nearly as much as the indirect losses caused by secession. Many of Dun's subscribers were wholesale merchants in New York, Philadelphia, Baltimore, Cincinnati, Louisville, Pittsburgh, St. Louis, and other northern cities who sold extensively in the South. The war not only stopped the flow of reports from the South, it also cut off the southern trade, and many of Dun's previous subscribers either failed or found their business so restricted that they dropped their subscriptions.

It would be unfair to attribute Dun's opposition to the war wholly to his economic losses. Soon after Fort Sumter he confided to his cousin Robert George Dun that the war distressed him as a patriot as well as a businessman. Dun argued that until southern independence was granted, "neither you nor I; nor any man living will see peace in our Country again."[42] To his sympathetic relatives in Ohio, Dun cited early southern military victories in support of his contention that the south could never be forced back into the Union, and added a warning not to tell anyone of his views, "for if expressed here would do me much damage—if not quarter me at Fort LaFayette for a while."[43]

Union victories depressed Dun because he believed they would only prolong the struggle by convincing the North that a military victory was possible. "No!" Dun wrote his uncle. "The

Table 5

R. G. DUN & CO.
PROFITS BY BRANCH OFFICES
1859-65

Office	Net Profits (Loss)					
	1859-60	1860-61	1861-62	1862-63	1863-64	1864-65
New York	$36,071	$11,168	$1,618	$2,025	($13,146)	($2,264)
Philadelphia	11,094	7,975	2,798	2,947	2,140	1,829
Pittsburgh	2,405	974	1,133	1,184	1,190	4,257
Chicago	314	1,470	(1,431)	543	22	(1,085)
St. Louis	518	(755)	(2,956)	(2,079)	(2,861)	392
Cincinnati	472	(2,824)	(2,397)	1,418	810	2,529
Louisville	1,858	1,866	(956)	(526)	(180)	(703)
Charleston	2,546	1,354				
New Orleans	3,836					
Detroit	1,482	1,364	828	12	8	1,322
Cleveland	682	819	1,088	1,464	624	1,382
Milwaukee	312	1,085	652	916	1,265	1,275
Montreal	6,483	6,146	4,310	9,954	12,811	9,403
Toronto	207	555	2,519	4,552	3,209	6,698
London	(1,020)	(2,219)	767	1,352	2,083	2,103

Source: R. G. Dun Letter Book, Vol. 3, reproduced in Owen A. Sheffield, "Dun and Bradstreet, Inc.: The Mercantile Agency Since 1841..." (1965), 11-5, 20A-20H. These
figures should be used with some care since the originals are faded and Dun's accounting appears at times inconsistent.

South can only be kept subdued by a standing army of a million
men."[44] The only hope lay with the peace Democrats. In October
1862 Dun congratulated his relatives in Ohio on the "glorious
Democratic victory" in that state, adding that if similar results
could be obtained in New York and other northern states, "the
war will stop even if separation is necessary to accomplish it
& the country will soon become prosperous again."[45]

As the war ground on and Dun helplessly watched his profits
slide, he became still more pessimistic. The North, he felt, was on
the verge of bankruptcy, and he predicted that the South would
win independence and become "the future garden spot of the

continent."[46] Union victories in 1863 simply prolonged the "final result of the war & that is Independence of the South."[47] In March of that year, Dun wrote to his brother-in-law, Senator Zachariah Chandler, soliciting Chandler's views on the future of the country so that Dun might better plan for the Mercantile Agency.[48] When Chandler confidently predicted an early Union victory, Dun wrote Benjamin Douglass that Chandler belonged in a "mad house."[49]

On the question of slavery, Dun explained to his brother, James, that he did not subscribe to Benjamin Douglass's "Divine origin" argument; nevertheless, he added, "It is plain that God intended the Negro to be the servant & slave of the superior race. This is as plain to me as that it is natural for the parent to govern the child; for the mind of the Negro is that of a child when compared with the Caucasian."[50] Still, Dun concluded that regardless of his faith in the South, he was tired of the war and "sick of politics & dont talk it anymore."[51]

In March 1864, in a long letter to his brother, Dun detailed his reasons for supporting the South, basing his argument on states' rights and the right of peaceful secession. Dun argued that the only hope to end the war before "you & I have hoary heads" would be the election of a peace party in the upcoming presidential election. He confidently predicted that "the peace element will be in ascendance by the time the election comes off."[52] The nomination of General George B. McClellan by the Democrats plunged Dun into despair, and he announced that if he voted at all, he would cast his vote for Lincoln. It was not that he liked Lincoln, but rather that he feared McClellan would galvanize and unite the North and might at the same time, by offers of peace, split the South.[53] Still, in December 1864 Dun confided to his brother-in-law, William James, that he had not voted for Lincoln because he had been sure that Lincoln would be elected by an overwhelming majority, and "I concluded not to dirty my hands by casting a vote for him."[54]

After Lincoln's election, Dun fell strangely quiet on the subject of the war. He never mentioned his reaction to the northern victory, except to comment that, unlike some businessmen, he did not expect a great demand for goods from the South, at least not for a year or so, because "the people of the South are not in a condition to buy much—nor will there be a disposition to buy from the Yankees if they could."[55]

Dun's silence did not reflect a change of heart. Rather he found himself increasingly occupied with Agency business and devoting more time and effort to planning for peace when it came. In the middle of the war, Dun had written Benjamin Douglass a long analysis of the Mercantile Agency's declining profits. Despite all his efforts, even cutting expenses so far as to omit reporting work vital to the future, he feared that if the struggle continued much longer, "I don't know what is to become of us."[56] Dun's fears were well founded. Profits for the New York office during the year 1862–63 barely exceeded $2,000, and, while profits from the branch offices exceeded $21,000, over $15,000 of that came from operations in Canada and the United Kingdom. The following year, 1863–64, business reached its nadir. The New York office, which usually accounted for about half the total profits, showed a loss of over $13,000, and total net income amounted to only $3,600.[57] The immediate cause of the precipitous decline of Agency fortunes lay in the demise of the *Reference Book* and the diminishing subscription list, but the major underlying factor was the general disruption of business, especially commerce, during the early years of the war.

R. G. Dun's first years as sole owner of the Mercantile Agency involved much more than simply reducing expenditures and marking time until the war ended and his business could return to normal. In spite of his administrative reorganization of the Agency, with Smith, Barlow, Boyd, and Reilly responsible for different areas, Dun still had to make a wide variety of detailed decisions in the day-to-day business. One problem in particular haunted him during his first years: finding honest, efficient, and talented managers for the branch offices. Matthias Smith's annual inspections provided Dun with better information than Douglass had been able to obtain in his visits. Smith stayed longer, audited the books more systematically, and made the tours more frequently than had Douglass.

Douglass's decision, which Dun continued, to involve the Agency directly in the collection business rather than referring all subscriber collections to corresponding reporters proved a constant source of trouble. For example, in the summer of 1860 during a routine audit of the Cincinnati office, Smith discovered that the manager had diverted nearly $3,000 of the collections to his personal use.[58] Dun immediately removed John Reilly as manager, but because Reilly promised restitution, he was willing to consider retaining him at a minor position elsewhere in the firm. Since Reilly neither made restitution nor showed the proper penitence, Dun instructed Smith to fire him immediately.[59] Even so, Dun declined to prosecute until Reilly made the mistake of joining the rival credit-reporting firm of McKillop & Co. in New York. Dun then told Stephen Gano, who had been appointed manager at Cincinnati, that Reilly was "an ungrateful scoundrel & should not go unpunished."[60] When William Reilly pleaded with Dun not to prosecute his brother because it would destroy their aged parents, Dun relented, but only after William agreed to make the debt good. John Reilly's departure only temporarily solved the Cincinnati problem, however. In January 1862 Dun angrily informed Stephen Gano that he would not tolerate "keeping back money" collected from subscribers as it should be immediately paid over. "You must not," Dun instructed Gano, "under any circumstances, use, even for a day, our client's money."[61]

Gano had violated one of Dun's standing instructions to branch managers, but Dun acknowledged that Gano had used the money to pay current expenses of the office and not for personal needs. In April 1863 during his annual inspection tour, Matthias Smith discovered that over a three-year period, the St. Louis manager had diverted to personal use over $6,000 collected for subscribers. The problem was compounded by the fact that Alfred McKay, the manager, had not entered the collections in his account books, and he had not required receipts from merchants when he had turned over to them money collected on their behalf. As a result, Smith noted, it was almost impossible to determine the exact amount owed to Mercantile subscribers. The news staggered Dun, and he advised Smith to use the utmost care in approaching clients about the status of their accounts, a warning that Smith assured him was not needed. Smith finally settled all claims against the Agency for slightly less than $4,000 and obtained title to some western land owned by McKay, which Smith assured Dun could be sold for enough to cover the loss.[62]

Smith's inspection tours served other purposes vital to the Agency. On his 1863 inspection tour, for example, he remained in Cincinnati for three extra days to help a new manager establish a bookkeeping system and to review local Agency policy. While in St. Louis, Smith had audited the local books, fired McKay and arranged to repay the money that the latter had diverted, and still had found time to "drop into the opposition office" to size up its operations, send Dun his views on general business conditions in the area, and consult with him about a replacement for McKay. Along the way from St. Louis to Chicago, Smith visited a number of corresponding reporters and even collected a subscriber's claim from a local attorney. He next visited Milwaukee, Detroit, and Cleveland before returning to New York. At each office he obtained an annual statement and took notes on any matter that he felt merited discussion with Dun.[63]

Occasionally Smith went far beyond his periodic inspections of branch offices and assumed the management of an office temporarily until Dun could find a replacement. For example, throughout the war, the Philadelphia office suffered from poor management and, finally, in October 1863, Dun relieved the manager and put Smith in charge. Smith audited the books, cancelled the previous manager's power of attorney, and appraised the competition. He found that previous managers had not actively solicited business ("No vigorous canvassing done here for a long time and Bradstreet had the field all to himself") and recommended appointing a vigorous manager who could outdo the rival firms.[64] After consultation with Smith, Dun agreed that M. P. Stacey, who had managed the Charleston, South Carolina, office before the war, had the proper qualifications and personal attributes for the position.[65]

The selection of managers was a major and enduring problem. Stephen Gano, who replaced John Reilly in Cincinnati in 1860, did not measure up to expectations, and Dun removed him after two years. He then offered the job in quick succession to several branch managers before he persuaded the Cleveland manager,

Arthur King, to take the position. After a year Dun told Benjamin Douglass that "King has developed as much talent for the management of the business as any man we have ever tried."[66] Unfortunately not all of Dun's choices proved to be as capable as King. Before he found a replacement for Alfred McKay in St. Louis, he offered the post to at least four candidates, and the Philadelphia office floundered under four different managers in as many years during the Civil War.[67]

Dun bombarded both new and old managers with instructions, suggestions, requests, and questions on a wide variety of topics. In October 1859, shortly after acquiring the Agency, Dun advised the Boston office manager to have a firm talk with an employee and urged that "you take a stiff ground."[68] In 1860 he reminded a young employee that being a manager "gives a young man position & makes him respected and looked up to."[69] In 1861, when he reduced managerial salaries as a wartime necessity, Dun told A. S. Peabody in Philadelphia that he was very disappointed at the latter's reluctance to accept the reduction for "the welfare of the business."[70] He informed William Hall in Montreal that changes in the New York office name—from Dun, Boyd & Co. to R. G. Dun & Co.—need not be a matter of concern since "Mr. Reilly, as is also Mr. Boyd [is] only a salaried partner, having no proprietary interest in the business of the Agency."[71] A month or two later Dun instructed his Detroit manager to push collection and asked about remittances promised in a previous letter.[72] In December of the same year, after taking Stephen Gano of Cincinnati to task for not following instructions on reports and collections, Dun complimented him for his high rate of renewals on subscriptions and reminded him that he welcomed frequent communications from his managers.[73] In any given month Dun's letters to his managers might cover such diverse topics as their own salaries, how much to charge bankers for subscriptions, and how best to arrange their office furniture. Most frequently he urged stronger efforts in soliciting and renewing subscriptions, careful attention to reporting, frugality, prompt remittance of all money collected, and patience until business conditions improved.

Dun scarcely needed to remind his managers of the disastrous impact of the Civil War on the Agency's income. Managerial salaries prior to the general cut in 1861 had ranged from $1,000 to $2,500, with provisions for profit sharing when net income at an office exceeded a specified amount. Dun's emergency reductions during the first year of the war averaged about 20 percent, to a maximum of about $500.[74] When Erastus Wiman, the Toronto office manager, pointed out that income from his branch had risen rather than declined, Dun replied that his business philosophy differed from that of his predecessor: "I have to look upon my business with its branches as a whole and govern my expenses and liberality accordingly."[75] Time and again during the war as other managers cited rising income from their branches in support of their requests for a salary advance, Dun's answer remained the same. His business consisted not of a series of semi-autonomous branches but was one firm doing business in a number of cities, and his decisions would be based on what was best for the whole.

In 1862 Dun again reduced the salaries of his office managers. In July he informed O. A. Hayes, his Chicago manager, that although he appreciated Hayes's spirit in accepting a previous reduction, a further cut, reducing Hayes's salary to $1,500, was now necessary and that similar reductions were in line for the other managers.[76] When Alex Armstrong, the Pittsburgh office manager, whose abilities Dun valued highly, protested at being cut to $1,000, Dun agreed to restore $200 but would go no further even though Armstrong eventually resigned. Dun insisted that business conditions left him no alternative.[77]

By the end of 1862, Dun found it impossible to retain or recruit experienced and capable personnel at the salaries being offered, much less consider any further wage cuts. In July 1863, in an attempt to solve the personnel problems at the Philadelphia office, Dun offered Daniel Webster, the former New Orleans manager, $2,000 per year in salary and 20 percent of all net profits in Philadelphia or a $2,500 salary, whichever proved the larger. Dun assured Webster that he could earn more as manager at Philadelphia than he was making by speculating in New Orleans cotton. Nevertheless Webster declined his offer. Dun finally persuaded William Hall from the Toronto office to take the position for $2,500 yearly and 10 percent of the net profits.[78] Salaries of most other branch managers were increased by $100 to $500, even though the Agency's profits scarcely justified such action.[79] When the financial condition of the Mercantile Agency improved in 1864, Dun negotiated a series of raises with the various branch managers.[80] His liberality was less a burst of generosity than it was a conviction that the branch managers were the key to profitable operations.

Part of Dun's generosity may have stemmed from his decision late in 1863 to reissue the *Reference Book* as quickly as possible. Like most of R. G. Dun's actions that sometimes seemed precipitous, this move had been reached only after prolonged study and discussions with his branch managers and partners. Dun had become convinced that the prosperity, if not the survival, of the Agency depended upon supplying the service to customers that only the *Reference Book* provided. Throughout the war, Dun had assured subscribers and branch managers alike that the *Reference Book* had been suspended only temporarily because of the general disruption of trade and concern that the publication under wartime conditions would fall below previous standards.[81] On January 1, 1864, in his annual circular to subscribers, Dun announced that because of "solicitation" from leading bankers and merchants, the Agency would issue a new volume "gotten up with that reliability and discrimination, our records warrant, and previous issues of the reference book have confirmed."[82]

As usual Dun's announcement to the business community was primarily self-serving. His decision to issue a new book reflected private necessity rather than public demand. In a revealing letter written in September 1863 to Benjamin Douglass, who had opposed the original book and had never changed his mind, Dun analyzed the limitations and advantages. There was no question that issuing a new volume immediately, as some of his branch managers were urging, would be extremely foolish. The reporting and posting of reports had lagged so much during the war that the cost of revising would be prohibitive. Dun worried also that with so many firms selling on restricted credit (cash or at thirty days), they would be tempted to purchase the book in lieu of subscribing to the Agency, thus reducing rather than increasing revenue.

The emergence of large specialized firms that Dun had perceived before the war had been accelerated by wartime. The more comprehensive railroad network in the North encouraged the development of a direct national market for many goods formerly handled by general wholesale or commission houses. The trend was toward a few large firms selling specialized goods directly to large numbers of small retail merchants. The changes in the structure of the market, which would require truly national credit-reporting, convinced Dun that a volume two or three times as large as earlier ones would be necessary if "we undertake to get out a book that will run out Bradstreet & others." Still, Dun acknowledged, there was a growing demand for a new *Reference Book*; "indeed," he told Douglass, "I sometimes think the whole agency bus[iness] must gradually merge into this mode of reporting. It is a galling confession, but I believe Bradstreet is making more money than we."[83] Nothing spurred R. G. Dun into action more than the thought of a rival, especially Bradstreet, making more money than he.

In late November 1863 Dun confided in William Morrison, the manager of the London office, that he had decided to publish a new edition of the *Reference Book* to be issued on July 1 of the following year. The new volume would have to be more "voluminous" than any previous edition and "without such rigid discrimination in the markings."[84] He solicited Morrison's opinions about the new rating scheme, as he did Edward Russell's and Erastus Wiman's, the Boston and Canadian managers. To these managers, whose judgment he valued most, Dun argued that any new volume, because of shifts in the market structure of the American economy, would have to serve not only bankers and commission merchants but also the many jobbers who were beginning to dominate U.S. commerce. No business with a large number of small customers could afford to visit the Dun & Co. offices for each transaction; they would need the information readily at hand. Thus the new book would have to be much more complete and the ratings much simpler. Dun proposed to drop the old triple ratings, which he felt were often inaccurate and confusing, in favor of a simple, clearly understandable rating with relatively few categories. Each firm would receive two

ratings: one for "pecuniary strength" and another for "mercantile credit."[85]

Dun originally proposed to use symbolic letters rather than
numbers to indicate capital worth, with his own name R-G-D-U-N
to be used as a key for five gradations, without publishing the
"estimate we base our markings on; for this would enable our
competitors to post their books in exact accordance with our
own."[86] At the urging of his managers, he finally adopted a key
using numbers for categories of capital worth and estimates of
credit standings. He instructed his managers to pick out eight to
ten businesses from their records, mark each for both capital
worth and credit, and then forward them for review by the head
office together with any suggestions, "to arrive at perfect
uniformity in this respect."[87] Dun's innovation — supplying
estimates of capital worth as well as credit standing — promised
to give his book a decided edge over those of his competitors,
none of whom attempted such estimates.

Table 6

R. G. DUN & CO.,
1864 RATING KEY

	Pecuniary Strength	General Credit
A1 +	$1,000,000 or over	A1 . . . Unlimited
A1	500,000 to 1,000,000	1 . . . High
1	250,000 to 500,000	1½
1½	100,000 to 250,000	
2	50,000 to 100,000	2 . . . Good
2½	25,000 to 50,000	2½
3	10,000 to 25,000	3 . . . Fair
3½	5,000 to 10,000	3½

Source: "Terms of Subscription" for 1864–65 *Reference Book* reproduced in
           Owen A. Sheffield, "Dun & Bradstreet, Inc.: The Mercantile Agency
           Since 1841 . . ." (1965), IV–13, 1C.

Committed to producing a *Reference Book* and convinced that the future of commercial credit-reporting lay in providing this service to subscribers, Dun threw himself into the preparation of the 1864 volume. To a relative in Ohio he apologized for failing to write, explaining that he had not left the office before 10:00 P.M. for the past month and did not expect to for the next six weeks.[88] Dun insisted that the branch office managers closely supervise the preparation of their ratings from information supplied by their corresponding reporters, and he urged them to be specific in their questions to their reporters. He pleaded with his managers in words that bordered on threats to complete their markings in time to meet his publication schedule.[89]

Although Dun had intended to issue the *Reference Book* on July 1, 1864, even the separately printed and bound Canadian section was not ready for delivery until August, and the volumes for the United States were delayed even further. The task of gathering reliable information on the capital worth of nearly 150,000 firms proved more difficult and time-consuming than Dun had predicted. Because of delays in securing ratings in the densely developed East, a separate western states volume was bound. Despite his strenuous efforts, the western and New England volumes did not go to the binder until mid-August, and it was late September before any general volumes were ready for delivery. When completed, the general volume contained credit-ratings for some 123,000 businesses, nearly five times the prewar total, and covered the United States except for the Far West and those parts of the South still in rebellion.[90] Since the Far West was not in the marketing area of most of his subscribers, Dun had not yet expanded the books to cover that region. He planned to issue at least a thousand copies, but by December only five hundred had been bound. On January 12, 1865, he informed the Philadelphia manager that he had run out of books and would have to go to press again. "The books we are now binding," Dun noted, "will be marked for 1865."[91]

Dun's prediction that the *Reference Book* would yield $20,000 profit on its first printing proved correct; his net income increased from approximately $3,600 in 1863–64 to more than $23,000 in 1864–65.[92] Part of the increase may have resulted from improved business conditions, but Dun attributed most of it to the new book. Still he admitted that in the rush to finish the volume, its accuracy and completeness suffered. Two complete trades in New York City had been omitted, and the city list had to be completely revised before the next printing. In January 1865 Dun published what was purported to be a new *Reference Book* for that year. Although it did contain the new city ratings and a few revisions completed by managers from their autumn correspondents' reports, this edition proved to be substantially the same as the earlier volume.[93]

Conceding that the July 1864 *Reference Book* had been rushed, incomplete, and all too often inaccurate and that the January 1865 edition represented little more than minor patchwork corrections of the previous deficiencies, Dun announced plans to issue a completely new volume for July 1865. The decision was affected by two separate but related factors. First, the Agency had traditionally revised its reports twice a year, and the shift to the *Reference Book* as the major vehicle for delivering this information to subscribers necessitated semi-annual revisions. Second, the tremendous growth in the number of firms being reported and the rapid acceleration of business transactions made it practically impossible to post changes to the book on a piecemeal basis for extended periods.

Dun's decision had important immediate consequences: it established a semi-annual schedule for the books, and although Dun encountered no serious delays in preparing copy for the new volume, the printers and binders again fell behind schedule, delaying delivery for more than a month and seriously hurting sales.[94] Most of this delay was attributable to the printer's lack of facilities to keep the book set in type between issues. To rectify this situation Dun decided that the Agency should do its own typesetting on a nearly current basis. By spending $15,000 on type and equipment, Dun was able to keep the type permanently set in the New York office. Changes and additions were posted currently so that new editions could be published with a minimum of delay.[95] In committing so much of his relatively meager capital in this, Dun demonstrated his conviction that the *Reference Book* was not merely an adjunct to the Mercantile Agency credit-reporting system but that it constituted the central and vital part of the business.

The growth in the size of the market, the development of large firms doing a high-volume business throughout that market, and the accelerating pace of business transactions, all trends in the American economy that Dun had correctly foreseen, necessitated changes in the techniques of providing credit information. Firms such as A. T. Stewart, selling to a multitude of small buyers, found it impossible to resort to the Agency offices for information on every credit transaction and demanded reliable information in a convenient package. The *Reference Book* met that need.

Perhaps even more important, although not so obvious, was the transformation from credit-reporting to credit-rating that Dun introduced in the 1864 *Reference Book*. The previous reports, available at the Agency offices, had been highly impressionistic, with emphasis placed on the character and moral habits of the businessman being reported. With information and reports coming from a wide variety of corresponding reporters, uniformity in language and credit estimates proved extremely difficult, if not impossible, to obtain. For this reason subscribers found themselves unable to make valid comparisons among applicants for credit or to establish meaningful guidelines for their employees to follow in granting credit. For firms doing business from a number of locations, as was increasingly true in the period, the ability to make general rules and regulations became vital to the conduct of their businesses. Dun's innovation in the 1864 *Reference Book* — the inclusion of capital worth as well as general credit ratings — transformed credit-reporting to credit-rating and allowed subscribers to make comparisons between firms and to adopt uniform rules and regulations on granting credit.

The increase in the emphasis upon the *Reference Book* in the Agency's overall operations forced Dun to modify the notification system and revise his basic pricing system. He reversed the Agency's previous policy by selling the book and reports as a package. Unlike the previous volumes, which had been sold separately for $200 cash, the 1864 edition could be purchased only by subscribers to the Agency. Dun instructed his managers never to sell the book to nonsubscribers, adding, "Our minimum rate of subscription with the privilege of the book will be one hundred dollars p.a. [per annum]."[96] Smaller concerns that did not want or could not afford the book could continue their subscriptions at the previous price. Although he later retreated slightly and sold the book separately to bankers and insurance companies who were mainly interested in the estimates of capital worth, Dun insisted that the *Reference Book* was intended not to replace the detailed reports but to serve as an auxiliary or convenience to larger houses, which could easily afford to pay for the entire service. Packaging the reports and the *Reference Book* allowed him to simplify the cumbersome notifications system used prior to the war. Dun decided to print a weekly notification sheet, which listed the names and location of firms on whom important and/or unfavorable information had been received. In some few cases where a rating change had been made, the new rating would be given. Since the merchants, manufacturers, and jobbers who purchased the *Reference Book* were also subscribers, those interested in firms listed on the notification sheet could call at the office to ascertain the details of the information. When Erastus Wiman proposed to print a much more detailed notification sheet for his Canadian subscribers, Dun objected: "The Book is not intended to be a complete thing disconnected from use of office."[97] When Wiman persisted, Dun replied that in justice to the Agency, Wiman must act on the instructions Dun had issued to managers.[98] Dun's insistence on keeping the notification sheet closely connected with the office and selling only to subscribers was a reaction to the changing structure of the American market.

Dun believed that the trend toward large firms selling to numerous buyers over an extended geographic area and often from multiple locations was certain to accelerate in the postwar period, creating a market for reliable credit information in a usable form for the entire national market. Manufacturers would become increasingly important as subscribers, dealing in larger transactions and needing fewer but more detailed reports on the credit-standing and net worth of customers. Dun felt confident that the combination of the written reports available at the Agency offices and the new *Reference Book* would enable his firm to "completely blot out every other work of the kind and have the field to ourselves."[99]

the Records of the Agency." Both the *Tribune* and the *Journal* offered particular praise of the ratings of capital worth in the *Reference Book*, which, coupled with the accuracy and completeness of the volume, the *Journal* concluded provided the subscriber "a succinct statement of capital employed in the various branches of trade, and of the general condition of mercantile credit, also showing at a glance the relative commercial importance of towns and cities."[5] What the business press failed to note was that the Mercantile Agency under Dun's direction not only reported on commercial credit; it also influenced the direction and volume of that credit.

Almost from its inception in 1858, the Agency's annual circular on business failures during the preceding year was widely accepted as the most authoritative statistical summary of business failures available. E. C. Kirkland has noted, "Since business downswings were also periods of liquidations, observers brooded over the figures of business failures, obligingly provided by a firm in which, no matter how titled, the name of Dun always appeared. Though quarterly and annual compilations did not include railroad or bank failures, Dun's reports were a significant measure of the mortality among American commercial and industrial enterprises."[6] Under Dun's management, the annual circular became less a simple statistical analysis and more a general commentary of economic and business conditions.

Even after the Civil War when the New York office assumed the responsibility for editing and printing all the circulars and headlined the reports with an analysis of the national economy, the circulars retained local information and data primarily of concern to subscribers outside New York. Each year Dun contributed an analysis of national economic trends. In 1865, for example, he noted that while the year had been one "of remarkable prosperity in all commercial pursuits," the good times were due largely to the "debt of the Government to the people" and hence must certainly be regarded as "an inflation." He also warned his subscribers that while the 530 failures in the northern states for 1865 had exceeded those of the previous year by only twenty, the total liabilities involved had jumped from slightly over $8.5 million to over $17.6 million. Dun attributed this rise to the high percentage of failures in urban areas where firms tended to be large, and to "reckless speculation" by a number of large business firms. Despite the inflation, Dun believed that if businessmen would exercise prudence, the outlook would remain bright.

Although Dun had always used his annual circular to explain abnormal fluctuations in the rate of business failures, before 1866 he had seldom offered advice or predicted the future performance of the economy. Even after the Civil War, most of his advice concerned commercial credit and factors relating to the granting of credit. He based his optimistic postwar predictions on the high world price for cotton, the increased immigration, and the natural economic development of the country. Never one to lose an opportunity to advertise the Agency, Dun concluded the 1865 annual circular by noting that in the United States, credit "is an essential." While both the amount and length of time for which credit should be extended should be conservative in periods of inflation, which might end suddenly, Dun felt that "men of character, of capital, of capacity, should be entrusted with confidence, and every means of obtaining information regarding them made available."[7]

In the 1867 circular, Dun argued that in spite of the increase in both the number and liabilities of failures, the business community could congratulate itself that during the previous year "no great calamity has befallen us." Dun thought that business was anticipating a severe crisis as a result of the suspension of specie payments and inflation. Noting that manufacturers, importers, and jobbers had experienced reduced profit margins during the previous year and had also been left with greatly expanded inventories, Dun deplored the dangerous tendency to expedite sales by granting too much credit. If merchants would be cautious in granting credit, manufacturers would keep in mind probable demand, and the Congress would "persist in the steady curtailment of the redundant currency," then Dun could see no reason for "any great catastrophe" during the coming year. "An opposite policy," he warned, "will hardly fail to precipitate a crisis which many expect, and all dread."[8]

It is impossible to measure the effect of Dun's advice to be conservative in granting credit on the credit market. Certainly the opinions of the most prestigious credit-rating and reporting firm in the country must have influenced manufacturers, importers, jobbers, and other commercial creditors considerably. When no crisis materialized, Dun's conservative advice became less urgent and then slackened. Unfortunately for his reputation as an economic forecaster, Dun failed to anticipate the panic of 1873, and he could only comment to his subscribers that *"when the financial skies are least overcast, danger is at hand."*[9] The unexpectedness of the panic notwithstanding, Dun's statistics on business failures, his review of the performance of the economy during the previous year, and his cautious predictions continued to be the most authoritative information available and to exert considerable influence on commercial credit.

With the rapid postwar expansion into the trans-Mississippi West, credit-reporting agencies such as R. G. Dun & Co. fulfilled a vital function in the economy by providing the necessary information for creditors to make decisions on commercial transactions in a vast, varied, and often remote region. Of particular significance was the flow of credit from older, more established sections to the newer, more remote, and less well-developed regions of the country. In providing accurate and up-to-date information, R. G. Dun, and to a lesser extent other credit-reporting firms, lessened the reluctance of eastern investors to extend credit in the more remote and less developed areas. While the agencies could not augment the available capital resources, they did accelerate the flow of credit. R. G. Dun repeatedly emphasized the vital role of credit in American economic growth. He insisted that honest merchants had nothing to fear and everything to gain by supplying the Agency with sufficient data to enable creditors to make rational decisions. Credit-reporting agencies made credit easier to obtain for those who deserved it.[10]

Not only did R. G. Dun & Co. facilitate the flow of capital, but in a subtle and yet pervasive manner Dun's credit-ratings hastened the growing dominance of corporate and large firms in the American economy. The rating keys provided the much-praised instrument through which the Agency influenced credit flows to larger firms. Its only major rival, Bradstreet's, did not offer estimates of "pecuniary strength" or capital worth. In the *Reference Book* Dun claimed that "no absolute connection" existed between the left-hand column, which indicated pecuniary strength, and the right-hand column, which rated the general credit of the firm.[11] Theoretically it was possible for a firm with an AI+ ($1 million or over) capital worth to receive only a 3 or 3.5 (fair) general credit, and for a firm receiving only a 4 ($2,000–$5,000) pecuniary strength rating to have AI (unlimited) general credit. In fact, from the beginning a high correlation existed between the markings in the two categories. Indeed in the spring of 1866, Dun even instructed his branch office managers that markings assigned should exhibit a high correlation. "A number of very absurd ratings were sent by offices last time," he complained, "indicating a great lack of uniformity, and the need for more correct ideas."[12]

Dun argued that too many 3-1.5 or 2-A1 markings were being received by the New York office. "This should rarely occur," he warned. "There should be a constant effort to keep the credit marking in close relation to the capital marking."[13] Dun instructed his managers never to assign a firm with a capital worth of 2.5 ($25,000–$50,000) a credit rating of 2 (good) or a business with a capital of only $100,000 an AI (unlimited) rating. Part of the problem, Dun suggested, stemmed from the practice of allowing local correspondents to suggest ratings:

> It should always be borne in mind that they [local correspondents] have a very meagre understanding of the Key and are apt to think the men in their locality quite entitled to the highest markings they give them relative to each other, not relative to the rest of the world; thus a good trader worth $40,000, they will not hesitate to call AI, forgetting that this is the only marking we can give A. T. Stewart & Co., who is worth half as many millions.[14]

The solution was to keep in mind the difference between local and national standards of credit and for managers to tone down their markings to conform with those of the New York office.

These instructions tended to award higher general credit-ratings to the larger firms. However much he might occasionally remind subscribers that it was good business to extend credit to smaller firms that received ratings of "good" or even "fair," keeping in mind the capital worth as an indication of the capacity of the business, Dun's insistence upon tying the two ratings together undoubtedly militated against the smaller concerns.

The impact of the widely accepted rating key, together with Dun's instructions for managers to rate corporations separately from the personal management of the firms, had significant repercussions. By divorcing the moral character of the managers of corporations from estimates of the firms' capital worth and general credit standing, Dun helped to reduce the bias among creditors against corporations. Most important, the use of the rating key meant that larger firms would be more attractive to creditors, often to the point that they could obtain disproportionately higher credit at more favorable terms. The indirect effect was to accelerate the growth of large corporate firms in the American economy.

Although R. G. Dun undoubtedly knew and thought as much about credit and credit-rating as any other person in the period, it appears that he did not fully understand the reciprocal relationship between his firm and the flow of credit in the American economy. In the decade following the Civil War, Dun found himself occupied with other matters: the details of the *Reference Book,* geographic expansion of the Agency to match the needs of the economy, administrative reorganization of the business, efforts to consolidate the Mercantile Agency's leadership against increasingly aggressive rivals, and the multitude of routine problems associated with managing a national business. Thus he had little time, even if he had been so inclined, to discuss the impact of the Agency on American economic development.

On the heels of the triumphant debut of the 1866 *Reference Book,* Dun found himself faced with an administrative crisis. The resignation of William Reilly soon after his brother had been fired for irregularities in the Cincinnati office meant that the burden of administrative details fell on Robert R. Boyd and Charles Barlow, with Matthias Smith spending considerably more time auditing and supervising the branch offices. In June 1865, showing the strains of overwork, Boyd had threatened to resign, complaining, "I have been with the Agency 15 years and am no better off than when I entered."[15] Reminding Dun that he had been absent only one day in two years, Boyd informed his employer that he was going to the country to "recoup my health," which he implied had been injured by overwork on the *Reference Book*. During the next month while Boyd recovered his strength, Dun dickered with him over salary. In July Dun made a final offer to his errant partner, warning him that in case he refused the offer, "I have in view a party to fill your place." Dun admitted, however, "I don't like the looks of a strange face in the place where I am so accustomed to see your familiar one—nor do I like parting with old friends."[16] He offered Boyd a salary of four thousand dollars a year and, most important, broke precedent by also offering him a participating share of the profits. Previously Dun had steadfastly refused to consider his partners anything but salaried clerks.

Two weeks later, after learning that Boyd had made overtures to another credit-rating agency, Dun withdrew his offer, claiming that it had been made "more from personal considerations to you than from benefits I expected to derive from your influence or services."[17] Dun's outrage at Boyd for going over to a rival could not conceal the fact that he had lost a valued and trusted administrator because of his niggardly attitude toward his staff. Moreover, he knew that he must immediately replace Boyd.

Dun needed someone to take charge of the time-consuming and tedious job of preparing the *Reference Book* and managing the all-important New York office—the "city department." Matthias Smith, although trustworthy and experienced, was too valuable as an accountant at the headquarters and as an auditor of the branches, in addition to being too old in Dun's opinion to be shifted into Boyd's position. On the other hand, Charles Barlow, who would continue as Dun's senior partner during his lifetime, excelled as a manager who thrived on routine and systematic details and tended to shun innovation. Barlow's long acquaintance with corresponding reporters and his success in keeping the reports flowing into New York while maintaining a schedule and managing a farflung information-gathering service made it impractical to reassign him to a position for which he had neither the experience nor the temperament.

Although Dun told Boyd that he already had a replacement in mind, he did not. From the beginning he looked for someone with experience in the Agency and familiarity with printing and publishing. No one in the New York office seemed to fit his needs. Dun first offered the position to Edwin F. Waters, one of the top administrators in E. Russell & Co., the Mercantile Agency associate office in Boston. Waters's qualifications, in addition to experience in one of the larger offices in the Agency, included newspaper and printing work. In negotiating with Waters, Dun discovered that it would be necessary to include a participating partnership to attract the kind of man he wanted.[18] When Waters declined to move, Dun offered the position to Erastus Wiman, manager of the Canadian operations for the Mercantile Agency.

The thirty-one-year-old Wiman, a native Canadian with great energy and talent, had worked for the *Toronto Globe* as a reporter before coming to work for the Agency in 1860. Besides managing the Canadian operations, Wiman wrote promotional brochures for other businesses and participated in politics, both of which Dun attempted to discourage. Even one of Wiman's critics admitted that he was "a man of great capacity, nurtured by constructive imagination and bolstered by tireless energy."[19] Although Dun was aware of Wiman's extreme vanity and pride, he was determined to lure the energetic young man to New York.

In October 1865 Dun offered Boyd's position to Wiman and invited him to come to New York to discuss terms. Wiman asked for 20 percent of the net profits of the entire business, with a guaranteed minimum annual salary of $10,000. In November Dun replied, offering either 15 percent of the net profits of the entire business with a minimum annual guarantee of $7,500, or 10 percent of the net profits of the Agency with a minimum guarantee of $5,000 and Wiman to retain his current share of the Canadian business. Reluctantly Dun dropped his demand that Wiman abandon all outside interests. Anticipating Wiman's complaint that the proposal would not mean any substantial increase over his current earnings, Dun held out an additional lure: "If you have weighted this matter well in your own mind and considered your bright chances for the future of a considerable proprietary interest in the whole business, I think you will be willing to accept."[20] Wiman agreed to Dun's second proposition, and in January 1866 Dun, Wiman, Smith, and Barlow concluded a partnership agreement.

The agreement, to extend for a period of four years, granted each of Dun's partners participating shares in the Mercantile Agency. Barlow received 15 percent of the net profits, Smith 10 percent, and Wiman 10 percent. Each of the three was guaranteed a minimum of $5,000 per annum, and Wiman retained his interest in the Canadian business of the Agency. Although Dun had suggested to Wiman the possibility of a proprietary interest in the Agency, the partnerships were strictly participating, and Dun made it clear that the partners served at his pleasure in an employee-employer relationship.[21]

From Dun's view, the partnership arrangement worked well, and although the personnel and percentages changed, he retained the basic organizational structure for the Mercantile Agency thereafter. In 1870, when the original agreement expired, Dun offered to increase Barlow's share to 17 percent of the net profits and Smith's and Wiman's each to 12.5 percent for a period of three years. Still he refused to grant any proprietary interest. In a letter to his partners late in 1869, Dun explained that heavy expenses in opening branch offices in California and Australia had prevented him from saving any money during the previous agreement.

> This [expansion] has absorbed a large amount of what I might have saved had I been disposed to follow a more niggardly course— hence I have now but little to show as a margin on the four years' business; so, of course, I have no intention of relinquishing any part of my proprietary interest until this object is obtained.[22]

If the three partners would accept Dun's proposal, he expected at its expiration "to be in a position to treat more generously with you."[23] The partners agreed to the new arrangement.

It is doubtful that Dun intended to share proprietary interest in the Agency. In 1872 when the renewal of the partnership came up for discussion, Dun's proposal contained no mention of proprietary interests. Indeed, while Dun agreed to increase Barlow's

interest to 20 percent of the net profits and Smith's and Wiman's
to 15 percent each, he also lectured his partners on the necessity
of their devoting all their attention during business hours "to the
business of the M.A. [Mercantile Agency]."[24] Moreover, Dun
made it clear that he considered his offer extremely liberal.
Profits from the Agency had steadily increased (see table 7) and

Table 7

R. G. DUN & CO. NET PROFITS,
1866-77

	Agency Net Profit	Partners' Share[a]	Dun's Net Return
		35%	65%
1866	$ 39,479	$ 15,000	$ 24,479
1867	70,954	24,834	46,120
1868	94,898	33,243	61,655
1869	87,025	30,458	56,567
		42%	58%
1870	145,675	61,183	84,492
1871	151,601	63,672	87,929
1872	172,939	72,634	100,305
		50%	50%
1873	252,830	126,415	126,415
1874	313,653	156,826	156,826
1875	253,363	126,681	126,681
1876	208,973	104,486	104,486
1877	211,621	105,810	105,810

[a]*Guaranteed minimum income of $5,000 each.*

Source: *Compiled from Owen A. Sheffield, "Dun and Bradstreet, Inc.: The Mer-*
cantile Agency Since 1841 . . ." (1965).

so had the salaries of Barlow, Smith, and Wiman. Still Dun explained that he wished to be generous as he intended "to feel more absolved from personal attention to the business," which would mean more work than before for the partners.[25]

In November 1877, as the expiration of the five-year agreement approached, Smith, Barlow, and Wiman appealed to Dun to make good his promise of a propietary interest in the firm. Actually Wiman had already broached the subject to Dun in an earlier discussion about Benjamin Douglass's debts to the firm. Dun wrote Douglass, "I have always had my doubts of his sincerity, but I am now more convinced than ever of his deep intrigury [sic] and deceit."[26] What actually infuriated Dun was the suggestion that his partners deserved a proprietary interest. He informed the three men that he wished to have some time to consider their request but that "the only debatable question in my mind has been whether by proposing a renewal on the same terms as heretofore I would be doing even-handed justice to some other employees in the Agency who have so long and faithfully served."[27]

In late November 1877, after consultation with his attorney, Chester A. Arthur, Dun replied to his partners. His November 22, 1877, letter to Barlow, Wiman, and Smith and another written a month later to Benjamin Douglass clearly delineated his philosophy of business and management. "As to your proposition that I should donate to you a one-half proprietaryship in a business yielding ten percent on *two and a half million dollars annually*," Dun could only reply that it was "too absurd for a moment's consideration."[28] He noted that he had no desire to disparage the talents, skills, efficiency, or faithfulness of his partners. Like the proprietor of any large business, he needed and valued his assistants, but "the talent employed has been liberally rewarded."[29] He pointed out that with no risk to themselves, in a period of twelve years their incomes had increased from less than $2,500 a year each to over $50,000 on the average during the last five years for Barlow and over $35,000 each for Wiman and Smith. To Douglass, who complained that Dun paid his partners too much, Dun argued that he had been well satisfied with Barlow and Wiman, and while Smith might be overpaid as an accountant, "I don't think I could have better men in their places."[30]

Dun willingly conceded that his partners' talents greatly enhanced the Agency, but he did not "by any means attribute the *entire* success of the bus[iness] to their instrumentality."[31] To his partners he claimed, "The bus[iness] is one, as you know, long established and has been from its beginning growing in usefulness, influence and power until it has become an indispensable Institution of Commerce and is bound to continue so with proper men to conduct it."[32] With or without his partners, either individually or collectively, Dun argued, the business under his direction would continue to prosper.

Not only would Dun not entertain the request for proprietary shares in the Agency, he refused to increase his partners' participating shares, saying that under no consideration would he "share more than one half my profits with any partners."[33] To their argument that Dun's policy of financing the expansion of branch offices and permanent investments in the Agency unfairly reduced their shares, Dun replied that they were compensated by a guarantee of a minimum fixed income. When, on the other hand, Douglass charged that too large a portion of profits was taken from the business and not enough capital invested for future growth, Dun exploded, "You must admit that I should be the best judge":

> Your idea seems to be that we should spend more fully all out profits in perfecting the bus[iness]. I have got too old for doing this simply for the glory of it and building up a vast pyramid of strength at my own sacrifice for the benefit of others and I mean to take a good profit out of the bus[iness] every year I remain in it and the profits will justify me. I don't know of any Agency bus[iness] that is not conducted with a view of making money, even year by year and there are certainly no other Agency which disburses one half nor one third we do. Then why should we not make money, if any is to be made in the bus[iness].[34]

Dun continued to hold out to his partners the hope of a proprietary share, but for the most part this represented no more than an attempt to keep his valued employees loyal to the Agency. If Dun had ever had any intention of sharing proprietary interests in the Mercantile Agency, that notion had rapidly vanished. As his returns from the Agency increased, so did his expenditures.

Perhaps it was his growing up in Chillicothe, Ohio, as a poor relative in a wealthy family that produced in R. G. Dun a love of grandeur and luxury. Once he had acquired a sizable and dependable income, he was determined to live as did other successful businessmen of the period. His new residence at 261 Madison Avenue, which he purchased in 1870, was situated in what was rapidly becoming *the* residential neighborhood for New York's wealthy elite. Dun's home, two blocks from J. P. Morgan's, was lavishly furnished and maintained by a staff of some fourteen servants. In his mansion, Dun displayed in specially designed rooms an art collection valued at his death at over $250,000. Even his private carriage drawn by one of the finest teams of horses in the city and driven by a uniformed attendant seemed designed to rival the ostentation of Morgan and Cornelius Vanderbilt.[35]

In addition to his townhouse, Dun built in the 1880s a large and pretentious country home, "Dunmeres," at Narragansett Pier, Rhode Island. An avid game-bird hunter and fisherman, Dun had been attracted to Narragansett by the excellent bass fishing, and after the death of his first wife built his home. It was not as large or pretentious as Vanderbilt's "Breakers" just across the bay at Newport or some of the other lavish summer homes built by Gilded Age business leaders, but it nevertheless was a visible indication of Dun's wealth and success.[36]

Dun's art collection, which he started in 1869 on one of his trips to Europe, symbolized his rise to opulence. As Vanderbilt, A. T. Stewart, Rockefeller, and other robber barons assembled art collections, so did Dun. Unlike many of the other newly rich of the period, Dun selected most of his own paintings, rarely resorting to agents. Except for some pieces by Joshua Reynolds, Benjamin Constant, Corot, and Henri Rousseau, Dun's paintings were for the most part by second-rate artists of the French romantic school. Dun's purchases were hardly surprising. The romantic school, with its heavy emphasis on pastoral and

8. "Dunmere," the R. G. Dun summer home at Narragansett, Rhode

9. Mary (Minnie) Bradford Dun, 1848-1910, second wife of R. G. Dun and the daughter of a sister of the first Mrs. R. G. Dun. This photograph was probably taken about the time of their marriage, October 1, 1884, by L. Alman of Newport, Rhode Island, and New York, New York. *Original in Ross County Historical Society, Chillicothe, Ohio. Courtesy of Dun & Bradstreet, Inc.*

domestic animal scenes, was supported by the Academy and was considered the accepted art for wealthy American collectors. In Dun's case his selections seem to have been based not only on being of a safe and accepted style; the subject matter evoked memories of his own rural Ohio beginnings.[37]

Dun's magnificent homes, fine horses, and valuable art collection were complemented by what must have been one of the finest wine and liquor cellars in the city. On his frequent trips abroad, Dun personally selected wines for his cellar. While traveling in France in 1869 he spent some $1,500 on wines, an amount that surprised even him.[38] Dun's personal taste ran more to bourbon than wine, however. When he acknowledged the Christmas greetings of his Louisville manager, Dun noted that sometimes he forgot to answer letters but added, "You know what will always be gratefully acknowledged and that is a bottle of such choice whiskey as you sent me for Christmas. I had the pleasure of taking the first drink out of it with the *President of the U.S.* [Chester Arthur] . . . he pronounced it *very* good."[39] In 1894, already suffering from cirrhosis, Dun instructed his Pittsburgh manager "to send me the ten cases of whiskey you have stored for me. The half barrel of the same which you have also stored I beg to leave with you a little longer."[40]

Dun also undertook a series of investments in railroad stocks, western mining ventures, ships, telephone companies, real estate, and other ventures. Most of these, however, constituted little more than a drain on his resources. Still, Dun's frailties and foibles, which he shared with so many of his contemporaries, should not obscure the fact that he undoubtedly had one of the finest managerial minds of the late nineteenth century.

Dun's refusal to grant his partners a proprietary share of the business was not merely selfishness but stemmed in part from his conception of the nature of the Agency. Despite his statement to Douglass that he was in the business to make money and not to build an empire, his actions were not always consistent with this concept. On more than one occasion Dun referred to the Agency as an "institution." When dealing with A. T. Stewart and Co. during the Civil War, he lamented that his subscribers seemed to "care nothing for the institution," and he frequently encouraged his branch managers to do their best for "Our Association." In late 1889 when Dun was divesting himself of outside investments, he refused to consider an offer to sell the Mercantile Agency, replying, "Now as to my Mercantile Agency plant—I think I should have to get into a very high tantrum to want to get away from it, in fact it would be an almost impossible thing to do while I live . . . it would be like selling out a man's family almost."[41]

Several years after Dun's death, Francis L. Minton, his personal attorney and one of the executors and trustees of his estate, argued that Dun held a clear notion of the public trust of the Agency and that he had emphasized its responsibility to its clients—not only to its subscribers but to the firms it reported on. The very nature of the Agency, Dun felt, demanded that it not be controlled by a soulless corporation but by a single person or a few persons acting jointly who were not subject to veto or pressure from a group of stockholders.[42]

At the same time Dun realized that the Agency's farflung international operations and diverse activities could not be adequately or practically managed by him personally. He had modified Tappan's and Douglass's basic geographic structure of the firm under which individual branch managers exercised specific responsibility for definite geographic areas and reported directly to the owner. He had added an administrative structure of three partners, each responsible for different segments of the business and with their incomes dependent upon the total performance of the Agency. The partners exercised both line and staff functions, each supervising some activities of the branch office managers and advising Dun about specific areas and the general conduct of the business. This structure allowed Dun to assign specific responsibilities and, while retaining flexibility, to adapt to his strategy of rapid geographic expansion in an expanding economy —at the same time outdistancing his rivals.[43]

Only a small part of Dun's effort during the decade following the Civil War centered on developing an effective administrative structure for the Agency and staffing it with talented people. The decision to resume publishing the *Reference Book* in 1864 proved to be the turning point in the Agency's fortunes. During the ten years following the Civil War, profits rose rapidly (table 7). Dun far outdistanced his rivals in the credit-rating business, and his opportunities, both within and outside the Agency, multiplied.

Dun's earlier decision to tie the *Reference Book* to a subscription to the Agency services for subscribers other than bankers and insurance companies would have required the Agency to expand geographically. The rapid growth in demand for the *Reference Book*, its expanded coverage, and the accelerated pace with which new branch offices were opened reflected the rapid expansion of the American economy and the development of a national market. With the exception of a small branch office in Nashville, Tennessee, opened in 1860 and quickly closed by the outbreak of hostilities, Dun had concentrated his efforts during the war on survival rather than on expansion. Nevertheless he realized that to serve its customers, the Agency had to match its expansion with that of its subscribers' market. The development of a fairly comprehensive railroad network soon after the war accelerated sales of jobbers, wholesale merchants, and manufacturers in a growing national market.

In 1866, after eight years without any geographical expansion, Dun established a branch at Buffalo, New York, and in 1867 he opened another in Memphis, Tennessee. During the thirty-four years following the Civil War, the Agency opened 120 new offices — 108 in the United States, 7 in Canada, and 1 each in Glasgow, Scotland; Paris, France; Melbourne, Australia; Mexico City, Mexico; and Havana, Cuba. With the exception of the Canadian branches, the foreign offices provided their subscribers with information on merchants in the United States and Canada and did not attempt to report on the country where they were established. William Morrison, the London office manager, and Benjamin Douglass both argued that the Agency should expand its reporting at least to the British Isles, but Dun refused, fearing that it would be too expensive and would provoke too much local hostility, which could result in harmful legislation or regulation. For the most part Dun was content with slowly expanding domestic coverage. Except for 1872 when a record nineteen branch offices were opened, the usual pattern consisted of three or four new ones each year. Typically the new offices either filled in existing coverage or reflected the westward expansion and increased urbanization of the United States. In 1874, for example, offices were added in Atlanta and Savannah, Georgia; Denver, Colorado; Williamsport, Pennsylvania; and Gloversville, New York. Fourteen years later the Agency established nine new offices: Shreveport, Louisiana; Topeka, Kansas; Fort Smith, Arkansas; Tacoma, Seattle, and Spokane, Washington; Wilmington, North Carolina; El Paso, Texas; and Wilmington, Delaware.[44] Branch offices provided not only the reporting service, a necessary adjunct to the *Reference Book* for subscribers; they also strengthened and broadened the information-gathering process.

The expansion of branch offices necessitated recruiting or transferring managers from one office to another. In 1865, in a letter to Erastus Wiman, Dun noted that Charles Murray, whom Wiman had recommended for a vacancy in Milwaukee, would have to be content with a southern office since a manager had already been assigned to Milwaukee. Dun suggested that his brother-in-law, Jay Lugsdin, be moved to Toronto as assistant manager to gain the necessary experience for managing a major office.[45] A year later Dun suggested to Lugsdin that he take the Montreal office, and he assigned Murray to Pittsburgh and George Minchener to Detroit. As part of his search for managerial talent, Dun usually solicited recommendations from his branch managers before promoting their assistant office managers.[46] In January 1867 Dun wrote to William Scarlett, the Baltimore manager, that a managerial candidate Scarlett had recommended seemed "'too much adicted [*sic*] to liquor.'" Not that Dun objected to an occasional "nip," but being "pretty well saturated" in the early afternoon did seem a bit too much. Still Dun did not want to be unfair and sought additional information before rejecting the man.[47] To supplement the recommendations from the branch office managers, Dun sought the opinions of his partners and often conducted personal interviews. Managerial salaries varied widely according to the importance of the office, and although branch managers never reached the salaries of his partners, Dun did pay them much better than he did rank-and-file employees. Usually Dun's judgment proved accurate; only rarely were managers dismissed.

Table 8

BRANCH OFFICES ESTABLISHED, 1858–76

Toronto, Ont.	1858	Grand Rapids, Mich.	1872
Buffalo, N.Y.	1866	Kansas City, Mo.	1872
Memphis, Tenn.	1867	Mobile, Ala.	1872
Portland, Me.	1868	Quincy, Ill.	1872
Halifax, N.S.	1868	St. Joseph, Mo.	1872
Toledo, Ohio	1868	Scranton, Pa.	1872
Albany, N.Y.	1868	Syracuse, N.Y.	1872
San Francisco, Cal.	1869	Utica, N.Y.	1872
Norfolk, Va.	1869	Worcester, Mass.	1872
Rochester, N.Y.	1870	Glasgow, Scotland	1872
Hartford, Conn.	1870	Paris, France	1872
Nashville, Tenn.	1871	Hamilton, Ont.	1872
Saint John, N.B.	1871	New Haven, Conn.	1873
Indianapolis, Ind.	1871	Atlanta, Ga.	1874
Newark, N.J.	1871	Denver, Col.	1874
Portland, Ore.	1871	Savannah, Ga.	1874
Providence, R.I.	1871	Williamsport, Pa.	1874
Columbus, Ohio	1872	Gloversville, N.Y.	1875
Davenport, Iowa	1872	Dallas, Tex.	1875
Dayton, Ohio	1872	St. Paul, Minn.	1875
Dubuque, Iowa	1872	Houston, Tex.	1875
Erie, Pa.	1872	Binghamton, N.Y.	1875
Evansville, Ind.	1872	La Crosse, Wis.	1876
Galveston, Tex.	1872	London, Ont.	1876

Source: The Mercantile Agency Directory (New York: Dun & Bradstreet, 1934).

Even after the administrative reorganization and the rapid expansion of branch offices, Dun supervised his managers closely.
In mid-1868, for example, he advised Alex Armstrong of Chicago

that the latter's practice of renewing subscriptions at low rates was the major cause for declining profits at the branch. "The price must be either advanced," Dun wrote, "or their subscriptions cut off."[48] Two years later he informed Jay Lugsdin, then in San Francisco, that it was good business to allow important merchants to subscribe at low rates occasionally to lure them into the Agency. After a long lecture to Lugsdin on sales and pricing policy, Dun urged his brother-in-law to "exercise your judgment."[49]

If Dun was quick to criticize his managers, he was also quick to praise, and at times he displayed admirable patience. Immediately upon returning from a trip to Europe in February 1869, Dun wrote J. H. Smith, the manager at Buffalo, and sent him a gold watch as a "token of my appreciation of your successful efforts in crowning yourself as champion of the association."[50] Some years later, when the St. Louis manager, A. J. King, repaid a personal loan that Dun had granted, Dun wrote a long letter thanking him for his efforts on behalf of the association. A few years later Dun promoted him to partner in the New York office.[51] Few managers misinterpreted Dun's personal interest and frequent kindnesses; the relation remained that of employer-employee. When William Scarlett objected to the terms of a new contract and admonished Dun that he should treat his partners more generously, Dun quickly replied, "As for your being a resident partner in Baltimore, you know it is a mere nominal thing."[52] For the most part Dun confined his supervision to branch managers and occasional discussions with his partners as the organization in the decade following the Civil War had outgrown any possibility of personal management even if Dun had been so inclined.

In 1860 the *New York Illustrated News* estimated the number of clerks in the New York office at 150.[53] By 1876 the demands of additional recording, collecting, corresponding, responding to inquiries, preparation of the *Reference Book,* and other duties had more than doubled this number. Although the number of reporters, salesmen, and clerks employed at the branch offices varied considerably, they ranged between fifteen and thirty-five, with the exception of major branches like Boston, Philadelphia, and New Orleans. By the late 1870s, when approximately 10,000 correspondents submitted reports on over 700,000 firms, R. G. Dun & Co. employed a staff of more than 2,000.[54] By the last quarter of the nineteenth century, the Mercantile Agency had become big business.

Table 9

FIRMS REPORTED ON IN THE *REFERENCE BOOK*

Year	Number of Firms	Year	Number of Firms	Year	Number of Firms
1859	20,268	1868	350,000	1884	933,159
1860	31,278	1870	430,573	1886	1,025,000
1861	25,260	1872	532,000	1888	1,103,299
1862	not issued	1874	594,189	1890	1,176,988
1863	not issued	1876	680,072	1892	1,239,424
1864	123,000	1878	713,420	1894	1,299,091
1865	123,000	1880	764,000	1896	1,320,251
1866	141,750	1882	848,000	1898	1,251,314
				1900	1,285,816

Source: Compiled from Edward N. Vose, *Seventy-five Years of the Mercantile Agency: R. G. Dun &Co., 1841–1916* (New York, 1916), p.98. There is no reliable estimate available of the total number of firms in operation for the period. Part of the problem lies in the lack of an entirely satisfactory definition of what constitutes a firm. U.S., Bureau of Census, *Historical Statistics of the United States, Colonial Times to 1970* (Washington, D.C., 1975), part II, pp.909-911, based its estimate of the number of concerns on the number of firms reported in R. G. Dun & Co.'s *Reference Book* but acknowledged that this was a far from satisfactory or complete solution. The definition employed for inclusion was not always consistent, several important types of businesses were not reported, and the coverage in some regions was not always complete.

The geographic expansion and growth of the economy naturally resulted in an increased number of firms doing business and
hence greatly increased the reporting requirements for the Agency. The number of firms rated in the *Reference Book* increased
steadily (see table 9). Only in 1873 did the volume decrease, and
while it would be tempting to blame the decline in the number of
firms rated to the large increase in business failures following the
panic that year, actually a disastrous fire in the Agency printing
plant delayed and shortened the volume.[55] In the July 1873 edition Dun announced that thereafter the book would appear four
times a year: January, March, July and September. This increase
from two to four editions yearly was in recognition of the inability of the firm to keep the book reliable for six months through
notification sheets. Data in the preface to the July 1874 edition
illustrated the problems of keeping credit-ratings current during
a period of rapid change and growth in both size and number of
firms. In the four-month period from March to July 1874, there
were approximately 160,000 changes averaging more than 1,300
daily: 53,984 new firms had been added to the volume and 36,279
dropped, 52,788 had been raised or lowered in credit-rating, and
16,830 firms had changed their names.[56] While the weekly notification sheet had sufficed when the number of firms reported on
remained relatively small, by 1873 the magnitude of the changes
among more than a half-million firms swamped the notification
sheet and made the *Reference Book* obsolete within a short time.

In addition to the stepped-up publication schedule for the
book and the accelerating number of firms covered, Erastus
Wiman and Dun periodically added new features to strengthen
it. The January 1880 *Reference Book* carried population estimates for each town or city, with an indication of its banking
facilities or, if none, the name of the nearest banking town. The
same edition also listed over 40,000 U.S. post offices, as well as
some 65,000 railroad stations in the United States and Canada,
and the names of the express companies serving each station. Six
years later in response to "the need of ready reference to the
immediate locality of places and their geographical location,"
state maps were included.[57] The March 1885 volume introduced
a new feature, a column, "Trade Classification," in which businesses were arranged in twenty-four categories on the basis of

materials and products with no reference to function, and arbitrary symbols such as *, /, and = were assigned to enable subscribers to determine the trade classification from a key in the preface. Dun noted that the new feature resulted from repeated requests by subscribers for lists of the trades in which they had a "direct interest so they could address circulars and draw off lists of names for the use of traveling salesmen."[58] Despite the admitted difficulty of categorizing some businesses, the trade classification proved a popular feature of the *Reference Book* and remained essentially intact until 1950 when the U.S. Census Bureau's standard industrial classification system replaced the scheme Dun had introduced sixty-five years earlier.[59]

Dun's emphasis upon improving the *Reference Book* reflected his conviction that it was the major vehicle through which the Agency served the commercial community. Many of the changes, revisions, and additions reflected Dun's perception of the transformation occurring in the American economy.

Rapid expansion of the Agency's branch offices was required to keep pace with the westward movement of the population and the growth of a national market. In 1877 Dun pointed out to his subscribers that his firm had in operation more branch offices than his two leading competitors combined.[60] The inclusion of the names of post offices and maps reflected the needs of manufacturers and jobbers serving a growing and often unfamiliar market. Dun's trade classifications, crude as they were, reflected the increased specialization of manufacturers, importers, and jobbers. All of the improvements Dun made in the *Reference Book* relected his conviction that the proper role of the Mercantile Agency in the American economy was not simply "to enable its patrons to avoid the hazardous and unsafe, but to strengthen their confidence where confidence is deserved — in other words, to promote as well as to protect trade."[61]

In addition to broader coverage, more information, and more frequent editions of the book, Dun made the ratings available to subscribers in smaller regional books, which contained information on specific areas, usually a single state. These smaller books, measuring about three by six inches, fit into the pockets of traveling salesmen and enabled them to make credit decisions while calling on potential customers.[62]

Dun also offered a variety of service publications to subscribers. The annual circular of the Mercantile Agency on business failures started prior to the Civil War became a semiannual and then a quarterly publication that discussed not only failures but economic conditions and prospects in the nation and in the various locales served by the Agency. In 1867 Dun published *The Mercantile Agency United States Business Directory for 1867*, which contained the names and addresses of business firms reported by R. G. Dun and Co. throughout the United States. However, it proved unprofitable and was not issued again.[63] Ten years later he started the *Mercantile Agency Annual*, which contained information on legal, business, and other subjects of interest to businessmen, as well as extensive advertising, which Dun sold. After it acquired a printing plant, the Agency increased its publishing output. In 1879 it sent its subscribers a *Synopsis of the Laws Relating to Assignments, Insolvency & etc. in the Various States of the Union*. Advertisements of banks and insurance companies appeared at the front and back of this volume. Prominent among these was a notice calling the attention of the business community "to the facilities possessed by *the Mercantile for the collection* of past due debts."[64]

Dun could proudly advertise the collection facilities of the Agency had full-time resident reporters, debts were occasionally credit-rating firm in the United States and the largest commercial credit-collection agency. None of Dun's competitors had extended collection services to their subscribers since Bradstreet had discontinued it during the Civil War.[65] By the time Dun started advertising the Agency's collection facilities, it had over 10,000 corresponding attorneys whose only remuneration for reporting was the fees they received for collecting past-due debts for subscribers.[66] Dun continued the practice of his predecessor, Benjamin Douglass, in handling the collection business through the Agency. In some areas, particularly larger cities where the Agency had full-time resident reporters, debts were occasionally collected by the office managers. In the country, where the Agency depended on corresponding attorneys, accounts owed to subscribers were forwarded to the attorneys for collection, and the Agency levied a modest fee for handling the transaction and transferring the money collected.

Since branch managers' salaries depended in part upon their profits, they were often tempted to bypass the local corresponding attorneys by collecting debts themselves, but Dun repeatedly warned them against this practice. In 1874 he reminded them of his previous instructions to refer all claims to local attorneys and expressed annoyance that some managers had disregarded his orders. Dun warned the offenders that in the future he would "accept no excuse."[67] Five years later, the Agency felt compelled to repeat the warning. Further, managers were to make every effort to secure as much claim business as possible for corresponding attorneys. "We care comparatively little," the Agency explained, "as to whether the claims come through our collection department or not. What we want is that the local correspondent should get the collection business and thus stimulate him to future exertions in our favor."[68]

These remonstrances were aimed at more than keeping the vital reporting system healthy. The collection department of the Mercantile Agency returned sizable profits, which promised to increase. In early 1876 Dun sent corresponding attorneys a circular letter assessing the status of the collection business. Swarms of local collection agencies had sprung up since the Civil War, indicating the quantity of such business then available, and Dun believed that the Mercantile Agency was in a position to bypass such local concerns and direct most of the claims business to its correspondents. All the latter needed were "charges as low as others and efficiency in doing the work."[69] Unlike the "petty collection offices," which advertised uniform fees for collection services, the Agency's corresponding attorneys charged the standard local rate in their respective area, and this tended to vary from locale to locale. The solution to this problem, Dun argued, would be for all corresponding attorneys to agree to the fee schedule that he proposed, and the Agency would then advise all its subscribers of the uniform rates.[70]

Although Dun did not inform his corresponding attorneys, he had already planned measures to introduce the needed efficiency into his administrative structure. Formerly the collection department operated as part of the New York office and had no separate identity. In January 1877 Dun turned the management of the collection business over to the law firm of Douglass & Minton (Benjamin Douglass, Jr., Dun's nephew, and Frances L. Minton, his personal and business attorney), agreeing to pay the firm 60 percent of the fees received for collecting New York City claims and $17,500 annually for handling all country collections.[71] Although Dun never maintained separate profit figures for the collection department, one authority has estimated a minimum average net profit of $30,000 annually for the period 1876–1900.[72] This estimate is, in all likelihood, too conservative. By 1900, the year Dun died, collection profits came to more than $107,000, or about 25 percent of the Agency's net profits. During the eight years after 1900, the collection profits consistently accounted for 20–25 percent of the total profits. It seems probable that collection profits for the period 1876–1900 averaged between 18 and 20 percent of the net profits of the Mercantile Agency, making it an extremely important adjunct to the credit-rating business.[73]

Not all of the subsidiary activities in which Dun sought to involve the Agency proved as profitable or as legitimate as collecting subscribers' past due claims. Addressing circulars for subscribers, which had produced a net profit of $8,770 in 1860, declined during the war, and by 1866 Dun no longer maintained separate accounting for the activity. During the decade following the war, he allowed that phase of the business to die out and never made any effort to revive it.[74]

Driven perhaps by visions of failure, Dun in early May 1864 had contacted Colonel H. G. Olcott, special commissioner for the War and Navy departments in Philadelphia, suggesting that Olcott's office should purchase copies of the *Reference Book* for use at the various quartermaster offices.[75] A few months later Dun wrote to M. P. Stacey, the Agency's Philadelphia office manager: "It occurs to me that an arrangement with the Internal Revenue Department might be made of much greater magnitude than that of the Quarter Masters, (i.e.) our book might be used as a basis for taxation & should be in the hands of the assessors at all important places. By the use of it Gov't income might be increased many million dollars."[76] Regardless of his efforts Dun had strong reservations about the policy of serving the government, and he worried about possible misuse and abuse of the information in the hands of politicians.[77] Dun insisted that any arrangement with the government would have to be "strictly confidential," and he warned Stacey not to inform the Agency employees, for "many who now show us their hands fully would be very shy hereafter."[78]

Notwithstanding the fact that Secretary of War Edwin Stanton was an old friend who had served as a corresponding attorney, the government refused to accept Dun's proposal. Perhaps because he realized the impropriety of such an arrangement and the irreparable damage it would do to the Agency's reputation, Dun never again approached any branch of the government. Clearly this was outside the range of activities available for the Agency's exploitation.

During the decade following the Civil War, Dun had relatively few precedents to follow, and he seemed to be searching out the proper limits of the Agency's income-producing activities consistent with the good name of the firm. The proposed contract with the government lay outside these limits. When the newly organized National Telegraph Company proposed in 1867 that the Mercantile Agency should market the stock of that company, Dun agreed. In September 1867 Charles Barlow, with Dun's approval, signed a memorandum agreement to undertake to sell "through our instrumentalities" $5 million of the stock in return for a 1.5 percent commission in cash and 1.5 percent in stock.[79] Eighteen months later, in May 1869, George B. Walters, secretary of the National Telegraph Company, asked permission to nominate Dun for the board of directors and executive committee of the company.[80] Dun immediately refused. Even before being asked to serve on the board, he had become suspicious of the possibilities of success for the National Telegraph operation and privately expressed his doubts to his New Orleans manager.[81] Dun never indicated how much, if any, of this stock the Agency had marketed. For the Mercantile Agency, however, the significance of the venture lay outside the amount of stock sold or the success or failure of National Telegraph. When the agreement was made, neither the forty-one-year-old Dun nor anyone else in the credit-rating business had the experience to grasp the impropriety of Agency participation in stock promotion schemes. To Dun's credit, after the abortive National Telegraph agreement, he avoided involving the Agency in such outside ventures.[82]

Dun did not yet understand that it was improper for him or his management personnel to engage in outside businesses. He frequently refused to serve on boards of directors when he thought he was being asked because of his connection with the Agency, but he was openly a director and substantial stockholder in the bankrupt Ozark Iron Company, which his brother-in-law William James had organized. He was the president and largest stockholder in the Caribou Consolidated Silver Mining Company, listed on the New York Stock Exchange, which he bought at a sheriff's sale in an effort to protect an unwise initial investment. Dun was also president of the Overland Telephone Company, which was forced out of business when the Supreme Court ruled that it had infringed upon the patents of the Bell Telephone Company.[83]

While Dun's outside ventures were, for the most part, financial disasters, there was nothing dishonorable in his actions. Yet he should have realized that his name was so intimately connected with the Mercantile Agency that it was impossible to disassociate his private ventures from the firm. Moreover the use of the Agency's or his name undoubtedly earned these companies a measure of confidence to which they were not entitled on their merits. Finally, having Dun's name associated with an unbroken string of business failures could not have been good advertising for a firm that specialized in alerting businessmen to the quality of credit-risks. Since the Agency sold information and service to its subscribers, its products were valuable only if they were trustworthy. It held no patents, controlled no sources of supply, and produced nothing that its customers could not obtain a substitute for elsewhere. Dun knew that the Mercantile Agency's preeminent position in the credit-rating business resulted from its comprehensive coverage and reputation for reliability.

Dun and his partners worried a great deal about competition and the host of rival credit-rating firms that sprang up after the Civil War. "No sooner had we 'weathered the Cape' of our diffic't. [difficulty] and it became apparent that the experiment was a success," Dun wrote a potential subscriber in November 1863, "than a pack of hungry imitators took up the idea and attempted to enter into competition with us."[84] Lured by the prospect of making money with little or no capital investment and no experience, the rival firms enjoyed only a short life; however, "They keep up a spasmodic kind of existence for longer or shorter periods and as they pass away (as they all do) others come in and take their places."[85] Although Dun publicly dismissed the rival concerns as annoyances and expressed embarrassment that they sometimes adopted names such as the "Improved Mercantile Agency" and sold reference books in the same manner that "cookery receipts books are peddled," he privately worried about competition and kept close track of his rivals.[86]

By the Civil War, all but a few of the numerous credit-rating agencies that had burgeoned had withered and died. Enticing though the business appeared, it was deceptively difficult, and few had the capital and talent to succeed. The war hastened the demise of marginal firms, and at its end the business was dominated by four credit-reporting agencies: R. G. Dun & Co., the largest and certainly the most prestigious; John M. Bradstreet & Son, Improved Mercantile and Law Agency, Dun's major competitor; the Commercial Agency, an older but declining firm, which had done business under a variety of names; and L. Ballard & Co., soon to fail.

The Commercial Agency, founded some three years after the Mercantile Agency, had presented the most formidable competition until Bradstreet forged to the front in 1857 with the publication of his reference book. Following the Tappan scheme of securing reports from corresponding attorneys, the Commercial Agency opened a number of independent branch offices and seemed to prosper. However, after the Civil War, the firm changed owners rapidly, and by 1872, when it was reorganized as McKillop & Sprague, it had undergone at least four changes in name. The branch offices were only loosely connected, the coverage was incomplete, and the firm, an imitator rather than innovator, failed in 1879. While Dun absorbed some of the business, Bradstreet actually bought a number of the branch offices and secured a fairly significant portion of the Commercial Agency's previous subscribers.[87]

Among Dun's leading competitors in the immediate postwar period, L. Ballard & Co. was the smallest and presented the least competition. Like the Commercial Agency, Ballard imitated rather than innovated. In 1858, following Bradstreet, Ballard published a reference book, but it covered only New York City. Ballard lacked the necessary sources of information to expand his book and often tried to pirate Dun correspondents. Never very successful, Ballard hung on until 1872 when he sold out to the newly incorporated McKillop & Sprague Co.[88]

The demise of Ballard & Co. and the Commercial Agency left only Bradstreet as a serious competitor to R. G. Dun & Co. Two years after founding his agency in Cincinnati, John Bradstreet had moved his head office to New York City where for the first few years he appeared to be simply one of a numerous assortment of rivals. Capitalizing on his legal background, Bradstreet specialized in the collection business. His sole innovation in the credit-reporting field was the publication of credit reports. Bradstreet's strength rested less with the quality of his reports than in the ease with which subscribers could use his system. Douglass and Dun and other credit-reporting agencies quickly copied Bradstreet's innovation. While Dun suspended publication of his own reference books during the war, Bradstreet continued to publish current editions. Dun claimed that Bradstreet's published information was incomplete, outdated, and useless, and he urged subscribers to obtain the most accurate information available in wartime by visiting his own offices. Bradstreet's subscribers could visit his office directly or obtain complete written reports upon request. While this offer proved to be an effective selling point, Bradstreet lacked the facilities to deliver any substantial number of individual handwritten reports. Nevertheless he remained Dun's major competitor.[89]

John M. Bradstreet's elder son, Milton, had returned to Ohio in

1856, leaving his father and brother, Henry, to manage the firm. In 1863, the same year that Dun confessed that Bradstreet was making more money than the Mercantile Agency, John Bradstreet died. Henry Bradstreet lacked his father's talents, and the firm's business began a slow, steady decline. Geographic expansion, declining profits, and mounting expenses forced Henry Bradstreet to borrow, and in 1876, Henry C. Young and E. F. Randolph, two of his principal creditors, along with Charles Finney Clark and Berkely Gorman, Bradstreet's Boston and Philadelphia managers, forced the firm to undergo reorganization and incorporation.[90] In the process Henry Bradstreet was forced out, and Charles F. Clark became president. Dun once more faced strong competition.

Dun always considered any competition formidable and acted accordingly. In May 1876 he wrote to the manager of the Philadelphia office that R. G. Dun & Co. had received numerous inquiries about Bradstreet but had refused to answer. Privately he considered the firm "rotten to the core," and while he could not determine what advantage they sought in incorporating in Connecticut, "there is a purpose in it no doubt."[91] Publicly, seeking to capitalize on Bradstreet's financial problems, Dun reminded his subscribers, "We are not a stock company, with mere nominal assets in stock certificates. We are a firm."[92]

In the post–Civil War period R. G. Dun's success and the early profitability of Bradstreet encouraged a large number of new firms to enter the credit-reporting business. Dun took special care to keep fully informed on all rivals.[93] Firms like the International Collecting Company and Mercantile Agency (1876), Jordan's Bonded Iowa State Collecting and Reporting Company, the Legal and Commercial Union, the Merchants Mutual Indemnity Association, and the Mercantile and Statistical Agency Association sprang up at what to Dun must have seemed an alarming rate. True, some of them, like the Phoenix Mercantile Agency in St. Louis, were quickly and publicly labelled "a commercial comedy,"[94] and others, like the Mercantile and Statistical Agency Association, soon closed their doors, with "the manager and promoter of the enterprise having been last seen in the company with the sheriff."[95]

At times Dun and his partners must have felt that rival firms were spawning spontaneously. In March 1879 Erastus Wiman sent a flyer from Bangert, Shaw & Company's Mercantile and Collection Agency in Philadelphia to the R. G. Dun & Co. office in that city with a note inquiring, "Who are these people?"[96] Although the Philadelphia office responded that the new rival did not "amount to anything," Wiman kept a close check on its operations.[97] At times various branch managers were also apprehensive about the competition. In April 1879, for example, the Chicago office warned that the newly organized American Mercantile Reporting Co. and its publication *The West* seemed well financed with "full, explicit reports, being well expressed and comprehensive."[98] Within three months a Missouri correspondent reported, "*The West* has collapsed and one of the proprietors is selling millstones in Minn."[99] The Buffalo, New York, office manager wrote to Wiman in 1880, "Agencies are getting thick as blackberries. We have 5 here now Dun's, Brads[treets], Mc & S [McKillop & Sprague], Fourse & Herschberger & Co. and the Buffalo Commercial Agency besides . . . small fry."[100]

The possibilities for rivals must have seemed endless to Dun. Each clerk who left or was dismissed from the Agency Dun and Wiman saw as a potential competitor. Disgruntled and discontented employees knew enough about the business to realize how easy it was to pirate information and often sought some cheap means of providing limited reporting and collection services at a reduced rate.

Dun obtained information about competitors through branch managers, friends, correspondents, and subscribers. From his position at the top of the field, he could well understand the difficulty faced by small concerns in the commercial credit-reporting business. Not only did large firms enjoy enormous economies of scale, but providing adequate service to subscribers selling in a national market required a national organization. Attempts by smaller concerns to specialize in one line of trade or in a specific area proved largely unsuccessful in the ever-expanding market. Dun estimated the Mercantile Agency's annual income in 1878 at more than three times the total of all the other firms in the business. In all probability Dun was conservative.[101] Even with a large income, Dun insisted that only by great care, economy, and efficiency did the Agency return a profit.

In November 1878 a New York journal, *The Public*, commented on the suspension of McKillop & Sprague Commercial Agency. *The Public* argued that there were too many firms in the credit-reporting business, noting that during the previous five years over forty such firms had been in operation in New York, and while a large number had failed "even today we are told, at least twenty Associations of this character" existed, all but a few of which "eke out a miserable existence."[102] The editor urged his readers to rely only on concerns "above the slightest suspicion" and conducted by men entirely "free from other engagements, so as to give the closest attention to the enormous amount of detail they must keep in command."[103] Money spent with smaller firms was, in *The Public* view, money thrown away.

The problem as Dun saw it was not simply that the entrances and exits of numerous small firms reduced his profits but rather that they threatened chaos. Pointing out that over forty-one agencies had taken bankruptcy in a few years, Dun argued that the millions of dollars lost in unfulfilled subscriptions and debts collected but unpaid could have been used instead for constructive purposes. There was, he insisted, ample demand and sufficient funds to do the reporting required by the business community. "But it is so divided up among different charlatans engaged in the business, as to destroy the object sought after."[104] For Dun the solution appeared obvious: prudent businessmen should prevent the needless cost and chaos by supporting only a reliable firm—the Mercantile Agency.

Dun particularly sought to dissociate the Agency from the "disgrace and contumely which such pretenders at the agency business have brought upon its very name."[105] Failures, scandals, and unethical and even dishonest conduct by the smaller credit-reporting agencies in his opinion threatened all such business. The public, always suspicious, now had their suspicions confirmed. Continued attacks from newspapers such as the *New York Commercial Advertiser, The Public,* and the *St. Louis Globe Democrat* required that the business reform itself or face outside regulation.[106]

As much as Dun fretted about chaotic competition, he worried even more about public attacks against credit-rating agencies, legal questions, and even potential legislative interference. These worries continued unabated as the Agency entered the last quarter of the nineteenth century, though Dun had to be pleased when he reviewed the progress of the Mercantile Agency since the Civil War. In ten years his profits had increased tenfold, and his agency now clearly dominated commercial credit-rating in the United States. He had developed the administrative structure of the Agency so as to free himself from routine duties and allow for more efficient and effective management. And he and his agency had gained national recognition.

5

The Coming of Age, 1876-94

During the last quarter of the nineteenth century R. G. Dun & Co. experienced the phenomenon of what E. C. Kirkland has labeled the coming of age of American industry.[1] As a business firm the Mercantile Agency reached maturity. Routines and informal operating procedures became formalized, manuals were published, flowcharts for information and reporting were developed, accounting forms were standardized, and institutional controls by the New York office were increased to ensure more efficient operation. The company pioneered in the adoption and utilization of the typewriter, which both symbolized and facilitated its modernization. New procedures and strategy required major modifications in the service offered subscribers and the philosophy of pricing. That Dun accomplished these tasks and enjoyed increased profits in spite of the lingering effects of the panic of 1873 and a major shakeup in top management was perhaps as much a tribute to his managerial skills as to the realization of the American business community and public that commercial credit-rating agencies were an integral part of the modern industrial economy.

In 1890 P. R. Earling, a leading authority on credit, noted that in the early years, credit-rating agencies were simply an adjunct of the credit system in the United States; "now," he concluded, "our present widely extended credit system is largely due to the labors of the Agencies," and "it is no longer a disputed question that they supply a want, and are indispensable to the public business."[2] Earling and other observers noted that the acceptance of credit-reporting agencies by business and the public had not come unchallenged.[3] In the last quarter of the century R. G. Dun & Co. survived and prospered despite a series of legal, political, and public attacks leveled against the concept of credit-rating agencies in the United States.

Much of the public prejudice against the Mercantile Agency and similar firms stemmed from what Earling called "the very nature of the institution and its inquisitorial functions."[4] Such attacks were not new. As early as 1854, the editor of a Baton Rouge paper had declared that financial reports were prepared by secret legal spies: "Talk of Vidocq or Fuche police—Japanese espionage—damnable leechers and hireling bloodsuckers; it is all honorable—legitimate—and proper in the place of this most villainous inquisition."[5] That same year a Franklin, Louisiana, paper attacked "Mercantile Spies" asserting, "No home will be secure, no privacy will be sacred from these harpian visitors. Neighbor will doubt neighbor & fear will check social intercourse. Let every honorable merchant cease business with wholesalers who use mercantile agents."[6] No doubt this hostility reflected the small-town morality of nineteenth-century America: while it was normal to know everyone's business, it was unseemly to pry. The nineteenth-century fear of secret conspiracies and monopolies added fuel to the public suspicion and hostility toward credit-rating institutions.

Public attacks on credit-rating agencies reached a high point in 1876 with the publication of Thomas F. Meagher's *The Commercial Agency "System" of the United States and Canada Exposed: Is the Secret Inquisition a Curse or a Benefit.*[7] Although Meagher did not single out R. G. Dun & Co., his former employer, but condemned all credit-rating firms equally, the Mercantile Agency received most of the publicity. Meagher denounced secret "inquisitions" and possible secret "black lists" of firms, which privately circulated "opprobrious matters" about firms that may have received favorable ratings in the reference books.[8] In addition he emphasized the danger of secret organizations, which allowed correspondents to bring "unnatural pressures" and "powerful secret influence" on every merchant in the land.

Meagher charged that the agencies even tampered with state legislatures in efforts to obtain favorable treatment. Most important, he charged that all agency reports were inaccurate, libelous, and gathered by incompetent correspondents. In short, the entire system was corrupt beyond the hope of redemption.

Dun chose not to fight Meagher's charges in public, but in March 1876 he issued a letter to his office managers offering "a general guide" to aid them in answering questions about Meagher's attack. The Agency had known about Meagher's book for the past year; the author had notified them of his intentions, "hoping, no doubt, that we might be induced to 'buy him off,' and, failing to get any recognition or notice from us, he now seems . . . to be resting on the hope that we will place an injunction on his book, and in this way aid him in bringing it into notoriety."[9] Nothing could be further from Dun's intention; no public notice was to be given by any managers. However, they were free to talk with subscribers.

"Thomas Francis Meagher *alias* Chas. F. Maynard, is," Dun noted, "as his real name implies, the son of Irish parents."[10] It was obvious that Dun believed that Meagher's Irish heritage would damn him as a liar. The circular noted that the Agency had employed Meagher in Montreal as messenger boy in 1862, promoted him to copyist, and finally placed him in charge of petty cash. He had migrated to New York in 1866 where the Agency had employed him "off and on" for several years as copyist and reader. In 1875 he had been dismissed for "dishonesty, and for attempting to corrupt the fidelity of some of his fellow clerks." In Dun's view such a person was not to be trusted nor his attack noticed except "by the public authorities, as an offense against good morals or catchpenny fraud."[11]

Dun dismissed Meagher's charges that the various agencies maintained a black list as a "tissue of lies," pointing out that the managers well knew that no such list existed or ever had existed in the Mercantile Agency. Much as it must have pained Dun, he even defended his rivals, claiming that none of the other agencies maintained such a list.[12] Like most of Meagher's attacks, the black list charge contained a shred of truth. The agencies maintained no secret lists, but the office reports did often contain derogatory and even libelous information not reflected in the *Reference Book*, and the merchants knew this.

No matter how much Dun and the other agencies might try to ignore Meagher's attacks or to dismiss them as "catchpenny fraud," the youthful Meagher clearly was a gifted writer who understood general business practices and finance and who was familiar with the operations of R. G. Dun & Co.[13] Moreover, he had a talent for exposing the system's most vulnerable weaknesses and for presenting his information about the Mercantile Agency in such a fashion that even when truthful, "it is so fragmentary, disjointed, and broken in its connection, as to become more fraudulent and deceptive than absolute untruth itself."[14] For example, in a long section, "Margin of Ignorance," Meagher underlined the discrepancies in the capital worth ratings assigned to the same firms by different agencies. Since Bradstreet did not assign ratings of capital worth, it escaped the "common pillory of comparison" with Dun and McKillop & Sprague Co. Using McKillop & Sprague's 1875 *Reports* and Dun's *Reference Book*, Meagher compared the capital rating on various firms. Obviously the estimates varied, but Meagher cleverly utilized the categories to overemphasize the variance. For example, a merchant Dun rated at from $50,000 to $100,000 might be rated by McKillop at from $100,000 to $250,000. Meagher listed the Dun rating at $50,000 and the McKillop at $250,000, and called the $200,000 difference the "margin of ignorance." Such distortions of the keys of the agencies, coupled with genuine differences in ratings, enabled Meagher to claim that the "margin of ignorance" on fourteen New York City merchants alone amounted to over $8,665,000.[15] Dun exploded to his managers that "such palpable perversion of the facts are hardly worth attention."[16]

Meagher's charges of inquisitorial tactics and secrecy touched a highly sensitive spot in Dun. It was, he insisted, "a sort of hallucination with many men, as it always seems to form the groundwork of attacks upon the Agency . . . the alleged *secrecy of its operations*."[17] The Agency, Dun argued, conducted its business as openly as any other business firm did. "We can always be found," he claimed, "everybody knows where to find us, and . . . we are ready at all times to see and converse with men who have reason to suppose that they have been misunderstood or misrepresented."[18] He inisted that this was done not as a "mere courtesy" but as an understood duty. True, the Agency, like all other businesses, tended to keep its affairs to itself, but if that constituted secrecy, "then every business man's afairs constitute secrecy." Moreover, the Agency stood in a unique relation to the reports it secured. Prudence demanded that reports, views, impressions, and knowledge communicated to the Agency with the understanding that it would be used for legitimate business purposes should remain confidential except for those legitimate purposes. Indeed, Dun argued that the Agency "may be said to be simply *custodians* of the reports," and as such, certain conditions necessarily attached to the interchange of information.[19] These simple procedures, designed to protect all parties involved, scarcely represented conspiratorial inquisitions or secrecy.

Meagher's attack on the secrecy of the credit-reporting agencies was not the first nor would it be the last to echo the charge. Thirteen years later Joseph Pulitzer's *New York World* repeated most of Meagher's accusations in a series of articles dwelling on the "secret inquisition." No doubt this reflected Pulitzer's penchant for sensationalism as much as his desire to reveal abuses by the agencies.[20] However, even the friendly critic, Earling, admitted that the American tolerance of credit-rating firms was unique: "It is paradoxical, for the free citizen of the United States is the only one on the face of the globe who tolerates it. It is a purely American institution and flourishes only on American soil."[21] In antebellum America, it was an uneasy tolerance, born of necessity and not acceptance; by 1890 it came from the conviction of the business community that credit-reporting agencies performed a vital function.

The almost total dependence of the Mercantile Agency on unpaid and untrained correspondents for credit information left it vulnerable to the charge leveled in the antebellum press, and echoed by Meagher and even by friendly critics like Earling, that the source of information was weak, contaminated, and untrustworthy. Dun himself admitted that the most serious charge Meagher made against the system was "that we are liable to be imposed upon by the incompetency or bad faith of others whom we employ to aid us in doing our work." He argued that the willingness of the Agency to consult with those merchants being reported helped to reduce the likelihood of error. Nevertheless he knew that the nature of the task made the Agency dependent on the correspondents and that beyond constant vigilance and cross-checking their information to test its accuracy, he could see little remedy for the situation.[22]

When Dun's close friend and frequent fishing companion, George Dawson, editor and publisher of the *Albany Evening Journal*, reviewed Meagher's book in his paper, he dismissed all of its charges against the Agency system except the need for better reporting.[23] Realizing the need to reform the system, Dun by 1880 had instructed his managers to use traveling reporters as much as possible for the semi-annual revisions of *Reference Book* data. In particular he instructed managers to code their revisions with a "large letter R" in red ink when done by a traveling reporter and in black ink when submitted by the local correspondent.[24] Throughout the 1880s Dun urged managers to use traveling reporters whenever possible and to "send out extra men from their staff of clerks" if necessary.[25] Managers themselves were instructed to do as much reporting in the cities as possible and to leave the details of the office "to less expensive help." Again and again Dun reminded his managers, "Our success and preeminence depend upon our getting first class Revisions, from good sources, by good men, and every energy should be bent in this direction."[26] By the end of the decade the New York office required all managers to furnish that office with a map of the districts under their charge, with the counties covered by traveling reporters colored in red, those reported by correspondents in blue, and those not visited left uncolored. The inference was clear. Dun expected to see a lot of red on the maps, and woe to the manager who submitted a map with many uncolored counties.[27]

Apparently Dun understood the widespread distrust of reports submitted by unpaid correspondents and, although he continued in some cases to rely on local attorneys for information, the Agency increasingly employed traveling reporters. By the late

1870s Dun was using "the increased and increasing extent of territory that we cover twice a year by *our travellers and reporters*" as a major inducement to prospective subscribers.[28] In 1885, after instructing managers to cut expenses, even to the point of reducing their staff, Dun specifically exempted increased expenditures that resulted from additional "traveling, reporting and canvassing."[29] By 1890 Earling could argue that the former dependence on unpaid correspondents had been remedied by the "better class" of agencies and could urge the business community to support agencies that "secure competent correspondents and pay and charge accordingly."[30] Although local attorneys were still utilized as unpaid correspondents to provide up-to-date information and to keep the Agency posted on new developments such as impending failures, reorganizations, or new firms, by the last decade of the nineteenth century much of the routine reporting and revisions were accomplished by paid traveling reporters.

The quality of reports improved, perhaps even more dramatically, as a result of the practice of asking firms to submit financial statements. As early as 1875 Agency reporters routinely identified themselves and asked for a statement of the capital assets and financial condition of the firm, which was then reported, along with the correspondent's remarks, to the Agency. The statements submitted by the firms took on an added significance when courts held that the firms were liable for "false representations" made by them. A court noted that statements made casually or from vanity that falsely or exaggeratedly estimated a person's financial means did not constitute fraud, but since the business of the credit-reporting agencies was so well-known,

> a person furnishing information to such an agency in relation to his own circumstances, means, and pecuniary responsibility can have no other motive in so doing than to enable the agency to communicate such information to persons who may be interested in obtaining it for their guidance in giving credit to the party; and if a merchant furnishes to such an agency a willfully false statement of his circumstances or pecuniary ability, with intent to obtain a

standing and credit to which he knows that he is not justly entitled,
and thus to defraud whoever may resort to the agency, and in
reliance upon the false information there lodged, extend a credit
to him, there is no reason why his liability to any party defrauded
by these means should not be the same as if he had made the false
representation directly to the party injured.[31]

Both of the major agencies, R. G. Dun & Co. and Bradstreet, were
already utilizing statements made by the firms being reported,
and the court decision simply accelerated the trend.

The courts had not always looked so favorably on credit-
reporting firms. Dun had, as had most other proprietors of credit-
reporting firms, worried constantly about libel, slander, and
damage suits. Indeed the Agency had faced what must have
seemed like a continual barrage of litigation and threats of legal
action throughout its existence, and it was not until the latter
part of the nineteenth century that a rather formidable body of
legal precedents had defined the legitimate sphere and modes of
operation for the agencies. Specifically the courts, after some reluctance, greatly extended the notion of privileged communications to cover relations between the agencies and their subscribers and restricted the liability of the agencies for the accuracy of the information provided.[32]

The earliest case involving the Mercantile Agency revolved
around the question of privileged communications between the
Agency and its subscribers and resulted in such a restricted definition that it threatened the existence of such firms. In 1851 John
and Horace Beardsley sued Lewis Tappan, claiming that his
Agency's report that they were about to fail constituted slander
and libel. The case achieved a good deal of notoriety when Benjamin Douglass refused to disclose whether the Agency had a
correspondent in Norfolk, Ohio, and he spent twenty days in jail
for contempt of court. Douglass's sentence had nothing to do
with the major issue—whether the use of clerks and correspondents destroyed the protection of privileged communications—and the court instructed the jury that if Tappan had
himself communicated the information to a client in good faith,
then the communication enjoyed privileged status; however,

recording the information in a place and manner that provided access to others and allowing clerks to communicate the information to clients removed the privilege. The jury returned a verdict of $10,000 for the Beardsleys.[33]

Tappan and Douglass appealed the verdict, and the U.S. circuit court, which upheld the lower court, agreed with the limitations on protection of privileged communications. Moreover Judge Samuel Nelson in the circuit court argued that legalizing mercantile agencies placed "one portion of the mercantile community under an organized system of espionage and inquisition" for the benefit of creditors. On the other hand the judge felt that not to legalize credit-reporting agencies would seriously restrict the right of merchants to inquire into the habits and standings of those seeking credit. Therefore, he concluded, "I am strongly inclined to think . . . the limitation attached to them by the court below is not unreasonable, to wit, that it must be an individual transaction, and not an establishment conducted by an unlimited number of partners and clerks."[34]

The limitation placed on the extension of privileged communications to the mercantile agencies, if allowed to stand, would have seriously jeopardized the future of the Mercantile Agency. On appeal to the U.S. Supreme Court, the case was remanded to retrial on error that had no bearing on the question of privileged communications. The Beardsleys never sought a retrial, and the status of privileged communication remained unsettled.[35]

No doubt the demonstrated need for and acceptance of credit-reporting agencies induced the courts to soften the hostile attitude expressed in *Beardsley* v. *Tappan*. Less than a decade later in the case of *Ormsby* v. *Douglass* (1858), the court dismissed a suit for slander after the plaintiff presented his evidence. In subsequent appeals the courts refused to grant a new trial. Reversing the view of the earlier court in *Beardsley*, in the New York Court of Last Resort, Judge Miller argued that the business of the Mercantile Agency "is sanctioned by the usages of commercial communities and the proof in this case fails to establish that he transgressed any rule of law in its transaction."[36] As to privileged communications, the court held that the number of persons involved in gathering and disseminating information had no bearing on

the status of privileged communications as long as they "associated for the purpose of gaining honest and truthful information."
The court concluded that the information that the Mercantile
Agency gathered and supplied to subscribers was indeed privileged as long as it was "made in a proper manner, without any
evil intent or malicious motive."[37]

Until after the Civil War lower courts had often displayed
hostility to mercantile agencies in holding them responsible for
misrepresentations, neglect, or false statements to subscribers.
Courts of appeal and superior courts had usually held the agencies not liable if commonly accepted methods of gathering
information were used and reasonable caution exercised to
ascertain its accuracy and reliability. Dun, as did other proprietors of credit-reporting firms, included in his contracts a
clause denying responsibility for losses and stating that the Agency was not responsible for the "verity or correctness of the said
information."[38] The law, of course, did not allow Dun or anyone
else to protect himself by contract against his own neglect. The
general rule applied was that when one was employed to per-
form certain services for another, he was assumed to exercise in
the employment "ordinary care and skill."[39] Dun, regardless of
contractual denials, assumed responsibility for negligence in the
exercise of his employment by subscribers if they proved he did
not use ordinary methods and skills.

By the 1880s favorable legal decisions, refinements in contracts with subscribers to take maximum advantage of the law,
and acceptance by the business community and the courts of the
credit-reporting agencies and their methods had severely limited
the possibility of legal action. Agency lawyers revised contracts
to make it clear that information was supplied subscribers as an
aid in determining the advisability of giving credit. The Agency
was "not [to] be responsible" for losses resulting from inaccurate
or false information and answers to inquiries were "strictly confidential."[40]

Noting that some branch offices signed or initialed the confidential sheets upon which inquiries were answered, Dun instructed managers to stop this "unnecessary and dangerous"
practice. The reason for omitting the signature was to take ad-

vantage of a Canadian statute, referred to as Lord Tenterden's Act and copied by many state legislatures, which provided that for the Agency to be legally liable, the report must be signed.[41] Despite Dun's approval of the statute, it did not, as he apparently thought, allow the Agency to avoid its responsibility. The legal test remained the degree to which the Mercantile Agency used commonly accepted methods of obtaining information and exercised reasonable diligence to ensure accuracy.[42]

Dun kept close watch over all suits, court decisions, and legislation concerning the Mercantile Agency and the credit-reporting business as a whole. He quickly modified practices and procedures to take advantage of favorable decisions and to avoid possible litigation.

For the most part Dun avoided politics and seldom pressed for favorable legislation. On the other hand he used every tactic available to defeat hostile legislation. Within a year of the panic of 1873, several legislatures attempted to push through measures making credit-reporting firms responsible for losses resulting from misinformation they had supplied. The *Commercial and Financial Chronicle* insisted that "various attempts at meddlesome law making by our State Legislature, and by the Legislatures of other States during the past winter" were nothing more than part of the general "mania for regulating by law."[43]

In May 1873 Dun dispatched Erastus Wiman to Ottawa, Canada, to lobby against a bill he called "prejudicial to our business," which would have required reporting agencies to post a bond to guarantee claims from damages resulting from false or inaccurate information.[44] Less than a year later Dun requested his brother-in-law William James in Missouri to use his influence to kill a bill introduced in that state's legislature, which he claimed "would virtually put the Agency out of business" in that state.[45] A month later Dun congratulated James for his success in stirring up opposition to the bill.[46] Measures introduced in most states would have required the agencies to post bonds to cover damage claims. A Pennsylvania measure, however, would have made misrepresentation a misdemeanor punishable by fines of $250 to $1,000, with half of the fine going to the informer.[47] The Pennsylvania house passed the measure, and a senate committee approved it. Dun prepared telegrams objecting to the measure and asking senators to vote against it, which were sent to each of the Pennsylvania branch offices with instructions to obtain the signatures of the most prominent merchants in each locale and forward the telegrams to the senate. Not surprisingly the senate soundly defeated the measure.[48] By the last two decades of the nineteenth century, attempts to enact hostile legislation had become increasingly rare. Legislatures thus reflected the growing acceptance of credit-reporting firms by the courts, the business community, and the public.

Generally legislative pressure and legal decisions had little effect on the operation of Agency business. Dun and his partners recognized not only their responsibility to work within the limits defined by the courts and legislation but their need to avoid adverse public attention. In March 1881, for example, the New York office admonished the branch offices to stop answering fire insurance inquiries asking if parties have ever been "burned out and what their general reputation is." Most important Dun insisted, "We must insist upon managers seeing that inquiries are confined to legitimate business people."[49] The Agency, Dun reminded the branch managers, made credit-reports on businesses, not individuals, and the practice of answering inquiries about or from parties not "in business at all, except as farmers or laborers," must stop immediately. Subscribers were to be instructed to confine their inquiries to legitimate business concerns.[50]

In the decade following the Civil War, the Mercantile Agency won widespread public and business acceptance and emerged as the leader in credit-reporting in the face of increased competition. In the same period R. G. Dun & Co. grew from fewer than twenty offices to an international organization with nearly sixty offices and enjoyed profits that rose from less than $40,000 to more than $300,000 per year.

The basic procedures Lewis Tappan had developed remained relatively unchanged throughout this period of rapid growth. Information was still gathered by local correspondents, although by the last quarter of the nineteenth century the efforts of unpaid local attorneys had been greatly supplemented by paid reporters. Data so collected were converted by the local office into a report that was copied in longhand into large record books. After sending the New York office a copy of the report, the original was forwarded to the nearest office desiring the information; after it was copied, it was transmitted in succession to whatever offices required information on the territory from which the report originated. Whenever a new office opened or the records of an office were destroyed, thousands of reports had to be copied into a new set of ledgers. As the number of reports multiplied, the copying became expensive and time-consuming, and indexing the information to make it readily available proved almost impossible. Because of their constant use, the ledgers soon became tattered and had to be replaced. Still, despite the growth of the Agency and the greatly increased demands for reporting, the basic system remained unchanged.

The typewriter enabled Dun and his partners to revise the entire Agency operation. Erastus Wiman in his book *Chances of Success* claimed credit for converting the Agency to the use of the new typewriter and asserted that the Agency's order for a hundred typewriters enabled the Remington brothers to keep their company in operation.[51] Although Charles Barlow, the senior and most conservative of Dun's partners, apparently was traveling abroad at the time the Agency tested and then adopted the typewriter, Dun was present and must have participated in the decision. After an initial trial in the New York office in 1874, a number of the machines, together with tissue paper, carbon, and instructions, were supplied to the branch offices. Within twenty years the Mercantile Agency had in use some fifteen hundred machines, and Wiman insisted that the typewriter had contributed more to the efficient operation of the Agency than any other development.[52]

On November 23, 1875, after testing the typewriters and allowing time for the branch offices to train operators, the company issued a manual containing rules and directions for preparing typewritten reports. In addition it included a set of distribution tables for the reports prepared at each of the sixty-five offices. In the past the original copy of a report, having been recorded in the office of origin, was circulated in succession to all

135.

T. R. McGURN.

STOREY CO., NEVADA.

VIRGINIA CITY & GOLD HILL.   GROCERIES, PRODUCE ETC.

JULY 1, 1885.

HAVE SETTLED WITH CREDITORS AT 50 CENTS ON THE DOLLAR IN 5 INSTALLMENTS COMMENCING JULY 15, 1885 NOTES HELD BY MAC ONDRAY &CO.

SEPT. 8, 1885.

GRANTED EXTENSION ON COMPROMISE NOTES, WHICH ARE NOW MADE DUE MARCH AND JUNE 1886.

T. R. McGURN.   VIRGINIA CITY & GOLDHILL.   GROC. PRODUCE &C.

DEC 3RD 1885.

HE SETTLED WITH CREDITORS AT 50 CENTS PAYABLE IN 5 MONTHLY INSTALLMENTS COMMENCING JULY 15TH 1885. HE PAID TWO NOTES OR 20 CENTS AND THE REMAINING NOTES OR 30 CENTS WAS EXTENDED TO DECEMBER 15TH 1885, MARCH 15TH 1886 AND JUNE 15TH 1886.

T. R. McGURN.   GOLD HILL &VIRGINIA CITY.   GRO. PROD. &C.

MAY 22ND 1885.

AT A MEETING OF CREDITORS HELD AT THE BOARD OF TRADE, SAN FRANCISCO HE REPRESENTED THAT TOTAL LIABILITIES WERE $49,000 & ASSETS $27,000 BUT GAVE NO DETAILS, IT WAS AGREED TO ACCEPT 50 CENTS PAYABLE IN FIVE MONTHLY INSTALLMENTS OF TEN PER CENT EACH, THE 1ST INSTALLMENT PAYABLE JULY 15TH 1885. AN AGREEMENT WAS CIRCULATED TO THAT EFFECT WHICH HAS BEEN SIGNED BY ALL THE SAN FRANCISCO CREDITORS EXCEPTING ONE THE STOCK BREWERY & THE AGREEMENT HAS BEEN SENT TO SACRAMENTO FOR SIGNATURE THERE.

T. R. McGURN   VIRGINIA CITY & GOLD HILL.   GRO & PRODUCE.

SEPT 22-86.

WHEN HE SETTLED AT 50 CENTS ON THE 18TH MAY 1885 HIS LIABILITIES AMOUNTED TO $28,207.00 THE SETTLEMENT NOTES AMOUNTED TO $14,103.80 PAYABLE IN 5 EQUAL INSTALLMENTS COMMENCING ON THE 15TH OF JULY 1885. THE FIRST TWO INSTALLMENTS WERE PAID & THEN HE GOT AN EXTENSION ON THE BALANCE HE HAS THUS FAR PAID HALF OF THIS BALANCE & STILL OWES ABOUT 15 PER CENT OR SAY $4,231.14 OF THE LD INDEBTEDNESS. HIS BUSINESS IS VERY MUCH CURTAILED FROM ITS FORMER DIMENSIONS & NOW CONSISTS IN SELLING FRESH FRUITS & C. THE GROCERY BUSINESS WHICH HE FORMERLY CONTROLED WAS BEEN VERY MUCH CUT UP. IT IS DOUBTED WHETHER THE SURPLUS LEFT HIM WITH ANY REAL SOLID SURPLUS ON WHICH TO CONTINUE THE BUSINESS & IT IS ALMOST CERTAIN THAT HE HAS NOT MADE ANYTHING SINCE THE SETTLEMENT WAS MADE. HE IS NOT IN A POSITION TO RECOMMEND FOR MUCH CREDIT.

T. R. McGURN   VIRGINIA CITY- &GOLD HILL-   GRO.

JANY. 14TH 1887.

THE GOLD HILL BUSINESS HAS BEEN GIVEN UP AND THE VIRGINIA CITY BUSINESS IS NOW RUN IN THE NAME OF HIS WIFE

MRS. T. R. McGURN   WHO HAS BEEN MADE A SOLE TRADER' THE HUSBAND HOWEVER IT STILL THE CONTROLLING SPIRIT IN THE CONCERN AND CAUTIOUS DEALINGS SHOULD BE THE RULE.

10. 1885 Report on T. R. McGurn, Storey County, Nevada. *Courtesy of Dun & Bradstreet, Inc.*

the offices interested in it. According to the manual's preface, the multiplication of offices brought about by the expanding market and the growth of a railroad network had made reliance on one original report impossible.[53] Typewriters, carbon papers, and tissue paper permitted the Mercantile Agency to duplicate the reports, thus permitting a rapid and simultaneous distribution of credit information throughout the firm. Although the technology for duplicating material existed prior to the typewriter, Dun had never utilized any of the various processes. With the accelerating velocity of transactions in the expanding economy, the capability provided by the typewriter was necessary if the Agency was to continue to meet the demands of its subscribers.

The adoption of the typewriter also forced a complete reorganization of the basic office routines. As information flowed into an office, reports were typed, duplicated, and distributed to other branches in accordance with the distribution tables contained in the instruction manual. Originally the New York office received a copy or "tissue" of every report, and the large offices in Boston, Philadelphia, and Chicago received copies of most reports from all the offices. Within a few years the flow of reports reached such a volume that the New York office requested the other branches not to forward the many thousands of copies on certain categories of small businesses that had no relation to the New York market. Most of the larger offices routinely screened incoming reports and discarded many that were of no interest to local subscribers.

Rather than copying reports in the large record books, the tissues at first were simply pasted in, but their fragility led to a change in procedure: they were pasted on thin but stiff manila sheets, about ten inches wide and fifteen inches long, with a separate sheet for each firm. Within its geographic area the originating office usually pasted such tissues for a single firm on both the front and back of a sheet, and when it was filled, sheets were added by the use of linen hinges, so that all of the reports on a single firm, often dating back several years, remained in one file. Tissues received on firms outside the district were pasted on similar sheets, but on these firms second sheets were never hinged to the original unless the current report made reference to previous information. To save space only single sheets were maintained on out-of-district firms. All of the sheets were trimmed to uniform size and put into binders, filed alphabetically by name and county or city. Each branch office used the identical office procedure and filing system. Indeed, by the last decade of the nineteenth century the procedures had become so routine, systematized, and uniform that at least one employee complained that managers were stifled in their attempt to introduce changes and improvements.[54]

The development of systematic and detailed routines to handle the flow of information proved only the first transformation of Agency practices engendered by the typewriter. Taking advantage of a major reorganization within the Bradstreet company and the bankruptcy of the New York office of his other major rival, McKillop & Sprague, Dun decided to undertake the first major alteration in credit-reporting agency operations since Bradstreet had introduced the first reference book some twenty years earlier.

Dun and Douglass had reluctantly adopted Bradstreet's innovation — a better delivery system for the information desired by subscribers — but Dun had retained Tappan's pricing philosophy. With only rare exceptions, he had refused to sell the *Reference Book* and the weekly notification sheets separately from the charge for the "privilege of the office," holding to Tappan's position that since the Agency had to prepare in advance to serve the needs of subscribers, the charge for a subscription should be based on the customer's potential, not the actual use. Even after returning to the publication of the *Reference Book* after the Civil War, Dun insisted on tying the use of the book to a basic charge for the privilege of the office, based on the dollar volume of the subscriber's sales. On rare occasions when Dun allowed managers to sell the *Reference Book* and notification sheets separately from a charge for the privilege of the office, it was in recognition that a single rate schedule no longer applied when the Agency moved outside the wholesale trade and began to enroll manufacturers, banks, commission merchants, and insurance companies as subscribers.

Dun's decision to retain a basic schedule of charges based on the subscribers' sales proved much sounder than Bradstreet's fixed charge to all subscribers regardless of size. True, Bradstreet made swift and deep inroads into the Agency's business during the years that Dun had failed to publish the book, but the revenue produced by the set charge was insufficient to sustain the quality subscribers demanded in credit-reports. In providing a reference book, Dun simply furnished in a more convenient form the information already contracted for. The extra charge for the book represented the cost of the convenience. Since the book could not be metered for the number of times used, Dun maintained that the subscriber's volume of business remained the fairest and soundest basis for measuring the value and potential value of the Agency's service.[55]

The development of the typewriter and its adoption by R. G. Dun & Co. offered opportunities beyond simply streamlining the flow of data. The new procedures worked so well that the Agency came to realize that the greatly increased volume of information being processed made the notification sheets inadequate to keep the *Reference Book* current. By 1876 book changes alone averaged nearly 5,000 a week. The national sheet, necessary to serve larger market areas such as New York and Chicago, was a folio with a capacity of fewer than 500 listings, or about 10 percent of the total changes. Actually the size of the notification sheet had little to do with its obsolescence. Few, if any, subscribers could effectively scan 5,000 names a week, identifying customers and selecting the items of interest. Even breaking the items down by trades and locale served little purpose for firms with a national market. Information was pouring into the New York and other major offices at a rate that threatened to swamp the delivery system.[56]

Since he had first joined the firm in 1854, Dun had tallied the number of reports read and follow-up notices on invitations to subscribers to call at the office if interested. Originally the tallies served to determine the profitability of each subscriber but were not used for billing. The adoption of the typewriter made it possible to provide individual written reports to subscribers and to charge accordingly.

The question Dun and his partners faced was whether to make written reports available on an unlimited basis as they did the oral service or to sell it on a report-unit basis as a separate service. Dun decided to sell the entire Mercantile Agency service on a unit basis, with privileges of the office, *Reference Book*, and notification sheets on a twice a week schedule plus a specified number of written reports. Apparently the shift in pricing and contracts took place as annual subscriptions were renewed. Although the September 1877 *Reference Book* contained a specimen contract that indicated a minimum of two hundred written reports, an advertising letter mailed to subscribers and potential customers in November mentioned no minimum. Indeed the flyer gave little indication of the significance of the shift, simply mentioning "written or printed reports . . . comprising in each case the material facts of the entire business history . . . down to a recent date" as one of a series of improvements being offered subscribers by the Agency.[57] The 1878 issue of the *Reference Book* contained a specimen contract with complete details of the new pricing scheme: (table 10). For the first time in the history

Table 10

1878 SPECIMEN CONTRACT

Reports		Reference Books	
		General	Sectional
100	with	2 - $75	2 - $50
100	with	4 - 125	4 - 75

Additional reports:
    Contracted in advance - $25 per hundred
    Excess, at the rate of $33 1/3 per hundred
Additional books:
    Generals - $25 each; Sectionals - $12.50 each.

Source: Compiled from Owen A. Sheffield, "Dun & Bradstreet, Inc.: The Mercantile Agency Since 1841 . . ." (1965), II-7, pp. 8-9.[58]

of the Mercantile Agency, R. G. Dun & Co. now sold things as opposed to service.

No doubt declining profits played a major role in Dun's decision to revise the pricing system and to offer written reports to his subscribers. Profits, which had displayed a slow but steady increase since the end of the Civil War, reached a high of over $313,000 in 1874, only to fall more than $100,000 in the next two years. Even though the smaller profits might well have been a short-run phenomenon reflecting nothing more than the residual effect of the panic of 1873, Dun's eye was always keen on the balance sheet. If reversing the sliding profit picture was not the determining factor in Dun's decision to shift the fundamental pricing and operational policies of the Agency, no doubt it provided the immediate incentive.

In retrospect Dun's decision proved flawed but not fatal. In basing subscription costs on the number of written reports and at the same time continuing to provide the *Reference Book* and weekly (sometimes semiweekly) notification sheets, Dun lost the protection against unlimited use of the *Reference Book*. Having made the decision to provide written reports on a unit basis for subscribers, Dun would have been well advised to have abandoned the notification sheets entirely (they had already proven inadequate) and to move immediately to continuous written report service for subscribers on selected lists of customers. Continuous service, which the Agency flirted with after adopting the new pricing schedule, would have secured better control of the Agency's information and would have greatly increased revenue. Declining profits, concern over the obvious inadequacies of the notification sheets, worry about the growth of trade-reporting associations that pirated most of their information from the reference books and notification sheets, and an inability under the old system to exploit the technological advances of the typewriter resulted in a decision that went either too far or not far enough in revising the Agency's operations.

The growth of giant enterprise in the late nineteenth century should not obscure the fact that a few large firms took their place over, not in place of, the 1.5 million small and medium-sized firms that constituted the bulk of American businesses.

Table 11

R. G. DUN & CO.
PROFITS, 1874-1900

Year	Profits Before Withdrawals by Managing Partners	Year	Profits Before Withdrawals by Managing Partners
1874	$313,653	1887	$371,762
1875	253,363	1888	389,503
1876	208,973	1889	432,954
1877	211,621	1890	430,293
1878	231,686	1891	471,569
1879	269,341	1892	432,063
1880	196,243	1893	484,768
1881	300,753	1894	597,912
1882	336,268	1895	615,151
1883	340,761	1896	522,463
1884	336,661	1897	517,807
1885	345,780	1898	519,356
1886	346,656	1899	425,626
		1900	493,531

Source: Compiled from Owen A. Sheffield, "Dun & Bradstreet, Inc.: The Mercantile Agency Since 1841 . . ." (1965), II-7.

Under the old subscription schedule a customer with $1 million annual sales paid a $1 per thousand or $1,000 base rate plus $50 for two books. To obtain the same revenue with the new price scheme, the same subscriber would have to take 4,000 reports at $25 per hundred, contracted in advance, plus two books. What Dun discovered was that the large firms did not necessarily have more customers, but they more often sold in larger lots. The same subscriber with 500 customers averaging $2,000 in annual purchases would net $1 million in sales but might require only $125 worth of reports plus $50 for two books, or a net reduction for the Agency of $875.[59]

On the other hand, Dun well knew that most of the Agency's subscribers were small businesses that often took the minimum subscription: $75 plus $50 for two books or a total of $125. Under the new scheme the minimum fell to 100 reports at $25 per hundred plus $50 for the two books, or $75 — a loss to the Agency of $50. Even medium-sized businesses with sales of $100,000 often contracted for fewer than 400 reports, with a resultant reduction in the subscription price. Most important, many firms now paid less for the books, notification sheets, privileges of the office, and the additional written report service than under the previous subscription terms. With no service charge or schedule, the Agency lost what little protection it had against large firms using the *Reference Book* and notification sheets without adequate compensation.[60]

The greatly increased number of subscribers successfully halted the declining profit picture during the two decades following the shift in pricing structure, but the average annual increase amounted only to 5.6 percent.[61] In the same period the number of branch offices grew from 76 to 136, and the number of firms reported in the *Reference Book* jumped from slightly over 690,000 to over 1,248,000. Although Dun's profits generally kept pace with the growth of offices and firms it reported on, and even with the growth of the national economy, the Agency failed to take the opportunity to dominate the credit-reporting business completely. Dun could hardly claim to have exploited the typewriter to gain greater earnings for the Agency.

In 1876 the time was propitious for Dun to make a major innovation in the credit-reporting business. Alone of all the major credit-reporting firms, R. G. Dun & Co. had adopted and integrated the typewriter into its operation. McKillop & Sprague was sliding rapidly into bankruptcy, and Bradstreet's was in the middle of a major reorganization. With his major rivals in disarray, the time was ripe for Dun to monopolize the credit-reporting business. By utilizing the technical capability provided by the typewriter, Dun could have offered his subscribers continuous reporting service on selected lists of customers. Such service would have revolutionized the delivery system for credit-reporting information to the same extent that Bradstreet's reference book had done some twenty years earlier.

Certainly Dun and his partners should have been aware of the potential of continuous service because within a few years, they were soliciting advice from managers regarding its introduction, both to prevent rival firms from pirating information from the notification sheets and to gain additional revenues. Dun and his partners proposed to "write out and send to each subscriber, every day, all the information we receive in which he is interested."[62] The new scheme would eliminate the need for the notification sheets, protect the Agency from "the wholesale robbery now practiced on us" by rivals, provide a vastly superior service to subscribers, and get a "better price for our services than the paltry sum we are now charging."[63] Dun left no doubt as to the source of his concern. New leadership, reorganization, the failure of McKillop, and the general good times had made Bradstreet "financially successful" and the Agency's only serious rival, but Dun had assured his managers that "after the battle was fought—and it would be a severe fight for one season—the victory would be ours."[64]

Managers were instructed to canvass each subscriber, explain the proposed change in contract, and determine the support for or opposition to the scheme. Subscribers were to be made to understand that the Agency wanted all of their business—or none. When subscribers sought to contract for fewer reports than the firm's business required, the contract should be refused. The "rub," as Dun expressed it, was that the new scheme, "if well and successfully worked . . . would be equivalent to doubling our rates." After making their survey, managers were instructed to make a careful evaluation of the chances for increased revenue.[65]

Apparently the reaction from subscribers proved negative, and so Dun rejected his plan. He had failed to act boldly and to capitalize on the weakness of the rivals. Dun's timidity and his unwillingness to risk even a temporary loss of subscribers and revenue cost the Agency an opportunity to gain almost a monopoly position in the credit-reporting business and delayed the introduction of continuous reporting service for nearly a half-century.[66]

Having failed to exploit his favorable situation in 1876, Dun would have been well advised to have retained some charge for the privilege of the office. The effect of the new pricing scheme was to reduce the minimum subscription charge. Probably Dun and his partners dropped the fixed charge of $1 per $1,000 sales in an effort to attract the large corporations that had become increasingly significant in the American economy. They hoped the larger firms, which too often hired internal credit managers, would be willing to pay for better service in the form of written reports on selected list of customers. Unfortunately the larger concerns with credit managers usually resorted to the Agency on only a small number of particularly bothersome credit risks: the result was that the income the Agency received from many of these firms was often not as profitable as Dun felt it should have been.[67]

While many of the nation's larger business concerns and banks were represented among the Mercantile Agency's subscribers, the "bread and butter" income came not from them but from the many smaller businesses, which often paid the minimum charge and depended entirely on the Agency for credit information.[68] The 1876-77 pricing decision, which reduced the minimum subscription charge, attracted more subscribers but at a lower unit income. Agency profits increased after the revisions in pricing and service policies, but neither Dun nor Erastus Wiman was satisfied. In 1886, a decade after the policy shifts, profits exceeded the 1874 high of $313,653 by only slightly over $30,000 — an increase of less than 1 percent annually in spite of greatly expanded coverage, the introduction of written report service, and a booming economy.[69]

Evidence of Dun's dissatisfaction appeared in a series of advertisements beginning in 1886 that supported the need for higher prices for his company's service as compared with those charged by rival agencies. These advertisements, which appeared in city directories, suggested that not only did the subscriber get better and more complete information from R. G. Dun & Co. but that higher rates and more income would enable the Agency to improve its services greatly with a minimum cost to the individual subscriber. Apparently Dun's pleas fell on deaf, if not altogether hostile, ears, and no rate increase followed until 1892.[70]

The increase in subscription prices in 1892, although following the suggestions outlined in earlier advertisements, seemed less motivated by a desire to improve service that by the need of both Dun and Wiman for larger profits to finance their outside business ventures. Essentially the new schedule raised the basic subscription price for two general reference books and one hundred reports by $25 regardless of the size of the firm. The year 1891 had been the most prosperous in the history of the Agency, with Dun and his partners' income amounting to over $470,000. Assuming no subscriber resistance to the higher prices, even with substantial sums devoted to the expansion and improvement of service, the new price schedule could potentially have more than doubled R. G. Dun & Co's profits. Dun and Wiman had not chosen a favorable time to institute a price rise, however. As the nation's economy slid into a severe depression, subscriber resistance mounted, and the Agency's income dropped nearly $40,000 in 1892. Because of the accrual system the increase on renewals would have carried over into 1893, and therefore the maximum increase, even assuming no loss of subscribers, would not have been realized until 1893, when profits exceeded the 1891 high, but only by slightly over $13,000.[71] Far from providing greatly increased profits, the impact of the 1892 price hike illustrated consumer resistance to the higher rates in the face of a declining economy.

As great as Dun's disappointment must have been in the failure of the 1892 price hike to produce greater profits, an even greater shock awaited him. In February 1893 he discovered that Erastus Wiman, his business associate for more than thirty years and his principal partner since Charles Barlow's death in 1880, had been systematically diverting Agency funds for his personal use.

Dun had been on one of his annual salmon fishing trips in Canada with Chester Arthur and U.S. Senator Roscoe Conkling in July 1880 when Barlow died. Summoned home by a telegram from Wiman, Dun assigned Barlow's duties and position to Wiman, retained Matthias Smith as auditor, named Arthur J. King, the St. Louis branch manager, partner and city manager in the New York office, and promoted his nephew Robert Dun Douglass to junior partner.

Wiman's promotion had not been accompanied by an increase

in salary, and when he complained, Dun replied that Wiman already received a salary as large "as is paid in the United States, not excepting that paid to managers for the heaviest corporations."[72] Wiman, always in need of funds to finance his grandiose outside schemes, persisted, and Dun decided that the next partnership agreement in January 1881 would increase Wiman's share to 20 percent, keep Smith's participation at 15 percent since "no further burdens have been thrown upon him," and that King would receive 5 percent and Douglass 3 percent.[73] In addition Wiman's name as senior partner would be included in the name of New York office—Dun, Wiman & Co.

After his promotion to what Wiman later referred to as "general manager" of the entire firm, he retained direct control over the *Reference Book*, printing, and purchasing departments. In December 1882 Dun requested Matthias Smith's retirement because of his "advancing years, long service and especially your well to do pecuniary position in life."[74] When Smith protested that he did not wish to retire just then, Dun agreed to allow him to "retain your desk after Jan. 1, '83 for a limited period of say six months on a fixed salary of one thousand dollars per month, to . . . have you instruct Mr. Robt. Douglass in all the matters in which you have had charge."[75] Having forced Smith into retirement, Dun neither replaced him as a partner nor transferred the accounting and auditing responsibilities to his nephew Robert Douglass, but decided to save $40,000 a year by hiring a young and inexperienced bookkeeper who would work under Wiman's supervision. Wiman was "in the saddle."[76]

Dun had never trusted Wiman, and on several occasions he had expressed concern about the latter's involvement in outside speculative ventures. In late fall 1881, Dun returned from an inspection trip of his Colorado silver mining property to find Wiman involved in some nasty publicity over the Mutual Telegraph Company. As a director of the Western Union Telegraph Company and president of the Great Northwestern Telegraph Company, Wiman was accused of bribing a former office employee of Mutual to steal him a copy of the contract between Mutual and its construction company, a contract suggesting that the construction company had paid substantial kickbacks to the promoter of the Mutual Company.[77]

Dun confessed to his brother, James, that the affair "angered me so much that he should drag my bus.[iness] into his dirty work that I was almost disposed to put him out entirely."[78] Instead, after several pleas from Wiman, a threat that Dun's actions might force him to resign, and intercession by Wiman's friends, Dun simply dropped Wiman's name from the firm in the United States, making it uniformly R. G. Dun & Co.[79] In return Dun extracted Wiman's written promise to withdraw from "all outside matters, especially from personal participation in the suit vs. the Mut.[ual] U.[nion] Tel.[egraph] Co. with the promise of giving entire attention to the M.A.[Mercantile Agency]," a promise that Wiman readily gave, with no intention of keeping.[80]

Far from confining his activities to the business of the Mercantile Agency, Wiman became even more deeply involved in outside ventures. In particular his efforts to promote Staten Island as a major deep-water port to compete with Manhattan led to his involvement in railroads, ferries, power companies, and a major real estate speculation on the island. With the collapse of an understanding with the Baltimore and Ohio Railroad, Wiman's haphazardly constructed financial empire began to crumble.[81] While Dun was vacationing in Florida, Wiman discounted a $25,000 note on R. G. Dun & Co. and deposited the proceeds to his account. In March 1887, after Dun's return and during Wiman's absence, the note, contrary to Wiman's instructions to the banks, was presented to Dun for payment. Horrified, Dun quickly instructed his Montreal manager to ascertain if Wiman had been doing the same thing in his native city.[82]

Failing to uncover additional cases of dishonesty and after Wiman had appealed to Dun's young second wife for mercy, Dun relented and allowed Wiman to retain his position.[83] In truth, Dun himself was so deeply involved in outside ventures, particularly in Colorado silver mining properties, that he failed to devote proper time and attention to the business. In addition his health was beginning to fail. These reasons and the fear that Wiman would transfer his talent and knowledge to some competitor, as much as his wife's intercession, caused Dun to settle for a promise from Wiman to repay the firm and to disassociate himself from outside ventures.

Wiman's promises were soon broken. Within a year Dun

returned from another trip to discover that a circular promoting the Cyclone Pulverizer Company, a firm promoting an ore-separating process, with Wiman listed as president and emphasizing his association with R. G. Dun & Co., was being distributed throughout the city. Infuriated, Dun insisted that Wiman comply with his agreement to divorce himself from outside ventures:

> My clear understanding with you, in consideration of mitigating your past offenses, was that you were to get out of all of these outside matters as quickly as possible and not in any way connect your name, in these matters, with that of the firm of R. G. D[un] & Co. & it is in this light that this matter is so annoying & objectionable. While you send the Cyclone circular as simply its President, by the accompanying paper you represent yourself as of the firm of R. G. D[un] & Co. & thereby use the influence of that name to float your private schemes & of course any odium attached to them would necessarily attach to the good fame and name of this firm.[84]

Dun demanded immediate assurance from Wiman that the latter was prepared to abide by the original agreement. Two months later Dun reminded Wiman that their partnership agreement expired on January 1, 1889. While not fully decided, Dun informed Wiman that he had been "considering seriously having no ostensible partners." In the meantime he demanded a written statement of Wiman's financial condition and "the names of all outside companies you are at present interested in, or connected with, together with amount of investment pecuniarily, in such companies."[85] Despite these threats, which by now Wiman must have realized were mostly idle, Dun renewed the partnership. The January 1889 agreement fixed Wiman's share at 17 percent, Arthur King's at 6 percent, and Robert Douglass's at 5 percent for a period of four years.[86]

Throughout the latter part of the 1880s, Dun spent increasingly less time in the actual management of the firm. In 1884 he had remarried, some two years after the death of his first wife, and the younger Mrs. Dun encouraged her husband to travel. Dun frequently spent some winter months in Florida, at least two months in the summer salmon fishing in Canada, and took periodic trips to the West to inspect mining properties. He and his wife also enjoyed touring Europe. The result was that Dun's absences from the office prevented him from exercising the same detailed supervision of the Mercantile Agency that he previously had. He devoted increasingly larger portions of his time to his private life and to outside ventures. Nevertheless he still managed to keep a close eye on the total income and on profits from individual branch offices. He also participated in almost all significant policy decisions.

Despite his long experience and his having a partner who had previously been caught diverting funds, Dun had not employed an independent controller in the firm or contracted for an outside audit. Apparently neither Dun nor the junior partners, King and Douglass, ever examined the books in any detail. Not even Dun realized how deeply involved Wiman was in outside ventures. Determined to weather his financial difficulties and save his personal fortune, Wiman began diverting funds almost immediately after having been restored to good graces in 1887. In July 1888 he drew $1,500 for his personal use and charged it to "legal expenses." During the next six years, using a variety of devices — including intercepting remittances from branch offices, drawing checks for suppliers and exchanging them for checks drawn to his name, charging personal expenses to the firm, and forgeries — Wiman diverted nearly a quarter of a million dollars for his personal use.[87] In February 1893 Dun, noticing the "very indiscriminate and loose way of drawing exchange checks to the order of parties with whom my firm have no business relations," instructed the cashier to hand each partner a check for the amount they were entitled to draw on the first of each month and to issue no other checks to their order and no exchange checks without Dun's personal consent.[88] Within a few days an independent audit had uncovered the extent of Wiman's diversion of funds. He was ousted from the firm and the evidence against him turned over to the district attorney. The investigation dragged on for over a year and the trial and appeals for another year. Though he was initially found guilty of forgery, Wiman was eventually freed on the technical point that as a partner he could not, by definition, commit forgery by signing the firm's name.[89]

In spite of the widespread publicity and the shock within the Agency, Wiman's ouster left little lasting impression on the business. Profits, which had been slowly increasing after the 1892 price adjustment, jumped nearly 24 percent in 1894 and the following year exceeded six hundred thousand dollars for the first and only time during Dun's life. But for R. G. Dun it had been a long, nasty, and disheartening affair, which taxed his already failing health and left him more determined than ever to right his house, withdraw from outside ventures, and leave the day-to-day management of the Mercantile Agency to men he could trust.

6

The End of an Era, 1894-1900

Dun's failing health would not have permitted him to reassume active management of the Agency after Wiman's dismissal even if he had been so inclined. For some time he had been systematically divorcing himself from the routine management, and in an effort to devote himself more to nonbusiness activities had even begun disposing of his outside investments and ventures. To replace Wiman, Dun promoted Arthur King to chief executive officer and designated his nephew, Robert Dun Douglass, as his only other partner and as heir apparent to the sixty-nine-year-old King. In choosing King and Douglass, Dun sought continuity, trustworthiness, and routine competency over agressive, expansion-minded, and vigorous leadership.

At the time of his promotion, Arthur King had been with the Mercantile Agency over forty years, serving as clerk in the New York office soon after his arrival from England. When Dun took over the Agency, he promoted King to manager of the newly established Cleveland office, then transferred him to Cincinnati, and finally to St. Louis. In each case King had assumed the management of branch offices in financial trouble and had proven hard working and trustworthy. In 1880 Dun promoted King to a partnership with responsibility for the New York City office. Although well liked and respected not only by R. G. Dun but throughout the Agency, the elderly King had neither the health, vigor, nor inclination to provide more than a caretaker management. On King's death in September 1896 Dun promoted Robert Dun Douglass to chief executive officer.[1]

Having assured himself of honest, competent management, Dun withdrew from active participation in Agency business. No longer was his letterbook filled with letters and memoranda to branch managers on a wide variety of business details; instead the lines of communications within the Agency were formalized, and the New York City office assumed a dominant position within the organization as the headquarters. During the last five years of his life, aside from regular checks on the overall profits, Dun assumed a direct role in management only to insist on institutionalization of procedures, to purchase the Boston office from his old friend and associate Edward Russell, and to plan and finance a new office building in New York City to house the city branch and headquarters of R. G. Dun & Co. The remainder and bulk of his time he devoted to those things in his private life he valued most: his family, his art collection, and fishing.

Within a year after dismissing Wiman, at Dun's insistence and under Robert Douglass's direction, the first *Mercantile Agency Manual* was issued to branch managers. While admitting that this first effort was "crude and imperfect," Douglass pointed out that the compilation of rules, suggestions, and special circulars issued since 1883 provided the managers with a nucleus that could be improved and adopted as the "standard Law for Agency government."[2] The *Manual* reflected Douglass's legal training, gave graphic evidence of the formalization of lines of responsibility and authority, and left no doubt that henceforth the operations of the Agency would be closely scrutinized and controlled by the New York office.

Matthias Smith's position in the New York headquarters had been formally renamed "general inspector of offices," and performance audits of all branches were routinely scheduled. As headquarters, the New York office insisted on uniform reports, forms, and procedures. It also checked the quality and performance of branch office corresponding reports. In October 1896, for example, New York headquarters informed the Hartford, Connecticut, office that simply forwarding the statement of the First National Bank of Winsted was not sufficient: "We must have the names of the officers and directors of the bank and also know something about the business of the bank and standing of those connected with it, in accordance with instructions set forth in the 'Manual' under the heading—'Reports of Banks.' "[3]

The New York office demanded compliance with the *Manual*, periodically questioned the accuracy of ratings assigned by branch offices, and insisted on full and up-to-date data. On a firm rated E-2.5 (capital worth $20,000–35,000 and general credit good) by the Troy, New York, office, the Agency headquarters requested a "fuller and more elaborate report" revised carefully since "our esteemed subscribers #457 . . . advise us . . . that the firm is not good pay."[4] On the other hand, when a branch office applied a too stringent rating, the New York office, after obtaining a full statement of the affairs of the firm, might grant higher ratings.[5]

The New York office, officially called the "city department," offered suggestions to the branches on everything from minor to major significance. At times it demanded details in reports, pointed out spelling mistakes to branch offices, corrected misinformation, and always sought to maintain quality control on the reporting. When a Canton, Ohio, firm defaulted on an anticipatory note, the New York office demanded to know how a firm with a D-1.5 ($35,000–50,000 capital worth and high general credit) rating in the July *Reference Book* could default in the same month.[6] Less than a month later the Pittsburgh office was informed, with a marked degree of exasperation, that simply reporting the inability to find a subject on whom a subscriber wished a report would not do. Since Pittsburgh had reported the same firm a year earlier, the New York office concluded, "It strikes us that if you could find him then you should be able to find him now."[7] When the Philadelphia office returned an inquiry with a note that the subject was not there and was not known either by the postmaster or assessor, headquarters replied that the report "was at variance with the facts," adding that it had ascertained that the subject was known by the assessor as a lifelong resident and a physician and that the postmaster rated the doctor Al in credit.[8] On the other hand, when the Buffalo office demanded to know why the city department had not forwarded information requested by a subscriber, headquarters responded with a lecture on proper policy. "For the very good and sufficient reason," the New York office replied, "that the report was an unfavorable one" and marked "B.D.," and subscribers were not to receive reports so marked. "We have therefore lived up to the 'Manual' in this instance."[9]

Only a minor part of the management changes under the New York headquarters office, the decline of personal management by Dun and his partners, the shift from semi-autonomous branch offices to an integrated, and more closely controlled organization resulted from Wiman's ouster. For the most part they reflected a process long in the making, and they paralleled similar developments in other large firms and industries throughout the American economy.[10]

For example, the opening of only three new branch offices between 1893 and Dun's death in 1900, after the firm had averaged opening over three new offices per year during the previous quarter-century, had little relationship to Wiman's departure. The more conservative management, the maturation of the Agency structure and organization, and the end of the geographic expansion of the American economy all influenced the decision to curtail the expansion of domestic offices. Even more important was Dun's desire to minimize capital expenditures in favor of short-run profits.

By far the most dramatic shift in the Mercantile Agency's operation was the growing significance of foreign reporting. While willing to establish overseas offices to serve foreign firms wishing credit reports on American businesses, Dun had always been reluctant to report on foreign firms. However, the increasing significance of overseas markets for American manufacturers made this policy obsolete. Firms such as the American Bicycle Company, the Palmer Pneumatic Tire Company, the American Clay Working Company in Bucyrus, Ohio, the National Cash Register Company, Eastern Kodak Company, American Tobacco Company, and the Hamilton Brown Shoe Company required reports on foreign customers.[11] If the Agency intended to continue to serve American manufacturers, it had to expand its overseas operations.

Even before Dun's death and probably without his explicit approval, R. G. Dun & Co. began reporting on foreign concerns. Overseas offices in London, Glasgow, Paris, and Melbourne, in

Table 12

R. G. DUN & CO.
BRANCH OFFICES, 1877-1901

Minneapolis, Minn.	1877	Melbourne, Australia	1887
Omaha, Neb.	1877	Shreveport, La.	1888
Peoria, Ill.	1877	Topeka, Kan.	1888
Springfield, Mass.	1877	Fort Smith, Ark.	1888
Des Moines, Iowa	1877	Tacoma, Wash.	1888
Saginaw, Mich.	1878	Seattle, Wash.	1888
Allentown, Pa.	1879	Spokane, Wash.	1888
Bangor, Me.	1879	Wilmington, N.C.	1888
Elmira, N.Y.	1879	El Paso, Tex.	1888
Little Rock, Ark.	1879	Wilmington, Del.	1888
Salt Lake City, Utah	1881	Bridgeport, Conn.	1889
Montgomery, Ala.	1881	Columbus, Ga.	1889
San Antonio, Tex.	1881	Jacksonville, Fla.	1890
Cedar Rapids, Iowa	1881	Fort Wayne, Ind.	1890
Sioux City, Iowa	1881	Lynchburg, Va.	1890
Winnipeg, Man.	1882	Augusta, Ga.	1890
Fort Worth, Tex.	1882	Washington, D.C.	1890
Reading, Pa.	1882	Vancouver, B.C.	1891
Waco, Tex.	1882	Winston-Salem, N.C.	1891
Lincoln, Neb.	1883	Trenton, N.J.	1892
Rockford, Ill.	1883	Quebec, Que.	1892
Springfield, Ohio	1883	Ottawa, Ont.	1892
Chattanooga, Tenn.	1883	Wilkes-Barre, Pa.	1892
Austin, Tex.	1883	Zanesville, Ohio	1893
Knoxville, Tenn.	1884	Charleston, W. Va.	1893
Duluth, Minn.	1884	Canton, Ohio	1895
Birmingham, Ala.	1885	Mexico City, Mexico	1897
Wheeling, W. Va.	1886	Havana, Cuba	1899
Wichita, Kan.	1886	Cape Town, South Africa	1901
Springfield, Mo.	1886	Sydney, New South Wales	1901
Macon, Ga.	1887	Guadalajara, Mexico	1901
Los Angeles, Cal.	1887		

Source: *The Mercantile Agency Directory* (New York: Dun & Bradstreet, 1934).

addition to supplying their subscribers with reports on American firms, began collecting data on local businesses. Overseas agents of American subscribers called on the company's offices abroad for reports on firms in their localities. In 1896 the Mercantile Agency advised prospective customers, "We can furnish reports from any part of the world, and have a contract covering such information, 50 reports for $100."[12] In locations where there was no branch office of R. G. Dun & Co., the New York office contacted three or four well-established business firms, attorneys, or banking houses for the required information. During the latter part of the 1890s, two or more reports per week were written on foreign firms on which no current information was available. The New York office handled all foreign reports, maintained all files on foreign concerns, and insisted that inquiries concerning foreign businesses be channeled through it. Furthermore headquarters required that all information be obtained from overseas sources and not from American firms doing business in foreign countries, since the latter were often unreliable.[13]

Two of the three branch offices opened between 1894 and 1900 were foreign — Mexico City and Havana. Nevertheless Dun's opposition to overseas reporting and his eagerness to maximize short-run profits stymied the expansion needed to keep pace with the development of international markets by American manufacturers. Of the 137 offices established by the Mercantile Agency from its founding until Dun's death, only seven were located outside the United States and Canada. In contrast, during the first sixteen years following Dun's death, an additional 104 new offices were opened — 77 of them overseas.[14] Fortunately, none of the rival credit-reporting agencies seriously attempted to compete on foreign reporting with the Mercantile Agency.

The demands for business information broadened during the latter decades of the nineteenth century. R. G. Dun realized that the quarterly *Business Outlook*, while read and respected in the business community, no longer filled the need for a publication designed to keep American businessmen abreast of changing economic conditions. The accelerated pace of business transactions in an economy characterized by frequent business cycles rendered the quarterly obsolete. In August 1893, less than six months after Wiman's departure, Dun replaced the older publication with the weekly *Dun's Review*. The *Review*, under Robert Dun Douglass's personal supervision, quickly established a reputation as the national authority on business conditions. It included much more timely information than the quarterly and offered much more comprehensive coverage. In addition to the usual compilation of business failures, the *Review* provided a summary of business conditions based on reports submitted by Agency managers throughout the United States and Canada. Features such as weekly and monthly data on bank exchanges, monthly inventories of building permits, an index number and other statistics on commodities prices, periodic reports on agricultural crop predictions, and an annual review of business conditions were added to the *Review* within a few years after its appearance.[15]

With the management reconstituted, the *Manual* published, and the new *Review* being well received by the business community, Dun once again retired from active management of the Agency. Now in his seventies and in declining health, he intervened actively on only two occasions prior to his death in 1900.

In the fall of 1897 Edward Russell, citing advancing age and a desire to retire from business after "fifty-three years of continuous service in the Agency," availed himself "of the friendly offer of Messrs. R. G. Dun & Co. to assume the business of his offices in Boston, Worcester, Lynn, Portland and Bangor."[16] Dun personally carried out the negotiations with his old friend and associate. For $142,000 he acquired the last of the independently owned Agency offices. While obviously pleased to complete his organization, Dun's letters to Russell contained a shade of regret to see his longtime associate depart from the business. "I thank you for the complimentary remarks you made of my fairness," Dun wrote, "and can certainly reciprocate them to yourself."[17]

At the time of these negotiations, Dun was planning and financing the construction of the Dun Building in New York. Completed and ready for occupancy in late 1898 at a cost exceeding $1 million, the building at 290 Broadway, at the corner of Reade Street, was one of the earliest steel-framed office buildings in

11. R. G. Dun Building at 290 Broadway, New York. *Courtesy of Dun & Bradstreet, Inc.*

New York City. By squeezing outside investments and by insisting that the Mercantile Agency delay other capital expenditures in favor of short-run profits, Dun financed the entire project without borrowing. The elaborate Dun Building represented far more than an investment to Dun; it was a prestigious home for his company and a monument to his name.[18]

His building complete and suffering from the debilitating effects of cirrhosis, Dun withdrew even more from the business. His only official act of 1898 had been to dismiss an office manager for misconduct. In March of that year, his brother, James Angus, died, and Dun felt the loss severely. Tired and ill, in early 1899 he authorized his brother-in-law William James to dispose of all the mining property in Colorado in any manner that James chose. In October of that year Dun wrote his last business letter, clearing up a small account in an unsuccessful Colorado silver mining venture.[19]

In the spring of 1900 his physicians suggested that Dun spend the summer convalescing at his country home, "Dunmere," at Narragansett Pier. For some years Dun had moved to the seaside for the summer, and apparently the fresh sea air proved beneficial. In the fall, as was his custom, he returned to his home in New York City. Still suffering from the progressive effects of cirrhosis, Dun remained at his home until his death on November 10, 1900, at the age of seventy-four.[20]

Newspapers across the country carried Dun's obituary. A cigar manufacturer rushed to register Dun's name and picture with *Tobacco Leaf*, a trade publication maintaining a registration of trademarks for brands of cigars, as a well-recognized symbol of integrity for his product. And during the next few weeks articles and editorials containing details of his will, estimates of his fortune, and appraisals of his significance appeared in numerous papers.[21]

When Marcus Daly, founder of the Anaconda Copper Mining Company and organizer of the giant ($75 million) Amalgamated Copper Company, and Henry Villard, one of the nation's leading railroad promoters, a founder of Edison General Electric Company, and controlling owner of the *New York Evening Post*, died within a few days of Dun, a number of newspapers carried an editorial comparing the three. Daly, a writer insisted, had left a great fortune, but it would soon be dissipated and his name forgotten. Villard, who at one time controlled transportation in the northwest United States, was dismissed as a newspaper reporter who "rose to control millions by manipulating railroads." "Neither," the editorial concluded, "has left anything behind him by which posterity will remember him."[22]

> With Mr. Dun it is different. He is known all over the world, and he has established an institution that will probably live as long as commerce lives. Emerson says that "an institution is the lengthening shadow of one man" and surely Mr. Dun's mercantile agency is the lengthening shadow of its founder.[23]

Flattering and in many ways truthful as these words were, it would be misleading to classify Dun with the business titans of the late nineteenth century (the so-called robber barons), Andrew Carnegie, John D. Rockefeller, James J. Hill, or even Marcus Daly and Henry Villard. Regardless of how much Dun may have aspired to membership, he would not belong even to that group of less well-known and less significant entrepreneurs that Glenn Porter has called "pocket robber barons."[24] It is not so much the relatively small scale of Dun's operations or the modest size of his fortune that precludes his inclusion, as it is his function and role in the economy that set him apart. Dun introduced no new products, opened no new resources, made no new combinations of materials, controlled no new sources of supplies or markets. He was not a heroic innovator acting in the role of the classical entrepreneur of the late nineteenth century. In the words of the Memphis, Tennessee, *Commercial Appeal*, "He was what is known as a safe, clear-headed business man . . . [who] by applying business methods to business" developed the Mercantile Agency into an institution whose name even today is synonymous with credit and credit-reporting throughout the commercial world.[25] In short he was a manager par excellence, and one suspects that if Dun is a fair example of the role of managers in the second half of the nineteenth century, that the contribution of the heroic entrepreneur may well be overdrawn and the significance of the managers may well be underestimated.

In the forty-two years that R. G. Dun owned and managed the Mercantile Agency, it grew from a small credit-reporting firm with fewer than twenty branches providing eastern wholesalers with information on country merchants into a large international organization, with over 135 branches, capable of furnishing up-to-date credit-reports on any business in the world. While Dun might insist that he was in business for profits and not to build an empire or create an institution, he had done just that. R. G. Dun & Co. was the largest credit-reporting firm in the world; it dominated the business and provided a standard to measure the performance of its rivals. Dun had lent more than his name to the firm; a half-century later Owen Sheffield would argue that many of the practices and procedures then being followed by Dun & Bradstreet stemmed from R. G. Dun and represented part of his legacy to the credit-reporting industry.

It had been Dun, who, to paraphrase Alfred Chandler, shaped an organizational structure to fit his strategy. Unlike his predecessors, Dun from the beginning had insisted that the Mercantile Agency was one firm doing business in a number of places. The good of the whole took precedence over any branch. Building on the basic organization of each branch manager responsible for all Agency activities and securing the necessary income to operate within his own territory, which allowed for easy expansion and great geographic flexibility, Dun instituted a central administration with both line and staff functions. Individual managers might receive instructions on reporting from Charles Barlow, report to Robert Boyd or Erastus Wiman on *Reference Book* sales, be audited by Matthias Smith, and process all collecting through Benjamin Douglass, Jr., and Frances Minton. Each of Dun's partners had the necessary authority for the responsibilities delegated to him, and all reported to Dun. By the last decades of the nineteenth century, these operating procedures were detailed in an agency *Manual*, which spelled out the proper channels of communications, delegated authority, and assigned responsibilities. The survival and prosperity of R. G. Dun & Co., in spite of Dun's death and a will that split the control of the Agency between participating and residuary heirs, is testimony to the soundness and flexibility of Dun's administrative structure.[26]

R. G. Dun's significance extended far beyond his own firm. Ownership of the largest and most successful credit-reporting Agency in the world meant that his innovations played a major role in reshaping the entire industry. Prior to Dun's 1866 *Reference Book*, with its emphasis on capital worth and statistical ratings, credit-reporting on the United States had been characterized by highly impressionistic reports with the emphasis on the business and moral character of the businessman being reported upon. By using statistical ratings and providing estimates of the capital worth of firms, Dun transformed the book from a convenient vehicle to disseminate information already contained in the Agency reports into a device to provide credit-ratings rather than credit-reports. The introduction of quantifiable measurements in Dun's rating key allowed subscribers to make valid comparisons among credit-seekers.

Dun's emphasis upon quantifiable measurements and his instructions to the branch managers to separate credit-ratings of corporations from the personal character of the corporate officers helped to increase acceptance of the corporate form of business organization in the late nineteenth century. In addition, by utilizing a credit-rating key that closely correlated capital worth and general credit standings, Dun encouraged businessmen to extend disproportionate credit to larger firms. Both of Dun's innovations promoted the growth of large corporate business organizations.

Finally, after successfully weathering the attacks upon credit-reporting agencies during the post–Civil War period, the Mercantile Agency and the credit-reporting business emerged in the last decade of the century in a strong and well-accepted position. The ability of the credit-reporting industry to withstand popular distrust, legal battles, legislative interference, and a high mortality rate among firms in the business illustrated the vital role it played in the economy. The continued preeminence of the Mercantile Agency was testimony not only to its significance in the American economy but to the ability of R. G. Dun.

Notes

Preface

1. Herman E. Krooss and Charles Gilbert, *American business history* (Englewood Cliffs, N.J., 1972), pp. 113–114.
2. Alfred D. Chandler, Jr., *Strategy and structure: Chapters in the history of industrial enterprise* (Cambridge, Mass., 1962).
3. For an excellent analysis of the role of managers versus the role of innovators in the economy, see Alfred D. Chandler, Jr., *The visible hand: The managerial revolution in American business* (Cambridge, Mass., 1977), pp. 1–12. Unfortunately Chandler's study appeared too late for me to incorporate his findings into my manuscript.
4. See James H. Madison, "The credit reports of R. G. Dun & Co. as historical sources," *Historical Methods Newsletter* (September 1975): 128–131.

Chapter 1

1. Roy A. Foulke, *The sinews of American commerce* (New York, 1941), pp. 49–50. For an excellent account of those relationships, see Bernard Bailyn, *The New England merchants in the seventeenth century* (Cambridge, Mass., 1955).
2. Ibid. pp. 49, 70–71.
3. Stuart Bruchey, *The roots of American economic growth, 1607–1681: An essay in social causation* (New York, 1965), pp. 75–76.

4. Ibid.
5. George Rogers Taylor, *The transportation revolution, 1815–1860* (New York, 1951), pp. 173–174.
6. Lewis E. Atherton, *The frontier merchant in Mid-America* (Columbia, Missouri, 1971), pp. 64–65, and Atherton, *The southern country store, 1800–1860* (Baton Rouge, 1949), p. 57.
7. Atherton, *Southern country store*, p. 113.
8. Ibid.
9. Quoted in ibid., 114.
10. For an excellent discussion of the evolution of merchant-capitalism and the role of sedentary merchants, see N. S. B. Gras, *Business and capitalism: An introduction to business history* (New York, 1939).
11. Glenn Porter and Harold Livesay, *Merchants and manufacturers: Studies in the changing structure of nineteenth-century marketing* (Baltimore, 1971), p. 16. I have relied heavily upon this excellent study for my discussion of nineteenth-century marketing practices. I am sure that an analysis of the subscribers to the Mercantile Agency would support Porter and Livesay's interpretation of the shifts in market structure in the late nineteenth century from merchants to manufacturers.
12. Ibid.
13. Lewis E. Atherton, "The problem of credit-rating in the antebellum South," *Journal of Southern History* 12 (November 1946): 535–536.
14. Ibid., p. 539, and Owen A. Sheffield, "Dun & Bradstreet, Inc.: The Mercantile Agency since 1841 — Serving the world of industry, commerce and trade and of finance and insurance: A private history" (1965), vol. 1 sec. 7. This is an unpublished four-volume study of the history of Dun & Bradstreet by Owen A. Sheffield, former secretary of Dun & Bradstreet, Inc. It is much more accurate and complete than either Edward N. Vose, *Seventy-five years of the Mercantile Agency; R. G. Dun &Co., 1841–1916* (New York, 1916), or Foulke, *Sinews of American commerce*. The first study is essentially a public relations tract written from internal sources and published by R. G. Dun & Co. The latter, a much more general study of commerce and credit by a Dun & Bradstreet executive to commemorate the one-hundredth anniversary of the company, is superior in many ways, but it nevertheless perpetuates many of the errors of the Vose study concerning the early history of the enterprise. Owen Sheffield spent over ten years working in the Dun & Bradstreet archives on his four volumes, which he then

deposited in the Dun & Bradstreet archives with the stipulation that they not be published. "I concluded," Sheffield wrote, "after well into the project that I would not attempt a final draft that might be considered suitable for publication. What I have done is to write without the restrictions and limitations that publication would impose, to have in three or more bound volumes what would serve as a base and guidance for others should Dun & Bradstreet ever wish to publish a history of itself." Although Sheffield did not always cite sources for his information, I found it exceptionally complete, detailed, and scrupulously accurate. He was a thorough and painstaking scholar who was completely candid in his opinions, and I have relied extensively on his study and his generosity. The study is paginated by sections, and the fourth volume consists mostly of documents and illustrations. Hereafter volume number will be given in Roman numerals, followed by the section and pages in Arabic.

15. R. W. Hidy, "Credit rating before Dun and Bradstreet," *Bulletin of the Business Historical Society* 13 (December 1939): 81.

16. Atherton, "Problem of Credit-rating," pp. 535–536.

17. Vose, *Seventy-five years*, p. 1.

18. Foulke, *Sinews of American commerce*, p. 288, restricts his claim to the United States. In fairness to Atherton, "Problem of credit-rating," pp. 534–556, and Hidy, "Credit rating before Dun and Bradstreet," pp. 81–88, both recognized at least primitive forerunners of Tappan's agency. More recent authors such as Bertram Wyatt-Brown, "God and Dun & Bradstreet, 1841–1851," *Business History Review* 40 (Winter 1966): 432–450, and James H. Madison, "The evolution of commercial credit reporting agencies in nineteenth-century America," *Business History Review* 48 (Summer 1974): 164–186, have, in the absence of contradictory evidence, assumed that Vose, Foulke, Hidy, and Atherton were correct in their assumptions.

19. Madison, "Commercial credit reporting agencies," p. 164. Madison argued, "When the Mercantile Agency opened its door in New York in 1841, it offered a new kind of service to American businessmen.

20. Griffen, Cleaveland and Campbell, 44 Wall Street, New York, to William Jessup, Montrose, Penn., June 9, 1835, in Dun & Bradstreet Archives, New York. Unless specifically noted, all manuscript material cited is located in Dun & Bradstreet Archives, New York.

21. Ibid.
22. Ebenezer Griffen, John Cleaveland, and William W. Campbell to William Jessup, "Confidential instructions for our correspondents," June 9, 1835.
23. Ibid.
24. Ibid.
25. Ibid
26. Lewis Tappan to S. M. Gates, April 19, 1841, copy in Sheffield, "Dun & Bradstreet, Inc.," IV–10, 1-f.
27. Edward E. Dunbar, *Statement of the controversy between Lewis Tappan and Edward E. Dunbar* (New York, 1846), p. 2.
28. For my description of Lewis Tappan, his background, and his character, I have drawn heavily on Bertram Wyatt-Brown's excellent study, *Lewis Tappan and the evangelical war against slavery* (Cleveland, 1969). I have concerned myself only with the aspects of Lewis Tappan's life and background that pertain to the Mercantile Agency. Certainly both the Tappan brothers deserve much more analysis than is possible to include in this study. The quotation is from ibid., p. 11. Sheffield, "Dun & Bradstreet, Inc," I-1, pp. 27–117, I-2, pp. 1–38, contains a good deal of information about Tappan's business career and the early operation of the Agency not elsewhere available.
29. Wyatt-Brown, *Lewis Tappan*, pp. 60–73.
30. Ibid., pp. 169–175.
31. Ibid.
32. Wyatt-Brown, "God and Dun & Bradstreet," p. 434.
33. *New York Commercial Advertiser*, July 20–31, 1841. A copy of the notice is reproduced in Sheffield, "Dun & Bradstreet, Inc.," I-2, p. 13A.
34. Vose, *Seventy-five years*, p. 14.
35. See, for example, Wyatt Brown, *Lewis Tappan*, p. 227.
36. Atherton, "Problem of credit rating," pp. 535–536. Reginald C. McGrane, *The panic of 1837* (Chicago 1924), offers the standard interpretation of the panic. For a more recent and more intriguing interpretation, as well as a summation of recent literature, see Peter Temin, *The Jacksonian economy* (New York, 1969).
37. Lewis Tappan to S. M. Gates, April 19, 1841, in Sheffield, "Dun & Bradstreet, Inc." I-1, p. 4A; *Biographical Directory of the American Congress, 1774–1949* (Washington, D.C., 1950), p. 1200.
38. Wyatt-Brown, *Lewis Tappan*, pp. 232–233, and Sheffield, "Dun & Bradstreet, Inc.," I-2, pp. 20–21. The memorandum book that Tap-

pan used as a subscription book simply contained the contract and terms of the agreement followed by the names of the subscribers. Starting with subscriber no. 91, individual contract blanks were used, and the name of the subscriber entered in the book by clerks in the office. The book continued in use as a subscription register through January 1852 and shows a total of 1,280 subscribers. This little memorandum book was in no sense a ledger; amounts of the subscription were not entered nor were "drops" or new or successor subscribers indicated, so it is impossible to arrive at an accurate number of active subscribers at any one date. Beginning in June 1854, B. Douglass & Co. maintained a ledger that indicated the amounts for each subscription, and "drops" and "new" subscribers were indicated.

39. Quoted in Sheffield, "Dun & Bradstreet, Inc." I-2, pp. 20-21.
40. Ibid., I-2, p. 21.
41. "Explanation of the objects and advantages of the Mercantile Agency," n.d. Internal evidence in the circular would date it in late 1842, certainly prior to the opening of the Boston office of the Agency. Tappan's problems arising from the obvious fact that merchants in the South were not covered is discussed below.
42. Ibid.
43. Ibid.
44. "Mercantile Agency—Terms of subscription," n.d. [probably late 1842].
45. Lewis Tappan & Co. to correspondents, circulars, September 25, 1845.
46. Lewis Tappan and W. A. Tappan to Thomas Fuller, Planesdale, Wayne County, Pennsylvania, July 20, 1843.
47. See "Circular letters of instruction to correspondents," 1842-58. The discussion of business conditions and public issues in the Agency circular letters greatly increased under Benjamin Douglass and R. G. Dun.
48. Wyatt-Brown, Lewis Tappan, pp. 233-235.
49. Sheffield, "Dun & Bradstreet, Inc.," I-2, pp. 15-16.
50. Lewis Tappan to Thomas Fuller, circular, Bethany, Wayne County, Pennsylvania, December 20, 1842.
51. Sheffield, "Dun & Bradstreet, Inc.," I-2, p. 17. The term branch office is somewhat misleading since during Tappan's ownership, they were either partly or even entirely owned by other parties, with Tappan taking a share of the profits for supplying the basic organization.

52. Sheffield, "Dun & Bradstreet, Inc.," I-2, pp. 15-37.
53. Both Wyatt-Brown, *Lewis Tappan,* pp. 232-235, and Sheffield, "Dun & Bradstreet, Inc.," 1-2, pp. 17-19, contain descriptions of the details of the Agency operation. Tappan had good reason to fear libel suits. See chapter 5 below.
of the Agency operation. Tappan had good reason to fear libel
s u i t s .
See chapter ·5 below.
54. Quoted in Wyatt-Brown, *Lewis Tappan,* p. 232.
55. Ibid., p. 227.
56. There is some question as to whether Tappan's decision was based solely on his antislavery sentiments, for at the same time he rejected affiliations with Britain or other foreign areas. Most important, within a short time Tappan would reverse himself and actively seek the southern market. It seems much more likely to me that his initial concern of the Mercantile Agency was limited to the New York market, and his vision shifted only under the pressure of his own success and the threat of competition.
57. Quoted in Dunbar, *Statement,* p. 10.
58. Ibid., pp. 10-12, and Sheffield, "Dun & Bradstreet, Inc.," I-3, p. 12.
59. Dunbar, *Statement,* pp. 12-13; Sheffield, "Dun & Bradstreet, Inc.," I-3, pp. 13-14; and Atherton, "Problem of credit rating," pp. 544-545. For a more complete treatment of rival firms, see chapter 4.
60. Lewis and W. A. Tappan to Thomas Fuller, circular, Wayne County, Pennsylvania, July 20, 1843.
61. Ibid.
62. Dunbar, *Statement,* pp. 9-11. Tappan sold Dunbar a one-fourth interest in the business.
63. Wyatt-Brown, *Lewis Tappan,* p. 238.
64. Lewis Tappan to Edward E. Dunbar, January 28, 1845, quoted in Dunbar, *Statement,* p. 14.
65. Dunbar, *Statement,* pp. 14-15.
66. Ibid, pp. 17-22.
67. Lewis Tappan to H. P. Watkins, Warsaw, Benton County, Missouri, circular letter, June 22, 1846.
68. Dunbar, *Statement,* pp. 22-23.
69. Quoted in ibid., p. 25.
70. Ibid.
71. Ibid., p. 26.
72. Sheffield, "Dun & Bradstreet, Inc.," I-2, p. 36.
73. Ibid., p. 84; I-2, p. 28.

74. Lewis Tappan to H. P. Watkins, circular letter, Warsaw, Benton County, Missouri, June 22, 1846.
75. Ibid.
76. Ibid.
77. For a discussion of Douglass's background, see chapter 2 below.
78. Quoted in Wyatt-Brown, *Lewis Tappan*, p. 240.
79. Atherton, "Problem of credit-rating," p. 556.
80. Wyatt-Brown, *Lewis Tappan*, p. 241.
81. R. G. Dun to R. E. Andrews, Hudson, N.Y., November 18, 1863, R. G. Dun Letter Books, vol. 2.
82. "The Mercantile Agency," *Hunt's Merchants' Magazine and Commercial Review* 24: (January 1851): 46–52.

Chapter 2

1. Bertram Wyatt-Brown, *Lewis Tappan and the evangelical war against slavery* (Cleveland, 1969), p. 241.
2. Quoted in ibid. Benjamin Douglass dominated the management of the Agency throughout the period of his and Arthur Tappan's partnership.
3. The information on the Douglass family come mostly from "*A brief sketch of the life of George Douglass*," n.d., file 4, Dun & Bradstreet Archives, New York; and Owen A. Sheffield, "Dun & Bradstreet, Inc.: The Mercantile Agency since 1841 — serving the world of industry, commerce and trade and of finance and insurance; A private history" (1965), III-1, pp. 42–60. Dun's characterization of George and Benjamin Douglass as religious fanatics was certainly not intended to offend them; he was very fond of both.
4. R. G. Dun to James A. Dun, June 2, 1862, R. G. Dun Letter Books, vol. 2.
5. R. G. Dun to William Carson, December 10, 1863, and to Wm. James, March 19, 1864, Dun Letter Books, vol. 2.
6. Sheffield, "Dun & Bradstreet, Inc.," III-1, pp. 61–62. Douglass never said how he came to enter the firm of Lewis Tappan & Co.; however, the then current dispute between Dunbar and Tappan undoubtedly became well known in the New York business community and Tappan undoubtedly knew Benjamin Douglass's father. In 1844 Douglass's sister, Letitia, married Zachariah Chandler, then a wealthy Detroit merchant who had been a long-

time business acquaintance of the Tappans. It seems likely that he brought Benjamin Douglass and Lewis Tappan together. Indeed, both the Benjamin Douglass family and Chandler and his new bride were then living with George Douglass in New York.

7. Quoted in Sheffield, "Dun & Bradstreet, Inc.," II-4, pp. 4–5.

8. Ibid. None of Douglass's letterbooks remain, and sources for the Mercantile Agency during his management are too thin to allow detailed analysis.

9. Stuart Bruchey, *The roots of American economic growth, 1607–1861: An essay in social causation* (New York, 1968), pp. 74–78.

10. Ibid., p. 79; J. G. Gurley and E. S. Shaw, "Money," in Seymour Harris, ed., *American economic history* (New York, 1961), p. 105. Robert Martin's series on real money supply has been considered to have overestimated the acceleration of economic growth after 1840; however, I am more concerned with the entire period, and this possible distortion has no impact on my conclusion.

11. Ross M. Robertson, *History of the American economy*, 3d ed. (New York, 1973), p. 237. Although there is widespread disagreement with Robert Martin's figures, there is general agreement that an acceleration of per capita income began about 1845. The question is whether the growth was really a sharp acceleration from the past rate or simply part of a secular pattern of recurring variations.

12. See semi-annual circulars to corresponding attorneys, 1851–59, Dun & Bradstreet Archives; Edward N. Vose, *Seventy-five years of the Mercantile Agency: R. G. Dun &Co., 1841–1916* (New York, 1916), pp. 46–56; and Sheffield, "Dun and Bradstreet, Inc.," II-4, pp. 6–7.

13. Vose, *Seventy-five years*, pp. 46–47, and Sheffield, "Dun & Bradstreet, Inc.," II-4, p. 7.

14. Quoted in Sheffield, "Dun & Bradstreet, Inc.," II-4, pp. 4, 12.

15. Semi-annual circulars to corresponding attorneys, 1851–59.

16. B. D. & Co., New Orleans, to correspondents, semi-annual circular, November 11, 1852.

17. Tappan & Douglass, New York, to correspondents, semi-annual circular, [early] 1852.

18. B. Douglass & Co., Cincinnati, Ohio, to correspondents, semi-annual circular, May 1854.

19. Wm. Goodrich & Co. to correspondents, semi-annual circular, December 10, 1854.

20. B. Douglass & Co. to correspondents, semi-annual circular, December 11, 1855.

21. Ibid., handwritten notes.
22. The gradual introduction of this information late in Douglass's tenure when he was heavily involved in extra-company affairs, coupled with the systematic development of business analysis in the Agency during R. G. Dun's ownership, suggests most strongly that it was Dun, not Douglass, who embarked on the activity of supplying subscribers with economic and business statistics and analysis.
23. "Mercantile failures in 1856," *Hunt's Merchants' Magazine* 36: (February 1857): 595.
24. B. Douglass & Co., New York, circular to our subscribers, January 1858. Vose, *Seventy-five years*, pp. 72–76. The analysis of business conditions increased, and in 1893 *Dun's Review* replaced the circulars.
25. Semi-annual circulars to corresponding attorneys, early 1852, and November 11, 1852.
26. Sheffield, "Dun & Bradstreet, Inc.," II-4, pp. 15–16. Dun's accounts indicate that he did expand both collections and addressing circulars to include the various branch offices, but the introduction of reference books allowed subscribers to select their own mailing lists.
27. Tappan & Douglass, New York, to correspondents, semi-annual circular, [early] 1852.
28. B. D. & Co., New Orleans, to correspondents, semi-annual circular, November 11, 1852.
29. B. Douglass & Co., Cincinnati, to correspondents, semi-annual circular, May 1854.
30. B. Douglass & Co., New York, to correspondents, semi-annual circular, 1855.
31. B. Douglass & Co., Pittsburgh, to correspondents, semi-annual circular, January 1, 1855. The various Mercantile Agency owners — Tappan, Douglass, and Dun — seemed unduly concerned about rival firms. For more information on rivals, see chapter 4.
32. Lewis Atherton, "The problem of credit-rating in the antebellum South," *Journal of Southern History* 12 (November 1946): 12, cites the case of a New York firm, stating that they had always found the Mercantile agency reports "too correct to doubt." For an excellent evaluation of the accuracy of the credit-reports, as well as their historical value, see James H. Madison, "The credit reports of R. G. Dun & Co. as historical sources," *Historical Methods Newsletter* (September 1975): 128–130.

33. Sheffield, "Dun & Bradstreet, Inc.," II-4, pp. 18–19.
34. *Key to Bradstreet's Book of Commercial Reports*, 1857, 1858; *Bradstreet's Book of Commercial Reports*, 1857, p. 72; both are reproduced in Sheffield, "Dun & Bradstreet, Inc.," IV-12, 2A-3A. Volume 4 of Sheffield's "Dun & Bradstreet, Inc.," consists primarily of reproduced documents collected from the Dun & Bradstreet offices throughout the organization.
35. Vose, *Seventy-five years*, pp. 49–50.
36. Ibid., and Sheffield, "Dun & Bradstreet, Inc.," II-4, p. 20.
37. B. Douglass & Co., Pittsburgh, to correspondents, semi-annual circular, January 11, 1855.
38. Ibid.
39. See table 2. Comparative figures for Bradstreet's profits and subscribers are not available.
40. R. G. Dun to James A. Dun, April 5, 1858, Dun Letter Books, vol. 1; R. G. Dun to B. Douglass, August 4, 1856, Dun Letter Books, vol. 1. It is impossible to determine exactly when or on what terms Dun became a participating partner, but the internal evidence, particularly the need for Douglass to have at least a nominal partner to avoid legal problems, indicates that Dun assumed the partnership immediately after Arthur Tappan left the firm.
41. Vose, *Seventy-five years*, p. 80.
42. *Mercantile Agency's reference book* (New York, 1859), preface.
43. Ibid., printed key pasted in the front of the book.
44. Sample contract for a year's subscription to the *Reference Book*, B. Douglass & Co., n.d.
45. Undated announcement of Bradstreet's forthcoming *Book of commercial reports*, John M. Bradstreet & Son, reproduced in Sheffield, "Dun & Bradstreet, Inc.," IV-12, p. 1-A; ibid., II-4, pp. 23–26.
46. Ibid., pp. 24–25.
47. Vose, *Seventy-five years*, pp. 81–83.
48. Sheffield, "Dun & Bradstreet, Inc.," II-4, pp. 23–24. Because of the limited manuscript material surviving in the Dun & Bradstreet archives, precise accounting is often impossible.
49. Ibid., II-4, pp. 24–26. In 1863, four years after assuming full ownership of the Mercantile Agency, R. G. Dun would confide in Douglass that as much as it hurt him to admit it, he believed that Bradstreet was making more money than he, Dun, and that he had to meet the competition.
50. "The Mercantile Agency System," *Banker's Magazine and State*

Financial Register (January 1858): 548.
51. R. G. Dun to B. Douglass, July 29, 1879, Dun Letter Books, vol. 8.
52. R. G. Dun to James Angus Dun, December 12, 1864, Dun Letter Book, vol. 3.
53. Ibid., November 22, 1865.
54. Sheffield, "Dun & Bradstreet, Inc.," II-4, pp. 28–29.
55. Ibid.
56. For a discussion of shifts in the structure of the nineteenth-century American economy, see N. S. B. Gras, *Business and capitalism: An introduction to business history* (New York, 1939), and Glenn Porter and Harold Livesay, *Merchants and manufacturers: Studies in the changing structure of nineteenth-century marketing* (Baltimore, 1971).
57. Glenn Porter, *The rise of big business, 1860–1910* (New York, 1973), pp. 17–19.

Chapter 3

1. R. G. Dun to James A. Dun, April 5, 1858, R. G. Dun Letter Books, vol. 1. Although only fragments of the incoming correspondence remain, almost all of R. G. Dun's outgoing correspondence, both business and personal, remains intact in eight letterpress volumes in the Dun & Bradstreet archives.
2. Robert Dun, Glasgow, to Walter Dun, care of John Graham, Richmond, Virginia, March 18, 1811, Dun Papers, Ross County Historical Society, Chillicothe, Ohio. The Dun papers in the Ross County Historical Society are an unusually rich collection of letters from the other brothers to Walter Dun covering a period of over twenty-five years.
3. Ibid., July 9, 1812.
4. Ibid., September 28, 1812.
5. Owen A. Sheffield, "Dun & Bradstreet, Inc.: The Mercantile Agency since 1841 — Serving the world of industry, commerce and trade and of finance and insurance; A private history" (1965), I-1, pp. 49–50.
6. George W. Dun to Walter Dun, January 28, 1833, Dun Papers.
7. Sheffield, "Dun & Bradstreet, Inc.," I-1, p. 50.
8. Land tract book, entry dated January 1, 1833, Dun Papers.

9. Sheffield, "Dun & Bradstreet, Inc.," I-1, pp. 50–51.

10. Robert Dun to Walter Dun, December 27, 1828, Dun Papers.

11. Ibid., July 29, 1830.

12. Ibid., January 26, 1835.

13. George W. Dun to Walter Dun, May 24, June 21, 1835, Dun Papers.

14. George W. Dun to John G. Dun, October 6, 1838, Dun Papers. Information about R. G. Dun's childhood is too meager to offer much explanation of his subsequent behavior.

15. Sheffield, "Dun & Bradstreet, Inc.," I-1, pp. 53–54. For a description of Chillicothe society during Dun's youth, see Isaac J. Finley and Rufus Putman, *Pioneer period and reminiscence of the early settlers and settlement of Ross County, Ohio* (Cincinnati, 1874).

16. James D. Norris, "A northern businessman opposes the Civil War," *Ohio History* 71 (July 1962): 138–139, and Lewis E. Atherton, *The frontier merchant in Mid-America* (Columbia, Missouri, 1971), pp. 13–58. Atherton notes that the position of clerk was considered a promising beginning for any ambitious young man who wanted to enter business and that many merchants had followed this pattern in their careers.

17. Sheffield, "Dun & Bradstreet, Inc.," I-1, pp. 52–53, and obituaries in *Chillicothe [Ohio] Gazette*, November 17, 1900, and *Cincinnati [Ohio] Tribune*, November 11, 1900.

18. Dun's marriage had the appearance of a marriage of convenience.

19. R. G. Dun to B. Douglass, August 4, 1856, Dun Letter Books, vol. 1.

20. Ibid.

21. Sheffield, "Dun & Bradstreet, Inc.," II-5, pp. 2–4.

22. Ibid., p. 4.

23. See Dun Letter Books, vol. 2, and M. B. Smith to R. G. Dun, drawer 3, file cabinet. See, for example, Smith to Dun, April 10, 1862, for examples of Smith's auditing duties. However, Smith's inspections of branch offices extended beyond mere audits into all areas of the Agency business. His annual visits resembled performance audits.

24. R. G. Dun to Daniel Webster, October 30, 1860, Dun Letter Books, vol. 1.

25. See chapter 2 above.

26. Preface of the 1860 *Reference Book* quoted in Edward N. Vose, *Seventy-five years of the Mercantile Agency; R. G. Dun & Co., 1841–1916* (New York, 1916), pp. 88–89.

27. Quoted in ibid., p. 89.

28. Ibid., pp. 89–90.

29. R. G. Dun & Co., circular to our subscribers, New York, January 1, 1862.
30. Ibid., January 1, 1863, p. 2.
31. Ibid., January 1, 1862.
32. Ibid.
33. Ibid., January 1, 1863.
34. Ibid., January 1, 1864.
35. Ibid., January 1, 1863.
36. R. G. Dun to W. Libby, December 20, 1862, February 15, 1864, Dun Letter Books, vol. 2.
37. By far the best work dealing with shifts in the structure of the market in the nineteenth century is Glenn Porter and Harold Livesay, *Merchants and manufacturers: Studies in the changing structure of nineteenth-century marketing* (Baltimore, 1971). See also N. S. B. Gras, *Business and capitalism: An introduction to business history* (New York, 1939).
38. R. G. Dun to James A. Dun, February 5, 1858, Dun Letter Books, vol. 1. Dun had supported Buchanan in 1856, but one suspects it was more to tease his brother than any serious political ardor.
39. Ibid.
40. R. G. Dun to David McKinlay, April 18, 1861, Dun Letter Books, vol. 1.
41. R. G. Dun to John Dun, September 25, 1861, Dun Letter Books, vol. 1.
42. R. G. Dun to Robert George Dun, September 1861, Dun Letter Books, vol. 1.
43. Ibid. Fort Lafayette in New York Harbor was used as a federal prison during the war.
44. R. G. Dun to John Dun, March 15, 1862, Dun Letter Books, vol. 1.
45. Ibid., October 20, 1862, Dun Letter Books, vol. 1.
46. R. G. Dun to Robert George Dun, January 27, 1863, Dun Letter Books, vol. 1.
47. R. G. Dun to John Dun, August 29, 1863, Dun Letter Books, vol. 1.
48. R. G. Dun to Hon. Zachariah Chandler, March 29, 1863, Dun Letter Books, vol. 2.
49. R. G. Dun to Benjamin Douglass, July 8, 1863, Dun Letter Books, vol. 1.
50. R. G. Dun to James Angus Dun, April 16, 1863, Dun Letter Books, vol. 1.
51. Ibid.

52. Ibid., March 24, 1864, Dun Letter Books, vol. 3.
53. R. G. Dun to John G. Dun, September 7, 1864, Dun Letter Books, vol. 3.
54. R. G. Dun to William James, December 2, 1864, Dun Letter Books, vol. 3.
55. R. G. Dun to John G. Dun, May 1, 1865, Dun letter Books, vol. 3.
56. R. G. Dun to Benjamin Douglass, August 8, 1863, Dun Letter Books, vol. 2.
57. Compiled from Dun Letter Books, vol. 3.
58. Dun, Boyd & Co. to John Reilly, June 21, 1860, Dun Letter Books, vol. 1.
59. R. G. Dun to M. B. Smith, July 12, 1860, Dun Letter Books, vol. 1.
60. R. G. Dun to Stephen Gano, March 2, 1861, Dun Letter Books, vol. 1.
61. Ibid., January 23, 1862, Dun Letter Books, vol. 2.
62. M. B. Smith to R. G. Dun, April 14, 15, 22, 28, May 1, 9, 11, 14, 23, 1863, drawer 2, file cabinet; R. G. Dun to M. B. Smith, April 24, 27, May 7, 14, Dun Letter Books, vol. 2.
63. M. B. Smith to R. G. Dun, April 22, May 26, 29, 1863, drawer 2, file cabinet.
64. Ibid., October 22, 1863, Dun Letter Books, vol. 2.
65. Ibid., and Sheffield, "Dun & Bradstreet, Inc.," II-5, pp. 16–17.
66. R. G. Dun to Benjamin Douglass, June 10, 1863, Dun Letter Books, vol. 3.
67. Sheffield, "Dun & Bradstreet, Inc.," II-5, pp. 16–17.
68. R. G. Dun to E. Russell, October 31, 1859, Dun Letter Books, vol. 1.
69. R. G. Dun to Stephen Gano, July 7, 1860, Dun Letter Books, vol. 1.
70. R. G. Dun to A. S. Peabody, August 15, 1861, Dun Letter Books, vol. 2.
71. R. G. Dun to William H. Hall, September 30, 1861, Dun Letter Books, vol. 2.
72. R. G. Dun to James Moore, November 26, 1861, Dun Letter Books, vol. 2.
73. R. G. Dun to Stephen Gano, December 12, 1861, Dun Letter Books, vol. 2.
74. R. G. Dun to A. S. Peabody, August 15, 1861, Dun Letter Books, vol. 2.
75. R. G. Dun to Erastus Wiman, June 12, 1862, Dun Letter Books, vol. 2.
76. R. G. Dun to O. B. Hayes, July 30, 1862, Dun Letter Books, vol. 2.

77. R. G. Dun to A. Armstrong, August 8, 26, 1862, Dun Letter Books, vol. 2.
78. R. G. Dun to Daniel Webster, July 13, August 28, 1863, R. G. Dun to William Hall, January 9, 1864, Dun Letter Books, vol. 2.
79. See, for example, R. G. Dun to J. L. Fonda, November 25, 1863, or R. G. Dun to E. Wiman, February 18, 1864, Dun Letter Books, vol. 2.
80. See R. G. Dun to George Minchiner, December 17, 1864, or R. G. Dun to J. L. Fonda, December 17, 1864, Dun Letter Books, vol. 2.
81. R. G. Dun to Stephen Gano, December 12, 1861, Dun Letter Books, vol. 2; *New York Daily Tribune*, December 30, 1862; R. G. Dun & Co., New York, circular to our subscribers, January 1, 1862, January 1, 1863.
82. R. G. Dun & Co., New York, circular to our subscribers, January 1, 1864.
83. R. G. Dun to Benjamin Douglass, September 4, 1863, Dun Letter Books, vol. 2.
84. R. G. Dun to William Morrison, November 30, 1863, Dunn Letter Books, vol. 2.
85. R. G. Dun to E. Russell & Co., March 3, 1864, Dun Letter Books, vol. 2.
86. Ibid.
87. R. G. Dun & Co. to E. Wiman, circular letter, March 30, 1864, Dun Letter Books, vol. 2.
88. R. G. Dun to John G. Dun, May 16, 1864, Dun Letter Books, vol. 2.
89. See, for example, R. G. Dun to J. D. Pratt, April 7, 1864, Dun Letter Books, vol. 2.
90. Vose, *Seventy-five years*, pp. 90–91, and Sheffield, "Dun & Bradstreet, Inc.," II-5, pp. 34–36.
91. R. G. Dun to M. P. Stacy, January 12, 1865, Dun Letter Books, vol. 4.
92. R. G. Dun to James A. Dun, December 12, 1864, Dun Letter Books, vol. 3.
93. R. G. Dun to E. Wiman, November 18, 1865, Dun Letter Books, vol. 4.
94. Sheffield, "Dun & Bradstreet, Inc.," II-5, p. 37.
95. R. G. Dun to E. Wiman, March 21, 1865, Dun Letter Books, vol. 4, and R. G. Dun to James A. Dun, November 22, 1865, Dun Letter Books, vol. 3.
96. R. G. Dun & Co. to E. Wiman, circular letters, March 30, 1864, vol. 4.

97. R. G. Dun to Erastus Wiman, September 17, 22, 1864, Dunn Letter Books, vol. 4.
98. Ibid.
99. R. G. Dun & Co. to E. Wiman, circular letter, March 30, 1864.

Chapter 4

1. R. G. Dun to Daniel Webster, March 26, 1866, R. G. Dun Letter Books, vol. 4.
2. R. G. Dun to Erastus Wiman, June 24, 1864, Dun Letter Books, vol. 4.
3. Quoted in Edward N. Vose, *Seventy-five years of the Mercantile Agency; R. G. Dun &Co., 1841–1916* (New York, 1916), pp. 93–94.
4. Ibid., pp. 94–95.
5. Ibid., p. 94.
6. Edward C. Kirkland, *Industry comes of age: Business, labor and public policy, 1860–1897* (New York, 1961), p. 7.
7. R. G. Dun & Co., annual circular to our subscribers, January 1866.
8. Ibid., January 1867.
9. Ibid., January 1874.
10. For an interesting analysis of some of the problems of the expanding American economy, see Thomas C. Cochran, "The paradox of American economic growth," *Journal of American History* 61 (March 1975): 934–937. Perhaps it would be better to say those deemed to deserve it by Dun's correspondents. Not only did the correspondents continue to emphasize the moral character of the businessman, they also made moral judgments about the type of business. Lyle W. Dorsett has called my attention to R. G. Dun & Co. correspondents' discrimination against saloonkeepers in Colorado, who regardless of their capital worth, credit-history, or personal character received low or no credit ratings.
11. R. G. Dun & Co., "Terms of subscription: *Reference Book*," July 1866 edition, drawer 3, file cabinet.
12. R. G. Dun & Co. circular letter to office managers, March 16, 1866 reproduced in Owen A. Sheffield, "Dun & Bradstreet, Inc.: The Mercantile Agency since 1841 — Serving the world of industry, commerce and trade and of finance and insurance: A private history" (1865), IV-8, pp. 3–4.
13. Ibid.
14. Ibid.

15. R. R. Boyd to R. G. Dun, June 24, 1865, drawer 3, file cabinet.
16. R. G. Dun to R. R. Boyd, July 13, 1865, Dun Letter Books, vol. 4.
17. Ibid., August 4, 1865.
18. Edwin F. Waters to R. G. Dun, September 13, 1865, drawer 3, file cabinet.
19. Sheffield, "Dun & Bradstreet, Inc.," II-5, pp. 23–24.
20. R. G. Dun to E. Wiman, November 7, 1865, Dun Letter Books, vol. 4.
21. Ibid.; R. G. Dun to Charles Barlow, September 14, 1872, Dun Letter Books, vol. 5.
22. R. G. Dun to E. Wiman (copies to M. Smith and C. Barlow), November 7, 1869, Dun Letter Books, vol. 4.
23. Ibid.
24. R. G. Dun to Charles Barlow (copies to E. Wiman and M. Smith), November 22, 1872, Dun Letter Books, vol. 4.
25. Ibid.
26. R. G. Dun to Benjamin Douglass, May 29, 1877, Dun Letter Books, vol. 6.
27. R. G. Dun to Charles Barlow (copies to E. Wiman and M. Smith), November 14, 1877, Dun Letter Books, vol. 6.
28. R. G. Dun to Charles Barlow, E. Wiman, and M. Smith, November 22, 1877, Dun Letter Books, vol. 6.
29. Ibid.
30. R. G. Dun to Benjamin Douglass, December 29, 1877, Dun Letter Books, vol. 6.
31. Ibid.
32. R. G. Dun to Charles Barlow, September 14, 1872, Dun Letter Books, vol. 6.
33. Ibid.
34. R. G. Dun to Benjamin Douglass, December 29, 1877, Dun Letter Books, vol. 6.
35. See file 13, Dun & Bradstreet Archives, New York, for copies of the obituary in newspapers throughout the country.
36. Sheffield, "Dun & Bradstreet, Inc.," I-1, pp. 94–98.
37. The *New York Evening Post*, December 1, 1900, carried a list of Dun's paintings, which were left to the Metropolitan Museum of Art, New York City. I am indebted to conversations with my colleague Professor Paul Corby Finney for a better understanding of Dun's paintings and their artists.
38. R. G. Dun to Zachariah Chandler, February 23, 1869, Dun Letter Books, vol. 4.

39. R. G. Dun to W. T. Rolph, December 29, 1881, Dun Letter Books, vol. 7.
40. R. G. Dun to W. J. Friday, October 23, 1894, Dun Letter Books, vol. 8.
41. R. G. Dun to James W. Fox, December 27, 1889, Dun Letter Books, vol. 8.
42. Sheffield, "Dun & Bradstreet, Inc.," II-7, pp. 15–17. Sheffield gained most of his impressions from conversations with numerous employees in the Agency who had known Dun personally, particularly Francis Minton, who served as company counsel and as Dun's personal attorney.
43. See Alfred D. Chandler, Jr., *Strategy & structure: Chapters in the history of industrial enterprise* (Cambridge, Mass., 1962), for a general discussion of the topic. Dun's organizational structure was not original, yet there is no evidence that he knowingly copied it from other enterprises; indeed the evidence indicates that, as Chandler has suggested was the case with railroad and other firms, the organizational structure flowed from inward decisions about how to expand the Agency.
44. *The Mercantile Agency Directory* (Red Book) (New York: Dun & Bradstreet, Inc., 1934), pp. 31–34. In marginal notes Sheffield has corrected the dates of the establishment of some offices, and I have followed his corrections.
45. R. G. Dun to E. Wiman, September 18, 1865, Dun Letter Books, vol. 4.
46. R. G. Dun to Jay Lugsdin, July 12, 1866, Dun Letter Books, vol. 4.
47. R. G. Dun to William G. Scarlett, January 8, 1867, Dun Letter Books, vol. 4. Dun himself drank fairly heavily, even then.
48. R. G. Dun to A. Armstrong, June 17, 1868, Dun Letter Books, vol. 4.
49. R. G. Dun to Jay Lugsdin, August 17, 1870, Dun Letter Books, vol. 5.
50. R. G. Dun to J. H. Smith, February 11, 1869, Dun Letter Books, vol. 4. Smith's major reward, of course, came from his percentage of the increased profits.
51. R. G. Dun to A. J. King, March 10, 1876, Dun Letter Books, vol. 5.
52. R. G. Dun to W. G. Scarlett, March 23, 1876, Dun Letter Books, vol. 5.
53. *New York Illustrated News,* March 24, 1860.
54. James H. Madison, "The evolution of commercial credit reporting agencies in the nineteenth century America," *Business History*

Review 48 (Summer 1974): 174–176. My estimates are based on a sample of employment records taken from files 7 and 34.

55. R. G. Dun to William James, January 6, 1873, Dun Letter Books, vol. 5.

56. "Prospects for the fall trade," circular to subscribers, R. G. Dun & Co., June 25, 1875, file 13.

57. Quoted in Vose, *Seventy-five years*, p. 100.

58. "Preface and explanatory key to classification of trades," in R. G. Dun & Co., *Reference Book* (January 1885).

59. Sheffield, "Dun & Bradstreet, Inc.," IV-8, pp. 14–15.

60. R. G. Dun & Co., circular letter, November 1877, file 13.

61. R. G. Dun & Co., circular letter to managers [c. 1873], file 2.

62. File 43 contains a number of the smaller pocket books.

63. R. G. Dun & Co., *The Mercantile Agency United States business directory for 1867 containing the names of the merchants, manufacturers, and traders generally, throughout the United States* (New York, 1867). File 43 contains a copy of the publication.

64. R. G. Dun & Co., *Synopsis of the laws relating to assignments, insolvency & etc. in the various states of the Union also the dates of the setting of the courts* (New York, 1879), preface. File 4 contains copies of this publication and the *Mercantile Agency Annual.*

65. Sheffield, "Dun & Bradstreet, Inc." II-7, p. 48.

66. Madison, "Evolution of commercial credit reporting agencies," pp. 174–176.

67. "Collection of claims," circular letter to managers, Dun, Barlow & Co., November 13, 1874.

68. "To Managers," circular letter, Dun, Barlow & Co., November 13, 1879.

69. Dun, Barlow & Co., circular letter to correspondents, March 1876.

70. Ibid. The Mercantile Agency received a small fee for handling the transfer of funds, and local attorneys charged the prevailing rates for their locale.

71. Sheffield, "Dun & Bradstreet, Inc.," II-7, p. 48.

72. Ibid.

73. Ibid.

74. Ibid., II-6, p. 22.

75. R. G. Dun to Col. H. J. Olcott, May 9, 1864, Dun Letter Books, vol. 4.

76. R. G. Dun to M. P. Stacey, November 17, 1864, Dun Letter Books, vol. 4.

77. Ibid., October 25, 1864.

78. Ibid., July 18, 1864.

79. R. G. Dun & Co. to Geo. B. Walters, September 25, 1867, Dun Letter Books, vol. 4., and quoted in Sheffield, "Dun & Bradstreet, Inc.," II-6, p. 24.

80. Geo. B. Walters to R. G. Dun, May 5, 1869, Dun Letter Books, vol. 4.

81. R. G. Dun to Daniel Webster, July 1, 1869, Dun Letter Books, vol. 4.

82. Sheffield, "Dun & Bradstreet, Inc.," II-6, p. 26.

83. Ibid. Dun's outside business ventures are mentioned here simply to illustrate the range of his activities. Every indication in his letters is that not only was he scrupulously honest and honorable in his business and personal dealings, but that he insisted that no employee cast any doubt on the integrity of the Mercantile Agency. See Duane A. Smith, *Silver saga: The story of Caribou, Colorado* (Boulder, Colo., 1974), for a discussion of Dun's involvement in silver mining.

84. R. G. Dun to R. E. Andrews, November 18, 1863, Dun Letter Books, vol. 2.

85. Ibid.

86. Ibid.

87. Sheffield, "Dun & Bradstreet, Inc.," I-3, pp. 1–10.

88. Ibid., pp. 11–12.

89. Ibid., pp. 13–39.

90. Ibid., pp. 14–35.

91. R. G. Dun to M. P. Stacey, May 3, 1876, Dun Letter Books, vol. 5.

92. R. G. Dun & Co., circular letter to subscribers, December 1878, file 2.

93. For a discussion of business attitudes toward competiton, see Edward C. Kirkland, *Dream and thought in the business community, 1860-1900* (Ithaca, 1956), pp. 1-28.

94. *St. Louis Globe-Democrat*, October 22, 1886.

95. E. B. Russell to E. Wiman, November 22, 1879, scrapbook, file 34.

96. Information about rival firms is contained in scrapbook, Dun & Bradstreet Collection, vol. 5, Baker Library, Harvard University.

97. Ibid.

98. Ibid., April 28, 1879.

99. Ibid.

100. John H. Smith to E. Wiman [c. 1880], in ibid.

101. R. G. Dun & Co., circular letter to subscribers, December 1878,

file 2. In 1878 when Dun made the estimate, his net profit, before withdrawals by the managing partners, amounted to $231,000. Although he never recorded his sales, on several occasions he estimated sales at ten times the annual profits, or approximately $2 million. Both Owen Sheffield and I are convinced that Dun's estimate of sales was conservative. Bradstreet in 1878 reported net sales of slightly less than $500,000 and profits of only $26,589; however, those figures are after payment of managing executive salaries.

102. *The Public*, November 7, 1878.
103. Ibid.
104. R. G. Dun & Co., circular letter to subscribers, December 1878, file 2.
105. Ibid.
106. See clippings in scrapbook, file 34. In analyzing Dun's response to competition, I am much more impressed with his deep distrust of political intervention than with his concern over the chaos of competition. See chapter 5.

Chapter 5

1. Edward C. Kirkland, *Industry comes of age: business, labor and public policy, 1860–1897* (New York, 1961).
2. P. R. Earling, *Whom to trust: A practical treatise on mercantile credits* (Chicago, 1890), p. 304.
3. Ibid., and James H. Madison, "The evolution of commercial credit reporting agencies in nineteenth-century America," *Business History Review* 48 (Summer 1974): 164–186. Madison dealt extensively with the problems and acceptance of credit-rating institutions in the latter part of the nineteenth century.
4. Earling, *Whom to trust*, pp. 302–303.
5. Quoted in Lewis E. Atherton, "The problem of credit rating in the ante-bellum South," *Journal of Southern History* 12 (November 1946): 552.
6. Ibid.
7. Thomas F. Meagher, *The commercial agency "system" of the United States and Canada exposed: Is the secret inquisition a curse or a benefit?* (New York, 1876). Thomas F. Meagher's real name was Charles F. Maynard. Perhaps he chose the alias in admiration of the famous Irish exile, Thomas Francis Meagher, who had earlier visited New York.

8. Ibid., p. 167.
9. "An attack on the Agency," circular letter to managers, Dun, Barlow & Co., March 1, 1876.
10. Ibid.
11. Ibid.
12. Ibid.
13. Owen Sheffield, "Marginal notes and draft statement" on fly sheet of Meagher, *The commercial agency "system"* in the possession of the author.
14. "Attack on the Agency."
15. Meagher, *The commercial agency "system,"* pp. 121–133.
16. "Attack on the Agency."
17. Ibid.
18. Ibid.
19. Ibid.
20. Sheffield, "Marginal notes."
21. Earling, *Whom to trust*, pp. 300–302.
22. "Attack on the Agency."
23. "A sensible criticism," circular letter to managers (c. 1876), file 2. Dun simply reprinted Dawson's review with a few explanatory remarks and admitted that Dawson's reservations about unpaid correspondents were "conclusions that will strike every business man as reasonable."
24. Dun, Wiman & Co., circular letter to managers, December 10, 1880.
25. "Various matters to February, 1885," circular letter, R. G. Dun & Co., February 1885.
26. "Summer revisions," circular letter, R. G. Dun & Co., August 22, 1884.
27. "Districts photographed," circular letter, R. G. Dun & Co., November 7, 1889.
28. "Dear sir," circular letter, R. G. Dun & Co., November 1877.
29. "Various matters to February, 1885," circular letter, R. G. Dun & Co., February 1885.
30. Earling, *Whom to trust*, p. 32.
31. Joseph W. Errant, *The law relating to mercantile agencies: Being the Johnson prize essay for the Union College of Law for the year 1886* (Philadelphia, 1889), p. 47.
32. Madison, "Evolution of commercial credit reporting agencies," pp. 177–180. Since Madison has an excellent discussion of the general impact of the shifting legal status of reporting agencies, I have attempted to confine my analysis to R. G. Dun & Co.

33. Ibid., p. 22; Edward N. Vose, *Seventy-five years of the Mercantile Agency; R. G. Dun &Co., 1841-1916* (New York, 1916), pp. 47-50.
34. Errand, *The law relating to mercantile agencies*, pp. 22-23.
35. *Beardsley* v. *Tappan* in *Reports of the four leading cases against the Mercantile Agency for slander and libel* (New York, 1873), p. 264.
36. Errant, *The law relating to mercantile agencies*, pp. 24-26.
37. *Ormsby* v. *Douglass* in *Four leading cases against the Mercantile Agency*, pp. 184-186.
38. "An improved ticket," circular letter to branches, Dun, Barlow & Co., March 5, 1877.
39. Errant, *The law relating to mercantile agencies*, p. 56.
40. "An improved ticket."
41. Ibid.
42. Errant, *The law relating to mercantile agencies*, pp. 67-70. For a more general discussion, see also *Report of important cases against the Mercantile Agency as to their liability for representations honestly made in the course of their business* (New York, 1877); and Madison, "Evolution of commercial credit reporting agencies," pp. 178-179.
43. *Commercial and Financial Chronicle* 18 (April 4, 1874): 338. I am inclined to agree with Madison, " Evolution of commercial credit reporting agencies," pp. 180-181, that the timing of this sudden burst of activity by several state legislatures may have reflected a growing concern over court expansion of the concept of privileged information; most likely, however, it also reflected credit losses suffered by the business community during the panic of 1873.
44. R. G. Dun to Gordon Forbes, May 13, 1873, R. G. Dun Letter Books, vol. 5.
45. R. G. Dun to William James, February 5, 1874, Dun Letter Books vol. 5.
46. Ibid., March 4, 1874.
47. *Commercial and Financial Chronicle* 18 (April 4, 1874): 338.
48. Erastus Wiman, *Chances of success: Episodes and observations in the life of a busy man* (New York, 1893), pp. 257-260. Wiman usually exaggerated his role and significance in the Agency and its operation.
49. Circular letter to managers, March 5, 1881.
50. Ibid.
51. Wiman, *Chances of success*, pp. 160-163.
52. Richard N. Current, *The typewriter and the men who made it* (Urbana, Ill., 1954), p. 177; Wiman, *Chances of success*, p. 163.
53. Quoted in Vose, *Seventy-five years*, p. 126.

54. For a description of the changes, see ibid. pp. 126–129; Madison, "Evolution of commercial credit reporting agencies," pp. 175–176; and especially Owen A. Sheffield, "Dun & Bradstreet, Inc.: The Mercantile Agency since 1841 — Serving the world of industry, trade and of finance and insurance: A private history" (1965), I-6, pp. 55–58.

55. Sheffield, "Dun & Bradstreet, Inc.," I-7, pp. 1–6. Since Dun and his three partners did not keep minutes of their meetings, the reasoning behind many of the more important decisions during the last quarter of the nineteenth century must be surmised from much less evidence than I would have preferred. However, Sheffield began work with R. G. Dun & Co. in 1900, and many of the operational practices were still being followed. Most imortant, Sheffield knew and talked with members of the firm who remembered the decisions. For these reasons his work becomes increasingly important during this period. Moreover, after a lifetime of experience in the firm and the credit-reporting business, Sheffield acquired a wealth of information and understanding, combined with a surprising objectivity and high regard for historical accuracy. For these reasons, a heavy dependence upon his work becomes less objectionable.

56. Sheffield, "Dun & Bradstreet, Inc.," II-7, pp. 18–20.

57. "Dear sir," circular letter, R. G. Dun & Co., November 1877.

58. Sheffield found several contracts for the period after the shift in pricing policy written for less than the minimum number of written reports and books. These were all from branch offices and indicated that the control of the New York headquarters was still not complete enough to prevent branch managers from occasionally granting subscribers contracts not sanctioned by the New York office. See, for example, the contract written with the Mishawaka Woolen Manufacturing Co. by the Chicago office, dated October 1, 1891, which for $50 called for one *Reference Book* and fifty reports. Ibid., IV-6, p. 3.

59. Ibid. II-7, pp. 43–44.

60. Ibid.

61. The estimate is calculated on a five-year average centered in 1877 and 1898. The years are selected to exclude 1874, which had unusually high earnings and actually represented the upward bound limits of growth for the period.

62. "Confidential," circular letter, R. G. Dun & Co., November 22, 1883, reproduced in Sheffield, "Dun & Bradstreet, Inc.," II-7, p. 75A.

63. Ibid.
64. Ibid.
65. Ibid.
66. After Erastus Wiman's dismissal from the Mercantile Agency in 1893, he did experiment with a continuous reporting service in his abortive Mutual Mercantile Agency, but the attempt was so short-lived that it failed to make any serious impact on credit-reporting practices.
67. Sheffield, "Dun & Bradstreet, Inc.," II-7, pp. 99–100.
68. Exact subscription figures are unavailable. Owen Sheffield estimated about 23,000 in the mid-1880s, but I am inclined to consider this as too low, perhaps the downward limit. It is the figure Dun on occasion during the period to illustrate the effect of variations in subscription prices on income. Two lists of subscribers in the Dun & Bradstreet Collection, Baker Library, Graduate School of Business Administration, Harvard University, would indicate 15,000 to 16,000 subscribers for the New York office alone. I am inclined to place the total number of subscribers in the mid-1880s at closer to 40,000. See "Subscribers A–Z," firm vol. 1, and "Subscribers, Numerical record, Nos. 42–21, 921, firm vol. 2, Dun & Bradstreet Collection.
69. The profits of R. G. Dun & Co. do not reflect the fluctuations of business cycle during the last quarter of the nineteenth century. The three periods of business prostration—1873–78, 1882–85, and 1893–97—that E. C. Kirkland, *Industry comes of age*, identifies as having sweeping impact on the general business community affected neither Dun's profits nor the general expansion of branch offices and services.
70. Sheffield, "Dun & Bradstreet, Inc.," II-7, pp. 100–101.
71. Ibid. See also table 11 above.
72. R. G. Dun to E. Wiman, December 31, 1880, Dun Letter Books, vol. 7.
73. Ibid.
74. R. G. Dun to M. B. Smith, December 1, 1882, Dun Letter Books, vol. 7. In view of Smith's long and valuable service to the Mercantile Agency, Dun's letter asking for his retirement in which Dun told Smith, "It must be obvious to yourself, that you are not earning a tithe of the salary you are now receiving," seems unjustly blunt and cruel. The letter and Dun's subsequent action reveals an unpleasant side to Dun's personalty.
75. Ibid., December 6, 1882, Dun Letter Books, vol. 7.
76. Sheffield, "Dun & Bradstreet, Inc.," II-7, pp. 57–66.

77. Ibid. pp. 62–63.

78. R. G. Dun to James A. Dun, December 28, 1881, Dun Letter Books, vol. 7.

79. R. G. Dun to E. Wiman, December 16, 1881, Dun Letter Books, vol. 7.

80. Ibid.

81. *Life*, October 4, 1963, and Sheffield, "Dun & Bradstreet, Inc.," II-7, pp. 68-72. For an account of Wiman's real estate venture on Staten Island, see *Building and Loan News* (March 1892).

82. R. G. Dun to W. W. Johnson, March 21, 1887, Dun Letter Books, vol. 7.

83. Erastus Wiman to Mrs. R. G. Dun, March 31, 1888, reprinted in *New York World*, June 15, 1894 together with an account of the Wiman trial, in scrapbook, file number 1.

84. R. G. Dun to Erastus Wiman, October 29, 1888, Dun Letter Books, vol. 8.

85. Ibid., December 1888.

86. "Articles of association of R. G. Dun & Co.," January 1, 1889, Dun & Bradstreet Archives, reproduced in Sheffield, "Dun & Bradstreet, Inc.," II-7, pp. 104-A–104-K. Had Dun maintained his resolve not to have partners, Wiman could have ended up in the penitentiary. Wiman's case depended on the fact that partners cannot embezzle from themselves.

87. R. G. Dun to James Harrall, February 17, 1893, Dun Letter Books, vol. 8.

88. The information on Wiman's misconduct, arrest, trial, and subsequent freedom on appeal is taken from an eight-page letter: R. G. Dun & Co. to John Fallows, District Attorney, City and County of New York, February 13, 1896, in ibid., which was undoubtedly prepared by the Agency's attorney; and a seventeen-page letter: R. G. Douglass to H. P. Dwight, manager of the Toronto branch office and longtime friend of Wiman's, February 18, 1896, in ibid.; and accounts of the trial and appeals clipped form the *New York World*, June 15, 1894, and *Boston Herald*, March 15, October 31, December 19, 1895 in scrapbook, file number 1.

89. Ibid.

Chapter 6

1. Edward N. Vose, *Seventy-five years of the Mercantile Agency; R. G. Dun &Co., 1841-1916* (New York, 1916), pp. 141–142, and Owen A. Sheffield, "Dun & Bradstreet, Inc.: The Mercantile Agency since

1841 — Serving the world of industry, trade and of finance and insurance: A private history" (1965), 11-7, pp. 116-127.

2. *The Mercantile Agency Manual* (New York, 1894), preface.

3. R. G. Dun & Co., New York, to R. G. Dun & Co., Hartford, Connecticut, October 13, 1896, firm vol. 9, Dun & Bradstreet Collection, Baker Library, Harvard University. Sheffield, "Dun & Bradstreet, Inc.," III-8, p. 34, noted that the office of general inspector "existed prior to Dun's death."

4. R. G. Dun & Co., N.Y., N.Y., to R. G. Dun & Co., Troy, N.Y., September 30, 1896, vol. 9, Dun & Bradstreet Collection.

5. R. G. Dun & Co., N.Y., N.Y., to R. G. Dun & Co., Albany N.Y., October 10, 1896, vol. 9, Dun & Bradstreet Collection.

6. R. G. Dun & Co., N.Y., N.Y., to R. G. Dun & Co., Pittsburgh, July 27, 1895, vol. 6, Dun & Bradstreet Collection.

7. Ibid., August 2, 1895, vol. 6, Dun & Bradstreet Collection.

8. R. G. Dun & Co., N.Y., N.Y., to R. G. Dun & Co., Philadelphia, September 19, 1895, vol. 6, Dun & Bradstreet Collection.

9. R. G. Dun & Co., N.Y., N.Y., to R. G. Dun & Co., Buffalo, N.Y., September 30, 1896, vol. 6, Dun & Bradstreet Collection. Since the time of Benjamin Douglass's management of the Agency, unfavorable reports were marked with his initials as an indication that the information was potentially libelous and therefore strictly confidential — to be furnished subscribers only on an oral basis with no notes.

10. I have been largely persuaded by what Louis Galambos has referred to as the "organizational synthesis" in modern American history — that the rise of large organizations has been one of the dominant themes in modern American history: " . . . a shift from small-scale, informal, locally or regionally oriented groups to large-scale, national, formal organizations. The new organizations are characterized by a bureaucratic structure of authority." Louis Galambos, "The emerging organizational synthesis in modern American history," *Business History Review* 44 (Autumn 1970): 279–290, and Louis Galambos, with the assistance of Barbara Barrow Spence, *The public image of big business in America, 1880–1940*, (Baltimore, 1975), preface, chap. 1.

11. See vol. 2, 12, Dun & Bradstreet Collection.

12. R. G. Dun & Co., N.Y., N.Y., to Payne Lumber Co., Oshkosh, Wisconsin, September 26, 1896, vol. 9, Dun & Bradstreet Collection.

13. See vol. 9 and 12, and in particular R. G. Dun & Co., N.Y., N.Y., to R. G. Dun & Co., Atlanta, Georgia, March 23, 1897, vol. 12, Dun & Bradstreet Collection.

14. *The Mercantile Agency Directory* (Dun & Bradstreet, Inc., 1934), pp. 31–35, list of offices, chronologically arranged; Vose, *Seventy-five years*, pp. 137–139.
15. Vose, *Seventy-five years*, pp. 140–141.
16. Ibid., pp. 144–45.
17. R. G. Dun to Edward Russell, November 26, 1897, R. G. Dun Letter Books, vol. 8.
18. Vose, *Seventy-five years*, pp. 150–152; Sheffield, "Dun & Bradstreet, Inc.," I-1, pp. 93–94; and R. G. Dun to J. G. Burns & Sons, April 7, 1897, Dun Letter Books, vol. 8.
19. R. G. Dun to William James, c. 1899, and R. G. Dun to S. A. Griffin, October 1899, Dun Letter Books, vol. 8.
20. *New York Tribune*, November 11, 1900; *Cincinnati [Ohio] Tribune*, November 11, 1900.
21. Sheffield, "Dun & Bradstreet, Inc.," III-8, pp. 16–17, and "Scrapbook of R. G. Dun obituary notices," file 13, Dun & Bradstreet Archives.
22. *Commercial Appeal*, Memphis, Tennessee, November 14, 1900, photocopy in Sheffield, "Dun & Bradstreet, Inc.," III-8, p. 13A.
23. Ibid.
24. Glenn Porter, "A picture from life's other side: Pocket robber baron. A review of Robert Hessen, *Steel titan: The life of Charles M. Schwab*," *Reviews in American History* 4 (September 1976): 415–420, and Glenn Porter, *The rise of big business, 1860–1900* (New York, 1973), pp. 1–25.
25. *Commercial Appeal*, Memphis, Tennessee, November 14, 1900.
26. Dun's will excluded his wife as a residuary heir but provided that she was to receive 25 percent, her half-brother Dr. Walter Buchanan 2 percent, Robert Dun Douglass 10 percent, and Frances Minton 5 percent of the annual profits from his estate during her lifetime. The remaining 58 percent was to be paid pro shara to his residuary heirs, the children of his sisters, Elizabeth Dun Douglass and Lucy Dun James. This division between the participating and residuary heirs caused a natural conflict for the next ten years over the question of maximizing profits versus the need for expansion and capital investment. With the Agency control divided between Mary Bradford Dun and Buchanan, who insisted on maximum profits, and Douglass and Minton, who were much more concerned about the long-term welfare of the Agency, the administrative structure provided the stability for survival and prosperity.

Bibliography

Manuscript Sources

The archives of Dun & Bradstreet, 99 Church Street, New York, contain most of the available business records, accounts, and correspondence pertaining to R. G. Dun & Co. The eight bound volumes of Dun's letterpress books constitute the single most valuable source. Very early in his career Dun decided to have his letterpress books serve as a record for all his correspondence, personal and business, and as a permanent record of his business accounts.

Almost no incoming correspondence, other than credit-reports, survives, and Dun kept no minutes or records of his discussions with his partners. What might otherwise be a too heavy dependence on R. G. Dun's letterbooks is tempered somewhat by the availability of copies of circular letters to subscribers, corresponding reporters, and branch managers.

It will be obvious to the reader that the availability and lack of sources undoubtedly limited and shaped my treatment of R. G. Dun & Co. The lack of correspondence from the Douglass period, 1849–58, forced a heavy reliance upon circular letters to subscribers and correspondents. On the other hand, during R. G. Dun's first years as owner and manager, he assumed close personal supervision and control of the business, and his letterbooks are filled with detailed letters to subscribers and subordinates. By the last quarter of the nineteenth century, after Dun had erected an administrative structure, his letterbooks contained much less detail on business and more on family and personal information. Dun's continuing withdrawal from the day-to-day management of the business during the last decade of the century meant that his letterbooks became much less valuable as a historical source on R. G. Dun & Co. In short, the availability of Dun's letterbooks as the major source forced a more biographical analysis of the business than might have otherwise been the case.

This is not to suggest that the circular letters to subscribers, correspondents, and branch office managers are not extremely valuable; they are. Dun's letters to subscribers, which evolved into *Business Outlook* and eventually into *Dun's Review*, contained valuable data on the firm and the state of the economy. Circular letters to correspondents and branch office managers provide insight into the process of credit-reporting and the structure and management of the firm.

One of the most valuable sources in the Dun & Bradstreet archives is Owen A. Sheffield's "Dun & Bradstreet, Inc.: The Mercantile Agency since 1841 — Serving the world of industry, commerce and trade and of finance and insurance: A private history" (unpublished, 1965), 4 volumes. Owen Sheffield, former secretary of Dun & Bradstreet, Inc., spent over ten years gathering documents and material in the various Dun & Bradstreet offices. After working for years on his four volumes, Sheffield decided they should not be published but deposited in the archives "as a base and guidance for others." This decision not only permitted Sheffield to be candid but also to include a large volume of reproduced documents without worrying about the constraints of publication. Sheffield brought to his work a lifetime of experience in credit-reporting and painstaking scholarship. Any scholar interested in Dun & Bradstreet or credit-reporting would profit greatly by his efforts.

The Dun & Bradstreet collection in the Baker Library, Harvard University, contains more than 2,500 volumes, consisting mostly of R. G. Dun & Co. credit-reports from 1841 to 1890. The reports represent the product of R. G. Dun & Co. and, while they are one of the finest collections of material for mid-nineteenth-century America available to scholars, they are of limited value to the history of the firm. However, in addition to the credit-report volumes, there are several volumes consisting mostly of lists of subscribers and scrapbooks, which do provide some insight into the company's operations in the last decade of the century.

Information about R. G. Dun's early childhood may be gleaned from the Dun Papers in the Ross County Historical Society, Chillicothe, Ohio. Although the data on R. G. Dun are somewhat limited, the Dun Papers are a rich collection of unused material on mercantile and economic conditions in the United States covering a twenty-five year period after the War of 1812. The Walter Dun Papers, Ohio Historical Society, are of limited value on R. G. Dun & Co.

Books and Pamphlets

A brief sketch of the life of George Douglass. New York, n.d.

Atherton, Lewis E. *The frontier merchant in mid-America.* Columbia, Missouri, 1971.

— — —. *The southern country store, 1800–1860.* Baton Rouge, Louisiana, 1949.

Bailyn, Bernard. *The New England merchants in the seventeenth century.* Cambridge, Massachusetts, 1955.

Bradstreet's book of commercial reports. New York, 1857–1900.

Bruchey, Stuart. *The roots of American economic growth, 1607–1681: An essay in social causation.* New York, 1965.

Chandler, Alfred D., Jr. *Strategy and structure: Chapters in the history of industrial enterprise.* Cambridge, Massachusetts, 1962.

— — —. *The visible hand: The managerial revolution in American business.* Cambridge, Massachusetts, 1977.

Current, Richard N. *The typewriter and the men who made it.* Urbana, Illinois, 1954.

Dawson, George. *Pleasures of angling with rod and reel for trout and salmon.* New York, 1876.

Dunbar, Edward E. *Statement of the controversy between Lewis Tappan and Edward E. Dunbar.* New York, 1846.

Earling, P. R. *Whom to trust: A practical treatise on mercantile credits.* Chicago, 1890.

Errant, Joseph W. *The law relating to mercantile agencies: Being the Johnson prize essay for the Union College of Law for the year 1886.* Philadelphia, 1889.

Finley, Isaac J., and Putman, Rufus. *Pioneer period and reminiscence of the early settlers and settlement of Ross County, Ohio.* Cincinnati, 1874.

Foulke, Roy A. *The sinews of American commerce.* New York, 1941.

Galambos, Louis. *The public image of big business in America, 1880–1940.* Baltimore, 1975.

Gras, N. S. B. *Business and capitalism: An introduction to business history.* New York, 1939.

Harris, Seymour, ed. *American economic history.* New York, 1961.

Kirkland, Edward C. *Dream and thought in the business community, 1860–1900.* Ithaca, 1956.

— — —. *Industry comes of age: Business, labor and public policy, 1860–1897.* New York, 1961.

Krooss, Herman E., and Gilbert, Charles. *American business history.* Englewood Cliffs, New Jersey, 1972.

McGrane, Reginald C. *The panic of 1837.* Chicago, 1924.

Meagher, Thomas F. *The commercial agency "system" of the United States and Canada exposed: Is the secret inquisition a curse or a benefit?* New York, 1876.

The Mercantile Agency directory. New York, 1934.

The Mercantile Agency manual. New York, 1894.

The Mercantile Agency's reference book. New York, 1859–61, 1864–1900.

The Mercantile Agency United States business directory for 1867 containing the names of the merchants, manufacturers, and traders generally, throughout the United States. New York, 1867.

Porter, Glenn. *The rise of big business, 1860–1900.* New York, 1973.

———, and Livesay, Harold. *Merchants and manufacturers: Studies in the changing structure of nineteenth-century marketing.* Baltimore, 1971.

Report of important cases against the Mercantile Agency, as to their liability for representations, honestly made in the course of their business. New York, 1877.

Reports of the four leading cases against the Mercantile Agency for slander and libel. New York, 1873.

Robertson, Ross M. *History of the American economy.* 3d ed. New York, 1973.

Sheffield, Owen A. "Dun & Bradstreet, Inc.: The Mercantile Agency since 1841 — Serving the world of industry, commerce and trade and of finance and insurance: A private history." (1965.)

Smith, Duane A. *Silver saga: The story of Caribou, Colorado.* Boulder, Colorado, 1974.

Sobel, Robert. *Machines and morality: The 1850's.* New York, 1973.

Synopsis of the laws relating to assignments, insolvency & etc. in the various states of the Union: Also the dates of the setting of the courts. New York, 1879.

Temin, Peter. *The Jacksonian economy.* New York, 1969.

United States Government Printing Office. *Biographical directory of the American Congress, 1774–1949.* Washington, D.C., 1950.

Vose, Edward N. *Seventy-five years of the Mercantile Agency: R. G. Dun &Co., 1841–1916.* New York, 1916.

Wiman, Erastus. *Chances of success: Episodes and observations in the life of a busy man.* New York, 1893.

Wyatt-Brown, Bertram. *Lewis Tappan and the evangelical war against slavery.* Cleveland, 1969.

Articles

Atherton, Lewis E. "The problem of credit-rating in the antebellum south." *Journal of Southern History* 12:534–556 (November 1946).

Cochran, Thomas C. "The paradox of American economic growth." *Journal of American History* 61:925–942 (March 1975).

"Credit organizations and meddlesome legislation." *Commercial and Financial Chronicle* 18:338 (April 4, 1874).

Galambos, Louis. "The emerging organizational synthesis in modern American history." *Business History* 44:279–290 (Autumn 1970).

Hidy, R. W. "Credit rating before Dun and Bradstreet." *Bulletin of the Historical Society* 13:84–88 (December 1939).

Madison, James H. "The evolution of commercial credit reporting agencies in nineteenth-century America." *Business History Review* 48: 164–186 (Summer 1974).

— — —. "The credit reports of R. G. Dun & Co. as historical sources." *Historical Methods Newsletter*, 128–131 (September 1975).

"The Mercantile Agency." *Hunt's Merchant's Magazine and Commercial Review* 27:46–53 (January 1851).

"The Mercantile Agency system." *Bankers' Magazine and Statistical Register* 4:545–549 (January 1858).

"Mercantile failures in 1856." *Hunt's Merchant's Magazine and Commercial Review* 34:595 (February 1857).

Norris, James D., ed. "A northern businessman opposes the Civil War." *Ohio History* 71:138–147 (July 1962).

Porter, Glenn. "A picture from life's other side: Pocket robber baron. A review of Robert Hessen, *Steel titan: The life of Charles M. Schwab.*" *Reviews in American History* 4:415–420 (September 1976).

"Traits of trade—laudable and iniquitous." *Hunt's Merchant's Magazine and Commercial Review* 29:50–57 (July 1853).

Wyatt-Brown, Bertram. "God and Dun & Bradstreet, 1841–1851." *Business History Review* 40:432–450 (Winter 1966).

Index

Albany Evening Journal, 129
American Bicycle Co., 156
American Clay Working Co., 156
American Mercantile Reporting Co., 121
American Tobacco Co., 156
Anacondo Copper Mining Co., 161
Armstrong, Alex, Pittsburgh office
    manager, 81
Arthur, Chester A., president of United
    States, 99, 104, 147
Arthur Tappan and Co.
    advertises for customers, 6
    dissolutionment, 16-18
    location, 12
Atherton, Lewis, 8
A. T. Stewart & Co., 72, 73

Bangert, Shaw & Company, mercantile
    and collection agency, 121
*Banker's Magazine and State Financial
    Register*, 56, 89
Baring, Thomas, of London's Baring
    Brothers and Company, 9
Baring Brothers and Company, early
    credit-reporting, 9
Barlow, Charles, partner, 67, 68, 95-100,
    116, 136, 147, 163
Barney, Hiram, Lewis Tappan's son-in-
    law, 31, 33
B. Douglass & Co., 67. *See also* Douglas,
    Benjamin Jr.; Mercantile Agency

Beardsley, Horace, 131-132
Beardsley, John, 131-132
Beardsley v. *Tappan*, 52, 132-133
Bell Telephone Company, 117
Boyd, Robert R., partner in Mercantile
    Agency, 67, 68, 94-96, 163
Bradstreet, Henry, John Bradstreet's
    son, 120
Bradstreet, John M., competition to
    Mercantile Agency, 49-56, 79,
    119-120
Bradstreet, Milton, John Bradstreet's
    son, 119-120
*Bradstreet's Book of Commercial
    Reports*
    competition to Mercantile Agency,
    51-56
    issued 1857, 51
    rating key, 51
Branch Offices
    expansion, 109, 156-159
    instructions to managers, 80-81, 107-
    109
    New York office supervises, 154-156
    recruitment of managers, 77-81, 107-
    109
    salaries of managers, 81-82
    Tappan's relations, 169 n.51
Buffalo Commercial Agency, 121
Business failures, statistics, 46, 70-71,
    90-92

Business firms, reported on, 85, 110-112
Business Outlook, 158-159

Capital worth, estimates of, 83-84. See also Credit-reporting
Caribou Consolidated Silver Mining Company, 117
Chandler, Alfred, 163
Chandler, Zachariah, United States Senator, 76
Channing, William Ellery, influence on Lewis and Arthur Tappan, 16
Chas. Barlow & Co., 67
Church, Sheldon P., early credit reporter, 9
Civil War, impact on Mercantile Agency, 74-77
Clark, Charles Finney, president of Bradstreet Agency, 120
Cleaveland, Warren A., opens credit agency, 27
Collections
  Griffen, Cleveland, and Campbell, 10-11
  profits, 48-49, 113-116
  under Tappan, 22-24, 28
Commerce, growth in early nineteenth century, 4-8. See also Market
Commercial Agency, 27, 118-119
Commercial and Financial Chronicle, 134
Competition, 27, 48-49, 118-123
Conkling, Roscoe, United States Senator, 147
Correspondence. See Credit-reporting; Reporters
Corresponding attorneys. See Collections; Reporters
Credit
  Colonial period, 34
  during Civil War, 71-72
  function in economy, xiii
  influence of credit agencies, 92-94
  panic of 1837, 19
  post-Civil War, 90-92

prior to panic of 1837, 6
Revolutionary War period, 45
See also Credit-reporting; Dun, Robert Graham
Credit agencies
  attacks on, 125-135
  legal attacks on, 131-135
  Meagher's attacks on, 125-128
  political attacks on, 134-135
  See also Meagher, Thomas F.
Credit rating. See Credit-reporting
Credit-reporting
  attacks on, 125-135
  Bradstreet's Book of Commercial Reports, 51-56
  Colonial period, xiii, 34
  corporate firms, 94-95
  coverage under Tappan, 22, 25-27
  Dun introduces quantitive measures, xv, 83-84
  early national period, 8-10
  firms by Mercantile Agency, 110-111
  firms prior to Mercantile Agency, 9-12
  foreign firms reported on by Mercantile Agency, 156-158
  frequency of Mercantile Agency reports, 111
  frequency of reports, 111
  Griffen, Cleaveland, and Campbell, 10-12
  instructions to reporters, 23-24, 128-130
  legal attacks on, 131-135
  Mercantile Agency founded, 18-20
  New York office supervisor, 154-156
  notification system, 87-88 (see also Notification system)
  political attack on, 134-135
  privileged communication of, 131-133
  problems under Tappan, 29-31
  procedures, 24-26, 28-29, 49-51, 135-145
  rating keys, 70, 83-84, 92-94 (See also Reference book)

Reference Book, 52-53, 83-85, 89-91
  shifts in nature, 87-88
  use of financial statements, 130-131
  written reports, 139-145
Credit-reports. See Credit-reporting;
  Dun, Robert Graham; Mercantile
  Agency

Daly, Marcus, 161
Dawson, George, Albany, New York,
  publisher, 129
Douglass, Benjamin, 131-132
  acquires Mercantile Agency, 36, 40-41
  branch offices, 43
  contribution to Mercantile Agency,
  57-58
  decides to issue reference book,
  52-54
  Dun explains business philosophy to,
  99-101
  early business experience, 37-40
  enters Mercantile Agency, 34
  family, 36-37
  instructions to reporters, 44-47
  marries Elizabeth Dun, 40
  marries Julia Hayes, 66
  profits, 47
  recruitments of reporters, 44-45
  revises prices, 44
  sells Mercantile Agency, 56-66
  transforms Mercantile Agency, xiv
  views on slavery, 37, 76
  vision of Mercantile Agency, 42-43
Douglass, Benjamin, Jr., Robert
  Graham Dun's nephew, 115
Douglass, Elizabeth Dun, 59
Douglass, George, Benjamin Douglass's
  father, 36-38
Douglass, Julia Hayes, Benjamin
  Douglass's wife, 66
Douglass, Robert Dun, Robert Graham
  Dun's nephew, 147, 150, 153-154,
  159, 163
Douglass & Minton, 115
Dun, Boyd & Co., 67, 80

Dun, Elizabeth Douglass, Robert
  Graham Dun's wife, 59-60, 64
Dun, George William, Robert Graham
  Dun's uncle, 61
Dun, James, Robert Graham Dun's
  grandfather, 60
Dun, James Angus, Robert Graham
  Dun's brother, 59, 73, 161
Dun, Jane, Robert Graham Dun's sister,
  62
Dun, John, Robert Graham Dun's
  uncle, 61, 74
Dun, Lucy Worthan Angus, Robert
  Graham Dun's mother, 61-62
Dun, Robert, Robert Graham Dun's
  father, 60-62
Dun, Robert George, Robert Graham
  Dun's cousin, 74
Dun, Robert Graham
  analysis of economic conditions,
  70-73, 90-92
  art collection, 101-104
  collections, 77-79, 113-116
  compared to Robber Barons, 101
  death, 161
  decides to issue *Reference Book*,
  52-54
  Dun Building, 159-160
  early business experience, 63-66
  education, 62
  evaluates Tappan's contribution to
  Mercantile Agency, 34-35
  expansion of branch offices, 109,
  156-159
  family, 62-66
  homes, 101
  illness, 161
  influence on credit flows, 92-94
  instructions to managers, 80-81, 107-
  109, 129-130
  instructions to reporters, 128-130
  introduces quantitative measurements in credit reports, xv
  introduces written reports, 139-145
  investments, 104-105, 116-117

joins Mercantile Agency, 47, 63-66
modifies *Reference Book*, 68-70
partners, 153-154
partnership agreements, 96-100,
148-150
personal life, 101-104
profits, 68-69, 85-86, 98-99, 105-106,
114-115, 121-123, 135, 142-147
purchases Mercantile Agency, 57-59,
66
rationalizes Mercantile Agency
structure, 67-68, 95-100, 182 n. 43
recruitment of branch managers, 77-
81, 107-109
Reference Book revision, 82-85
responds to attacks on Mercantile
Agency, 126-135
revises reporting procedures, 138-145
significance, 161-164
shifts nature of credit-reporting,
87-88
statistics on business failures, 90-92
suspends publication of reference
book, 72-73
transforms Mercantile Agency, xv
views on competition, 118-123
views on slavery, 73-76
views on war, 73-77
vision of Mercantile Agency, 104-105
will, 192 n. 26
withdraws from active management,
154-155
See also Mercantile Agency
Dun, Walter, Robert Graham Dun's
uncle, 60
Dunbar, Edward E.
assessment of early credit-reporting
business, 12-14
disagreement with Lewis Tappan,
31-33
dissolves association with Tappan,
32-33
establishes branch in Boston, 28
joins New York Office, 29-30
Dun Building, New York, 159-160

"Dunmere," Robert Graham Dun's
home, 101, 161
Dun's Review, 159
Dusenbery, William Coxe, proprietor
of Commercial Agency, 27

Earling, P. R., 124, 125, 128, 130
Eastern Kodak Co., 156
Edison General Electric Co., 161
Edward E. Dunbar & Co., Boston branch
office, 28-29
Edwards, Alfred, member of Arthur
Tappan and Co., 17
E. Russell & Co., Boston branch office,
43, 96

Financial Chronicle, 89
Fourse & Herschberger & Co., 121

Gano, Stephen, Cincinnati office
manager, 78-80
Gates, Seth M., New York Congressman,
19-20
Goodrich, William, proprietor of Phila-
delphia branch, 29-30, 31, 33, 43
Gorman, Berkely, manager of Brad-
street's Philadelphia office, 120
Graham, Elizabeth, Dun's grandmother,
60
Graham, John, Dun's great uncle, 60
Grant, S. S., leather merchant, 55
Great Northwestern Telegraph Co., 148
Griffen, Cleaveland and Campbell
early credit-reporting agency, 10-14

Hall, William, Montreal office manager,
80-81
Hamilton Brown Shoe Co., 156
Hayes, O. A., Chicago office manager,
81
Hospenteller & Turner, Chillicothe,
Ohio, merchandising firm, 63
Hunt's Merchant's Magazine, 35, 46

International Collecting Company and Mercantile Agency, 120

James, Lucy Dun, Robert Graham Dun's sister, 63
James, William, Robert Graham Dun's brother-in-law, 63, 76, 134, 161
J. D. Pratt & Co., Baltimore branch office, 34
Jessup, William, Montrose, Pennsylvania, lawyer, 10-11
John M. Bradstreet & Son, Improved Mercantile and Law Agency, 118-120. See also Bradstreet, John M.; Bradstreet's Book of Commercial Reports
Jordan's Bonded Iowa State Collecting and Reporting Co., 120
Journal of Commerce, 89

King, Arthur J., partner, 80, 109, 140, 147, 150, 153-154
Kirkland, Edward C., 124

L. Ballard & Co., 118-119
Legal and Commercial Union, 120
LeRoy Gazette, 19
Lord Tenterden's Act, 134
Lugdin, Jay, Robert Graham Dun's brother-in-law, 62, 107

McClellan, General George B., 76
McKay, Alfred, St. Louis office manager, 78-80
McKillop & Sprague, credit-reporting agency, 118-122
Market
    changing conditions in nineteenth-century, 79
    expansion of, 41-42, 87-88, 91-92, 106, 107, 112-113, 156-159
    southern, 170 n.56
Maynard, Charles F., alias Meagher, Thomas Francis, 126

Meagher, Thomas F., attacks on credit agencies, 125-128
Mercantile Agency
    administrative structure, 95-100, 105
    attacks on, 125-135
    branch offices, 27-31, 81-82, 106-108
    business failure statistics, 70-71 (see also Business failures, statistics)
    claims to first credit-reporting firm, 10-12
    collection service, 77-79, 113-116 (see also Collections)
    competition, 48-52, 118-123 (see also Competition; Dun, Robert Graham)
    coverage under Tappan, 22, 25-27
    credit-reporting procedures, 23-26, 135-145 (see also Credit-reporting)
    decision to issue Reference Book, 52-54
    Dun Building, 159-160
    early competitors, 27
    early profits, 21-22
    early subscribers, 20-23
    expansion, 156-159
    expansion of branch offices, 109
    expansion under Douglass, 42-44
    expansion under Tappan, 32-33
    firms reported on, 110-111
    foreign firms, 156-158
    funding, xiv, 18-20
    growth, 135
    impact of Civil War, 74-77
    influence on flow of credit, 92-94
    instructions to managers, 80-81, 107-109
    instructions to reporters, 18-24, 128-130
    introduces written reports, 139-145
    legal attacks on, 131-135
    Meagher's attacks on, 125-128
    notification system, 87-88 (see also Notification system)
    number of employees, 109-110
    partnership agreements, 96-97, 98-100, 148, 150

political attack on, 134-135
pricing policy, 20-21, 26, 44, 54, 87-
88, 140-147, 158
problems of reporting southern states
under Tappan, 29-31
profits, 47-48, 68-69, 74-75, 77, 85-86,
98-99, 105-106, 114-115, 121-123,
142-147, 184-185 n.101
recruitment of managers, 77-81, 107-
109
Reference Book, 54-55, 82-85 (see
also *Reference Book*)
services to subscribers, 43, 48-49,
113-116 (*see also* Credit-reporting)
significance, 163-164
statistics on business failures, 46,
90-92
suspends publication of *Reference
Book*, 72-73
Tappan's contribution to, 34-35 (*see
also* Tappan, Lewis)
use of financial statements in reporting, 130-131
use of typewriter, 136-142
See also Tappan, Lewis
Mercantile Agency Annual, 113
Mercantile Agency Manual, 154-155,
159, 163
*Mercantile Agency United States Busi-
ness Directory for 1867*, 113
Mercantile and Statistical Agency
Association, 120
Merchants Mutual Indemnity Associa-
tion, 120
Minchener, George, Detroit branch
office manager, 107
Minton, Francis L., Robert Graham
Dun's attorney, 105, 115, 163
Morrison, William, London office
manager, 83
Murray, Charles, Pittsburgh branch
office manager, 107
Mutual Telegraph Company, 148-149

National Cash Register Co., 156
National Telegraph Company, 116

New York Commercial Advertiser, 17-
19, 122
New York Daily Tribune, 89
New York Evening Post, 161
New York Illustrated News, 109
New York Independent, 46
New York Office, supervises credit
reports, 154-156
New York World, 128
Notification system
strength of Bradstreet's, 54-56
weakness of Mercantile Agency, 54-
66, 88, 111
written reports, 139-149
See also *Reference Book*

Olcott, Colonel H. G., 115
Ormsby v. *Douglass*, 132-133
Overland Telephone Co., 117
Ozark Iron Company, 117
Ozark Ironworks, 62

Palmer Pneumatic Tire Co., 156
Partners, 96-100, 148-150, 153-154
Peabody, A.S., Philadelphia office
manager, 80
Phoenix Mercantile Agency, 120
Porter, Glenn, 58
Porter, Glenn, and Harold Livesay, 78
Pratt, Jubes D., established Baltimore
branch of Mercantile Agency, 32
Prices, 20-21, 26, 54, 87-88, 140-147, 158
Privileged communications, 131-133
Profits, 47-48, 68-69, 74-77, 85-86, 98-99,
105-106, 114-115, 121-123, 135,
142-147, 184-185 n.101
Public, The, 122
Pulitzer, Joseph, 128

Randolph, E. F., 120
Rating key. See *Reference Book*
Reference Book
decision to issue, 52-53
features, 111-113
frequency of publication, 111

modifications, 69-70
prices, 87-88, 142-147
profits, 68, 85-86
rating keys, 84, 89-90, 92-94
renews, 82-85
suspends publication, 72-73
written reports, 139-145
Reilly, John, Cincinnati office manager,
    78-79
Reilly, William, partner, 67-68, 94
Reporters
    instruction from Dun, 128-130
    recruitments by Griffen, Cleveland,
        and Campbell, 10-11
    under Tappan, 19-20, 32-33
    See also Credit-reporting
R. G. Dun & Co. See Dun, Robert
    Graham; Mercantile Agency
Russell, Edward, Boston branch owner,
    83, 154, 159

Scarlett, William, Baltimore branch
    office manager, 107, 109
Secrecy in credit agencies, 125-128
Sedy's, London credit-reporting firm, 53
Sewall and Salisbury, Boston mercantile
    firm, 16
Sheffield, Owen, 163
Smith, H. H., Buffalo branch office
    manager, 109
Smith, Matthias B., partner, 67-68
    77-80, 95-100, 147-163
S. P. Church & Co. sued, 52
Stacey, M. P., Philadelphia office
    manager, 79, 115-116
Stanton, Edwin, Secretary of War, 116
St. Louis Globe Democrat, 122
Subscribers
    credit services to, 22-26, 49-51, 135-
        140, 168-169 n.38, 189 n.68
    Tappan solicits, 20-23
    written reports to, 139-145
    See also Credit-reporting
Subscriptions
    number of, 168-169 n.38, 189 n.68

prices of, 20-24, 44, 54, 87-88, 140-
    144, 147 (see also Prices)
Synopsis of the Laws Relating to Assign-
    ments, Insolvency & etc. in the
    Various States of the Union, 113

Tappan, Benjamin, Lewis Tappan's
    father, 14-16
Tappan, John, Lewis Tappan's brother,
    16
Tappan, Lewis, 131
    business experience prior to Mercan-
        tile Agency, 16-20
    collection services, 22-24
    contribution to Mercantile Agency,
        34-35
    disagreement with Edward Dunbar,
        31-33
    dissolves association with Edward
        Dunbar, 32-33
    early life, 14-16
    early profits, 21-22
    founds Mercantile Agency, xiv,
        10-12, 14, 18, 20
    involvement in social reform, 16-17
    opens branch offices, 27-31
    pricing philosophy, 26
    problems of covering southern states,
        29-33, 170 n.56
    profits, 34
    recruitment of reporters, 22-24
    sedentary merchant, xiv
    sells Mercantile Agency, 34
    semi-annual circulars to reporters,
        23-34
    vision of Mercantile Agency, 25,
        27-28
Tappan, Sarah Homes, Lewis Tappan's
    mother, 16
Tobacco Leaf, 161
Toronto Globe, 96

Villard, Henry, 161
Vose, Edward, 10

Walters, George B., secretary of
    National Telegraph Co., 116
Ward, Thomas Wren, early credit
    reporter, 9
Waters, Edwin F., 96
Webster, Daniel, manager of New
    Orleans branch office, 68
West, The, 121
Western Union Telegraph Company,
    148
Wiman, Erastus, Mercantile Agency

partner, 81, 83-84, 96-100, 107, 134,
    136, 147-153, 156, 164
Whiting, W. E., member of Arthur
    Tappan & Co., 17
Whyte, Robert, Nashville lawyer, 8
William Goodrich & Co., Mercantile
    Agency Philadelphia branch, 31, 33
Woodward, William A., proprietor of
    Commercial Agency, 27

Young, Henry C., 120

About the Author

James D. Norris is professor of history at the University of Missouri, St. Louis. His previous books include *Frontier Iron, Politics and Patronage in the Gilded Age*, and *AZn: A History of the American Zinc Company*.

Recent Titles in
Contributions in Economics and Economic History
SERIES EDITOR: *ROBERT SOBEL*

The Age of Giant Corporations: A Microeconomic History of American
Business, 1914-1970
Robert Sobel

Samuel Gompers and the Origins of the American Federation of Labor,
1848-1896
Stuart Bruce Kaufman

Statistical View of the Trusts: A Manual of Large American Industrial and
Mining Corporations Active Around 1900
David Bunting

State and Regional Patterns in American Manufacturing, 1860-1900
Albert W. Niemi, Jr.

The American Banking Community and New Deal Banking Reforms,
1933-1935
Helen M. Burns

Gold Is Money
Hans F. Sennholz, editor

The Drive to Industrial Maturity: The U. S. Economy, 1860-1914
Harold G. Vatter

Individual Freedom: Selected Works of William H. Hutt
Svetozar Pejovich and *David Klingaman, editors*

Friedrich A. Sorge's Labor Movement in the United States: A History of
the American Working Class from Colonial Times to 1890
Philip S. Foner and *Brewster Chamberlin, editors*

Essays in Southern Labor History: Selected Papers, Southern Labor
History Conference, 1976
Gary M Fink and *Merl E. Reed, editors*

The Iron Barons: A Social Analysis of an American Urban Elite,
1874-1965
John N. Ingham

The Railroad Mergers and the Coming of Conrail
Richard Saunders